Nuclear Weapons and Aircraft Carriers

HOW THE BOMB SAVED NAVAL AVIATION

NUCLEAR WEAPONS ★★★★★★AND★★★★★★ AIRCRAFT CARRIERS

JERRY MILLER

SMITHSONIAN INSTITUTION PRESS
Washington and London

© 2001 by the Smithsonian Institution
All rights reserved

Copy editor: Tom Ireland
Production editor: Robert A. Poarch
Designer: Janice Wheeler

Library of Congress Cataloging-in-Publication Data
Miller, Jerry, 1919–
    Nuclear weapons and aircraft carriers: how the bomb saved naval aviation / Jerry Miller
      p. cm.
    Includes bibliographical references and index.
    ISBN 1-56098-944-0 (alk. paper)
      1. United States. Navy—Aviation—History—20th century. 2. Aircraft carriers—United States—History—20th century. 3. Nuclear weapons—United States—History—20th century.
    I. Title.
    VG93.M55 2001
    359.9′4′097309045—dc21   00-061886

British Library Cataloguing-in-Publication Data is available

Manufactured in the United States of America
06 05 04 03 02 01   5 4 3 2 1

∞ The paper used in this publication meets the minimum requirements of the American National Standard for Information Sciences—Permanence of Paper for Printed Library Materials ANSI Z39.48-1984.

For permission to reproduce illustrations appearing in this book, please correspond directly with the owners of the works, as listed in the individual captions. The Smithsonian Institution Press does not retain reproduction rights for these illustrations individually, or maintain a file of addresses for photo sources.

To Rear Admiral William S. "Deak" Parsons, U.S. Navy,
the Atomic Admiral (1901–1953). U.S. Navy photo.

Contents

Preface ix
Acknowledgments xiii

Introduction 1
1. The Beginning 10
2. Policy and Strategy 22
3. Weapons 40
4. Heavy Attack 77
5. Light Attack 120
6. Delivery Tactics 154
7. Ships 178
8. Testing the Capability 199
9. Targeting 206
10. The Past, the Present, and the Future 228
11. Reflections 236

Notes 263
Index 289

Preface

The aircraft carrier established itself during World War II. The U.S. Navy started the war with seven carriers and finished that war with almost a hundred of varying shapes and sizes. Considering the impact that carriers had on the outcome of the war, particularly in the Pacific theater, it was almost inconceivable at that time that their future would be seriously questioned. However, the atomic bomb changed all concepts of future strategies. The rapid demobilization following the war eliminated many carriers, but the future of naval aviation, and to some extent the Navy itself, were threatened by the impact of the atomic bomb on strategic thinking. Many national defense policy makers believed that future wars would be fought with atomic weapons: all that would be required for our national defense was a few such weapons, coupled with long-range delivery systems, such as big bombers. The United States had exclusive capability with the ultimate weapon—and nothing else was needed.

This view became prevalent in the newly created U.S. Air Force, the logical service to conduct such a war. Some elements of the Air Force not involved in the so-called strategic bombing would not even be of much use. Armies and navies, particularly naval aviation, would no longer be required. Consequently, some serious debates occurred with the Navy, particularly naval aviation, which was fighting for a role in the future. Louis Johnson, the secretary of defense under President Harry S. Truman, dealt the Navy a serious blow by canceling a new "super" carrier, the USS *United States,* on which construction had already started. The contest erupted into what was labeled by the press as "The Revolt of the Admirals." Though "revolt" was too strong a term, special offices were actually established in the Navy to counter the threat of extinction. Great leaders such as Adm. Arthur W. Radford and Capts. (then) Arleigh A. Burke and Donald C. Griffen, repulsed by the executive branch of our government, banded together to present the Navy's case to Congress, risking their careers for what they believed to be principles essential to our nation's defense.

The key figure in Congress was chairman of the House Armed Services Committee, the Honorable Carl Vinson, a Democrat from Georgia. Following a series of highly publicized hearings, Adm. Louis E. Denfeld, the chief of naval operations, was forced to take a position. He courageously supported the concepts of his subordinates, going against the popular view of the civilian authority. With that support from the uniformed leader of the Navy, Chairman Vinson ruled in the Navy's favor. The committee authorized a role for the Navy in strategic nuclear warfare. Admiral Denfeld was forced to retire immediately, and other recriminating actions were taken, such as the removal of Arleigh Burke from the flag officer promotion list. He was later restored to that list by President Truman.

Some Navy leaders paid a price with damaged careers, but they achieved their goal. The Navy was then in a position to play a role in the delivery of atomic weapons, which at that time meant using aircraft carriers and their embarked aircraft. While the Air Force had already demonstrated its capability with the Hiroshima and Nagasaki attacks, the Navy had no capability whatsoever. There ensued a great struggle to attain such a capability as quickly as possible and to create the systems and train the manpower for the mission that had been authorized by Congress. The fascinating story of that struggle, without precedent in the Navy, highlights the talents and accomplishments of many outstanding people. Ironically, while the bomb at first threatened the extinction of the carrier, a good case can be made that it eventually saved naval aviation.

Although several elements of the story have been covered as separate subjects in various publications, others, such as the targeting of weapons, have received little attention. It is my intent to give a complete account of how the Navy attained a nuclear weapons delivery capability for its aircraft carriers over a period of fifty years—a unique period in their history.

Acknowledgments

The need for narrating naval aviation's struggle to bring the aircraft carrier and the nuclear weapon together as a potent weapons system started as a dialogue with Vice Adm. Frederick "Dick" Ashworth, USN (Ret.). He supplied many source documents and imparted his personal knowledge of the events through his oral history and numerous reviews of portions of the draft manuscript. Capt. E. T. Wooldridge, USN (Ret.), an established author on naval aviation, provided guidance and exceptional editorial support, without which this work would not have been published. The main contributors, however, are the many exceptional individuals who played a role in the struggle, along with Dick Ashworth.

Nuclear Weapons and Aircraft Carriers

Introduction

It was not long after midnight in the spring of 1964 in the Aegean Sea south of Greece. A task force of U.S. Navy ships was engaged in re-supplying the combatant ships with food, dry goods, ammunition, and fuel, a procedure that had evolved from the early days of World War II, when U.S. Navy ships were forced to stay at sea for long periods. The replenishment ships steamed at a speed of about 12 knots, one behind the other, a few thousand yards apart. They held their course and speed as the ships being resupplied came up alongside, taking station from one hundred to two hundred feet abeam. After settling down at the same course and speed, lines necessary for transferring supplies were connected between the two ships. Helicopters were used to augment the operation, moving from one deck to another with their cargoes.

The approaches by the combatant ships to the individual supply ships were standard, usually starting with a U turn from abeam the supply ship. The officer controlling, or "conning," the combatant gauged the turn so that it would end up on a parallel course with the line of replenishment ships, slightly behind the one being approached. Then, using a higher speed, the combatant came up alongside the supplying ship, the speed of approach depending on the commanding officer of the combatant. For carriers, a speed of 25 to 27 knots was common. At the appropriate time, orders to the engine room were given to reverse the propellers. The carrier never actually went into reverse but merely reduced speed to the same speed as that of the supply ship. After the course and speed were stabilized, supply lines were passed between the ships, and transfer operations commenced. The cargo was oil, jet fuel, food, ammunition—whatever was needed. It was an impressive operation when done correctly, and for the officer successfully maneuvering the ship, it signified his qualification as a "capable mariner."[1]

The USS *Franklin D. Roosevelt* had recently received a new navigator on board, a talented young commander with considerable aviation experience, but unused to being on the bridge of a ship involved in replenishment maneuvers. So, on this wonderful moonlit spring night in the Mediterranean, he had been given an opportunity to practice. Under the commanding officer's supervision, he was conning the ship during the approaches to the replenishment line. After an approach was completed, the carrier would speed up, move out ahead, and circle around for another approach. The navigator was getting the hang of the operation very well—until he made a serious error in judgment.

On one approach, during his big U turn, he came in at an angle, rather than parallel, to the course of the replenishment ships. The proper and smart thing in such cases is to "wave off"—abort the approach and begin again. But it was late, and I wanted to get the maneuver completed. Therefore, I took the conn from him and attempted to save his bad start.

The *Roosevelt* had a deck-edge elevator on the starboard side for moving aircraft between the flight deck and the hangar deck below. It was usually folded in an upright position for replenishment operations, but for this practice exercise, it had been left down for the flight deck crews to use for their busy workload. The elevator protruded from the side of the ship by several feet, and if the *Roosevelt* were going to hit anything on that side of the ship, the elevator would be the first thing to make contact.

My failure to be prudent and "go around again" was a good lesson for the new navigator, but it was not very good for my ego or conducive to my future peace of mind, for I made an error in judgment during my attempt to salvage the approach. My mistake in judgment caused the deck-edge elevator to impact the mast rigging of the ammunition ship the *Roosevelt* was approaching. It narrowly missed the bridge structure but did snap a few turnbuckles on the ammunition ship rigging. Then, as I gradually turned the carrier away, the stern quarters of the two ships came together with a bump that caused an early reveille for the members of the crew trying to get some sleep. It was a collision caused by an overly confident sailor attempting to salvage a bad approach.[2]

Fortunately, no one was hurt. Some side plates of the *Roosevelt* were dented, and a fair amount of paint had been scraped away. A few minutes later, we were alongside another replenishment ship, continuing the night operations—but the damage to my ego was considerable. I remember standing on the bridge, looking out into the night and reflecting that this was a hell of way to terminate a naval career, one that I had enjoyed so. But, as usual, the crew was magnificent. With cutting and welding torches and a lot of paint, they had the evidence of the collision pretty well obscured by noon of the following day. Rub out the stain: it helps the pain go away.[3]

The incident would have had far greater significance had the media chosen to publicize the event. They could have made some sensational headlines, for there were a considerable number of nuclear weapons in each of the ships involved. In reality, however, the storage and security of these weapons were such that there was no danger of a nuclear incident.

The U.S. Navy played a large role in the creation of the atomic weapons capability of the nation, starting with the development and delivery of the first weapons. One of the major reasons for this Navy role was the "gun club," a collection of professional naval officers

Admiral William S. Sims, U.S. Navy, president of the Naval War College, 1919–1922. He said, "It's the shots that hit that count"—the creed of the Navy's elite gun club. Photo courtesy Naval War College Museum.

who chose to concentrate much of their interest and talent on weapons. They were all bright, dedicated, and professional. Many were Naval Academy graduates who developed an interest in ordnance and gunnery while at that institution. During tours as junior officers in ships—often large battleships—they became intrigued with the more sophisticated aspects of ordnance and gunnery. Making nine large 16-inch-diameter shells, fired from a battleship, land in close proximity to a target fifteen miles away was a challenge. Adjusting the pattern, or dispersion, of the shells was a fascinating science, requiring a knowledge of the construction of the guns, the turrets in which they were housed, the systems used to control their firing, and gunpowder.

One of the earliest gun clubbers of the twentieth century was Adm. William S. Sims, who commanded U.S. Naval Forces in European waters during World War I. Known for his intellect, he was the president of the Naval War College from 1919 until 1922. Sims was well respected for the philosophy reflected in the simple phrase, "The shots that hit are the ones that count." Near misses were of no interest to him. That philosophy had a major impact on the Navy's success in winning battles at sea and its emphasis on ordnance and gunnery, the "fist of the fleet."

Commissioned officers who took a liking to the ordnance and gunnery aspect of warfare usually attended three years of postgraduate school in ordnance engineering after a tour of three or four years in a "ship of the line" equipped with many guns—often big ones. Frequently the graduates of these programs would then accept changes in career patterns, becoming "ordnance engineering duty officers only." They would abandon the traditional path to the command of a ship at sea in favor of a career devoted strictly to ordnance and gunnery. However, some chose to pursue both career paths, concentrating on ordnance when appropriate but continuing on the road of the traditional mariner, hoping eventually to command one or more ships.

In the latter category were some outstanding individuals. One of the most senior was Vice Adm. W. H. P. "Spike" Blandy, a brilliant and personable leader. Before World War II, he expressed doubt that there was any future in naval aviation, believing that guns had served their purpose in the past and they would continue to do so in the future. He followed the tendency of many gun lovers to discourage promising young officers from entering naval aviation.[4] World War II apparently caused a change in his views, for he became a strong champion of naval aviation and a key player in helping it attain a nuclear weapons delivery capability. Early in the war, he headed the Bureau of Ordnance, which acquired much of the ordnance used by the

Navy and Marine Corps. Anyone working with naval ordnance and gunnery during World War II knew the name Blandy.[5]

Among others who chose the gun club route was Adm. Arleigh A. Burke, who headed the Navy for a record six years in the late 1950s and early 1960s. He is noted among other things for spearheading the introduction of the submarine-launched ballistic missile, Polaris.[6] Burke's belief in the significance of ordnance was expressed in a brief article published in 1984. Burke counseled that before an officer was carried away with sophisticated theories about strategy, tactics, and leadership, he had best be sure that he knew how to make his weapons work. "If the equipment doesn't work in battle, it doesn't make much difference how much else the officers know, the battle is lost—and so are the people in it. So, it can be right handy to be a good engineer first—and a brilliant theorist after."[7] A great leader himself, he preached that if your men believed that you knew your weapons and how to make them work, you would not have much trouble getting them to follow you into combat. Burke was so revered by the aviation community of the Navy that they made him Honorary Naval Aviator number thirteen. Burke's counsel would be strongly endorsed by all members of the gun club, who had a record for getting the job done by getting hits on the target.

Adm. Horacio "Rivets" Rivero was a prominent gun clubber who became involved in the development of U.S. nuclear deterrent capability. Rivero came into the nuclear picture immediately following the war as a charter member of the OP-36 office, the Atomic Operations Division in the Navy Department. One of his early assignments was as the representative of the Joint Chiefs of Staff at the Bikini tests.[8]

Another distinguished naval officer who looked back on his experiences in the ordnance field as particularly satisfying was Adm. Thomas H. Moorer. Moorer was a member of the Strategic Bombing Survey, which examined the results of bombing in the Pacific, including those at Hiroshima and Nagasaki. Though never assigned to formal postgraduate training, he was fortunate to have served as the executive officer at the Ordnance Test Facility at Chincoteague, Virginia, and at the ordnance station at Inyokern, California, where he received excellent experience in the more sophisticated aspects of ordnance. The schooling served him well in the years ahead, when he became the chief of naval operations and the chairman of the Joint Chiefs of Staff.[9]

Vice Adm. John Tucker "Chick" Hayward was a naval aviator who has to be categorized as a gun clubber, although, much to his chagrin, he was never ordered to formal Navy postgraduate studies in ordnance. Instead, he gained his knowledge of nuclear physics in graduate courses at the Moore School in Philadelphia and from close association with the scientific members of the faculty at MIT and Cal Tech. His several assignments to naval ordnance duties provided him an opportunity to contribute significantly to the Navy's achievement of a strategic nuclear capability.

Had a fourth atomic weapon been dropped on Japan, Comdr. (then) Thomas Walker would probably have been the "weaponeer," the scientific member of the crew. His role in developing tactics for delivery of nuclear weapons from naval aircraft was most significant, not to mention his later role in the development of the Polaris.

Undoubtedly the gun clubber most intimately and prominently associated with nuclear weapons was Rear Adm. William "Deak" Parsons.[10] He served as Robert Oppenheimer's deputy at Los Alamos, New Mexico, during the development of the atomic bomb. His responsibility was to "engineer" the weapon so that it could be delivered on target. Immediately following the war, he was the technical expert of the OP-36 organization in the Pentagon. He played a key role in the tests at Bikini and was the initiator and champion of early ideas on how the Navy could use nuclear energy and solve some of the problems that would be faced in the dawning nuclear age. In the days following the war, Rivets Rivero served as Parsons's alter ego, taking on many of the tasks that came before the Navy staff.

Parsons withstood great pressure to abandon his traditional line officer career pattern and become a full-time ordnance engineer. He resisted those pressures, feeling that it was necessary for him to work with the weapons in an operating environment so he could better understand and deal with the weapons-development process. His role with Oppenheimer was remarkable, setting an example of the experienced military professional working closely as a teammate with one of the most brilliant scientists of all time. Parsons turned the concepts of atomic weapons into practical products that could be delivered on an enemy target. He made the significant decisions and oversaw the creation of the vast logistic force that was required to accomplish the mission. It was fitting that although he was not an aviator, he served as the weaponeer of the crew that dropped the bomb on Hiroshima.

In his various assignments, Parsons was fortunate to gain the support and admiration of a wonderful civil servant, Dr. L. T. E. "Tommy" Thompson, who spent many years at the ordnance proving ground in Dahlgren, Virginia. It was the hope and dream of both Parsons and Thompson that sometime an ordnance laboratory could be developed that would bring together the civilian scientist/engineer and the professional naval officer, working as teammates for the joint development of useful ordnance.

Such a facility eventually came into being. Known as the Naval Ordnance Test Station (NOTS), Inyokern, California, it became the birthplace of many new ordnance improvements under the direction of a much-admired civilian director, William "Bill" McLean. The Sidewinder missile was a particularly significant product of NOTS and Bill McLean. It is still in service fifty years after its initial development. Many gun clubbers served at Inyokern, including Parsons, Hayward, Walker, Moorer, and his classmate, Tom Connolly.[11] The opinion of many who served with Parsons, particularly Admiral Moorer, is that the Sidewinder missile never would have been successfully developed had it not been for Parsons and his ability to persuade, based on his technical competence and gentlemanly manner.

The Navy can be proud of its gun club members, who exhibited a dedication to weapons and played crucial roles in achieving victory in World War II. The success of the atomic bomb in terminating the conflict with Japan is a testimonial to the validity of the gun club creed. Several members of the club were instrumental in the development of nuclear weapons, and more contributed later to the development of the capability of the Navy to attain a nuclear weapons delivery capability.

1. The Beginning

Vice Adm. Frederick Lincoln "Dick" Ashworth first learned about the atomic bomb in 1944. As a Navy commander, he reported to Los Alamos, New Mexico, chagrined that he had been suddenly ordered to a shore billet after a short tour of duty at the Naval Proving Ground in Dahlgren, Virginia. When he received his orders to Los Alamos, Ashworth was quite sure that the Navy personnel bureau had no knowledge of what he was supposed to do. They had just responded to a high-level order to transfer him to new duty, where he was to be intimately involved in not only the development but also the delivery of the weapon.[1]

The Manhattan Project, under the direction of Maj. Gen. (then) Leslie Groves, Army Civil Engineer Corps, was the organization established for the development of the atomic bomb. Groves built and presided over a vast empire that consisted of thousands of people involved in the myriad of duties that were involved. At Los Alamos, an assemblage of top-level scientists was serving under the direction of Robert Oppenheimer. There were a few regular and many reserve naval officers in the organization, recruited mostly for their special scientific skills. The most prestigious and scientifically astute was Capt. (then) William "Deak" Parsons, who was essentially Oppen-

Dick Ashworth, naval aviator, commanding Torpedo Squadron Eleven, Guadalcanal, early World War II. Ashworth collection.

heimer's deputy. Parsons's principal task was to take the product the scientists were developing and engineer it so that it could be delivered, in some manner, on an enemy target. Ashworth was ordered to report for duty to Parsons, an officer whom Ashworth described as "one of the most outstanding ordnance experts in naval history." Ashworth could not have been more pleased to serve as Parsons's backup. The gun club now had two prestigious members on the atomic team, and a good case can be made that naval aviation's entry into atomic weaponry started with Dick Ashworth's arrival on the scene.

Ashworth's duties were varied. Some of the critical flight tests for various components of the bomb were conducted at the Army air base in Wendover, Utah, utilizing Army Air Forces B-29 bombers. He was to supervise and coordinate these testing programs, although he could not see that the scientists and engineers in Los Alamos needed much supervision or coordination from a new Navy commander. He also served as a gofer for Oppenheimer and Captain Parsons, delivering messages to key personnel, such as Adm. Chester Nimitz, concerning progress on the weapon. He spent time in Washington, pressuring the services to order properly qualified personnel, commissioned and enlisted, to the project. This was not always easy, since the level of imposed secrecy prohibited personnel officers from realizing the significance of the work to be done and the priority it was to receive. However, the code name Silverplate was assigned to the project, giving it the highest priority. This had a significant effect, particularly within the Army Air Forces.

Ashworth's most important assignment had to do with the delivery of the bomb. He believed that General Groves was already looking ahead to the time when these bombs would be delivered on the enemy, whether Germany or Japan. Germany, certainly contemplated as a target, was defeated before the bomb was ready. It became clear later that General Groves wanted someone in the bombing aircraft reporting to him, someone who had been exposed to the bomb development and therefore would be able to make good technical and tactical decisions. Ashworth was sure that person was Captain Parsons. Since Groves always insisted on having a spare for everything, he needed a backup for Parsons, and that turned out to be Ashworth.

Ashworth had no special training in nuclear physics, so he was fortunate that Captain Parsons arranged for him to have a desk in his office in Los Alamos. Consequently, Ashworth was able to listen in on many important technical discussions between Captain Parsons and his associates in the laboratory. In addition, he was permitted to attend the colloquia that were held each week to discuss the week's technical problems and develop fixes for them. He was not able to absorb much of what went on but found it fascinating to watch Oppenheimer lead these meetings. The top scientific people in the lab always attended these colloquia—Niels Bohr, Eugene Wigner, Victor Weisskopf, Hans Bethe, and Isador Rabi—many of whom were Nobel laureates, or would be. The average age of the scientists was twenty-nine.

By listening and learning what they were trying to do, Ashworth began to understand the engineering tasks associated with the project.

Ashworth felt that someone with a background like his would probably provide a more pragmatic approach to the operational aspects than would be provided by the scientists and engineers in the lab. However, more important was the fact that the aircraft crews that would man these aircraft in combat operations simply did not have exposure to the technical characteristics of the bombs. Up until the night of the preflight briefing for the Hiroshima operation, no one in the 509th Bomb Group had any knowledge of the ultimate mission of the group except Paul Tibbets, the twenty-nine-year-old Army Air Forces colonel in command of the group. Ashworth felt that Tibbets had been given very little technical knowledge of the bomb design.

One of Ashworth's most significant duties was the selection of the site for basing the aircraft and support facilities for the delivery of the bomb. In February 1945 Ashworth was directed to carry a secret letter to Guam and hand it personally to Admiral Nimitz. This letter would inform Nimitz for the first time that an atomic bomb was under development and would be available to him in the Pacific about the first of August 1945.

Ashworth traveled from Washington directly to Guam wearing the ordinary cotton khaki uniform of that period. He carried the letter in a money belt around his waist. When he arrived, he went directly to the headquarters of Admiral Nimitz, who was amused to see Ashworth open his uniform jacket and unbutton his shirt to extract the money belt. After the long trip, the belt was a bit the worse for wear, and its contents a little stained and damp from sweat. However, it was in good enough shape for the admiral to open and read it.

The letter was addressed "Dear Nimitz" and signed "King"—Adm. Ernest King, the chief of naval operations. It informed Nimitz that the explosive yield of the bomb would be about eight thousand tons of TNT equivalent, the best estimate at the time of the expected yield; that support of his command would be required; and that he was authorized to inform only one officer on his staff about the venture.

When Nimitz had finished, he rang for the chief of staff, Adm. Charles H. "Soc" McMorris, and handed him the letter. He told Ashworth to tell Admiral King that he could not provide the services that he knew would be required by this project without his operations officer, Capt. Tom Hill, being aware of the program. Then he pointed out that it was now only February. Didn't they know back there that he had a lot of war to fight before August? Why couldn't he have the bomb now?

Ashworth described briefly the status of development of the weapons and told Nimitz that August first was selected by General Groves as the first realistic date that the bomb would be ready for delivery. Nimitz turned in his chair, looked out the window for several seconds, then turned back and said, "Thank you, Commander. I guess that I was born just about twenty years too soon." Ashworth felt that Nimitz sensed the magnitude of the bomb. Perhaps he also saw that the bomb might hold a possibility of ending the war.

Included in the King to Nimitz letter was the statement that Ashworth would be exploring the western Pacific area for space that would be occupied ultimately by the 509th Bomb Group and the Los Alamos scientists and engineers who would soon take the project into the forward area. Nimitz was to provide Ashworth with the support needed to do this part of his job. The selection of the island was easy for Ashworth. Guam was too far south; Saipan was the most northern suitable site but did not have the air operations facilities that were available on Tinian. Most importantly, Japan was within range of Tinian, and the buildup of the B-29 bombing against Japan from that area was increasing in intensity. Therefore, Tinian was selected as the site for the forward base. Captain Parsons never questioned Ashworth's decision.

Many questions have been asked over the years about why naval officers, Parsons and Ashworth, were included in the crews of the aircraft that delivered the bombs on Hiroshima and Nagasaki, since it was essentially an Air Force delivery mission. Parsons and Ashworth were to be designated "weaponeers," a term dreamed up by Parsons to define the duties of General Groves's Los Alamos representative,

Tinian Island, 1945. Ashworth collection.

who would be on board the aircraft carrying the bomb. General Groves was concerned about the possibility of crises that might develop during the actual bombing operations, crises that would require decisions by someone who could evaluate the situation from a technical and tactical point of view — tactical because it was possible that the situation might dictate deviations from the delivery plan. To the best of Ashworth's knowledge, he and Parsons were the only officers at Los Alamos that fit Groves's requirements. Only Colonel Tibbets had been briefed about the mission of the 509th Bomb Group, and that briefing was comparatively superficial. General Groves did not want the bomb treated as "just another bomb." Maj. Charles Sweeney, the pilot of the B-29 that dropped the bomb on Nagasaki, had learned something about the bomb because it was his organization that provided the B-29 services for the tests at Wendover. However, he had no firsthand knowledge of the technical details. After the Hiroshima

The Nagasaki cloud. Ashworth collection.

bomb was dropped, the secret was out, and the airmen were well aware that they were doing something special.

Parsons was the obvious choice for this weaponeer job. It was always Groves's policy to have spares of everything throughout the project. Since Ashworth met the criteria, he became the spare for Parsons. Just before the Hiroshima operation, Groves told Parsons and Ashworth that they would alternate on each tactical mission. Ashworth believes that Groves's rationale was the anticipated need for more than two bombing operations. Ashworth doubted that anyone involved had any idea that only one or two bombs would do the job.

Historians have often asked the question, "How many bombs did we have?" Ashworth recalls that Groves's answer was always, "Enough." Plutonium was being created in amounts that would make another bomb available about the first of September. By that time, the war would be over.

In his book, General Groves tells about a message that was sent on 29 May by Gen. Lauris Norstad, who was in charge in Washington of all B-29 operations throughout the world.[2] This message said in effect that the bomb-carrying aircraft would have two officer specialists on board, the senior of whom would have final judgment should decisions be required as a result of deviations from the tactical operational plan. The second specialist would be an Army technical officer who would assist by operating the "black box" that monitored the status of all electronic parts of the bomb en route to the targets. Obviously, command relations were extremely important on these missions.

In mid-June the Los Alamos contingent of scientists and engineers who were to constitute the overseas party began arriving at Tinian. A squadron of fifteen specially configured B-29 aircraft arrived under the command of Colonel Tibbets, who was to pilot the *Enola Gay,* the aircraft slated to drop the gun-type Little Boy on Hiroshima. The second bomb, the implosion-type Fat Man, was to be dropped from a B-29 piloted by Major Sweeney. The squadron had been training at Wendover in Utah and later from Batista Field in Cuba, practicing long over-water navigation flights.

On 16 July 1945 a major test of the Fat Man was conducted at Alamogordo, New Mexico. The test was called "Trinity." Results exceeded all expectations of those who were there to see it fired. The fateful bomb deliveries were beginning to materialize.

History is replete with accounts of the dropping of the bombs. Ashworth's personal account is probably one of the best and most accurate. He was very much a part of the scientific as well as the operational aspects of the entire operation. He points out that the Manhattan Project was not recruiting personnel or planning for just two bombs. This was to be an ongoing operation. There seemed to be no limitations to how many bombs might be required—General Groves's philosophy at work. The project did things in a big way and left no loose ends.

Although only two bombs were dropped, plans for future weapons centered on the Fat Man–type of bomb because it was more efficient. That concept emerged with the success of the Trinity shot at Alamogordo and was confirmed with the success of the bomb dropped on Nagasaki.

The entire effort was scheduled to be complete by the first of August 1945, when General Groves had said that all should be ready for the combat operations. This was an educated estimate with input from all parts of the project that would be involved in meeting the date. The target date was met. However, a small typhoon near Japan precluded any bombing operations, and the weather forecasters believed that it would be five or six days before the disturbance cleared out and bombing would be possible. Thus, the target date for the Hiroshima attack was set for the sixth of August.

A report to General Groves on the results of the mission was transmitted as soon as the crew was debriefed, and it was at this time that President Harry S. Truman was informed of those results. He was on his way home from the Potsdam conference on board the USS *Augusta*. The public announcement was made from the ship—and the secret was out. The United States had attacked Japan with an atomic bomb, and the mission had been most successful.

While the Hiroshima mission with the Little Boy bomb had gone smoothly, such was not the case with the mission to Nagasaki. Starting with a fuel problem that required the first modification of the flight plan, things began to get worse. Confusion in communications at the rendezvous point with the supporting aircraft added to the difficulties, resulting in concern about the possibility of a fuel shortage and the chances of completing the mission without landing in the water. Another concern was the weather over the primary target, Kokura. Following three abortive attempts to drop the bomb, the city was saved by the weather, and Nagasaki became the target. Even there, the weather almost prevented a drop. The approach to the target was made on radar, and only the last few seconds of the bombing run provided sufficient visibility for a visual identification of the target. Then came a tense, low-fuel state flight to the nearest airfield in Okinawa. The mission was completed successfully. Fat Man showed that it could be the bomb design for the future, but it had not been an easy flight. Dick Ashworth has lived with the story for the more than fifty years since its occurrence and has told it many times in various formats.

Following the filing of their action report by the crew of the *Enola Gay,* it was just a matter of refueling and flying back to Tinian. The radio operator had the intercom system plugged into the radio, and the crew could listen to music and news reports. It was then that they learned that the Soviets had joined the war against Japan and that the Japanese had approached the Swiss with a request for them to explore the possibilities of peace arrangements with the Allies. In the flush of the excitement, they could not help feeling that they had won the war.

Obviously, the war had been won long before the two atom bomb operations, but the Japanese had refused to surrender. In the final analysis, Ashworth believed that it was safe to say that the bomb attacks ended the war, for this gave the emperor the leverage with the War Council to demand that surrender terms be offered to the Allies. These considerations invariably lead to questions of whether we should have used the bombs from a strategic standpoint and whether it was morally right to have done so.

When asked, "Do you have any regrets about your part in these operations?" Ashworth's answer has always been, "No, this was war to be pursued to unconditional surrender, a policy established by the Combined Chiefs of Staff long before these operations took place. How much different were these attacks than the fire raid on Tokyo in March 1945 when probably 100,000 people were killed and more than sixteen square miles of the city destroyed? That does not make it any better. But it was wartime."[3] Ashworth had this to say about the future:

I cannot conclude this discussion of the Nagasaki mission, the last use in wartime of an atom bomb, without saying a few things about the future. I think that it is safe to say that no one involved in the development of the bombs from the highest command levels to us working folks had any realistic concept of the magnitude of the devastation one of these so called nominal 20,000-ton energy equivalent bombs would cause. Oppenheimer might be one who did. From the Bhagavad-Gita in Sanskrit that he could recite from memory, "Now I have become death, the destroyer of worlds."

However, when one reads the recorded impressions of those who witnessed the Trinity test, particularly the scientists most closely involved in the development of the bomb, you find that their reaction was concentrated on the awesome technical magnitude of the thing. On the other hand General [Thomas] Farrell's first remark to General Groves was "The war is over," what one might expect from a military man.

Remember, we had yet to understand the magnitude of the devastation of an atom bomb explosion in terms of the total destruction of a city's infrastructure, the total elimination of the fire and police departments, elimination of the medical and hospital facilities and people, total destruction of all communications and yes, the magnitude of the results of the prompt and residual radiation. Had we understood that degree of devastation at the time, the question as to the use of the bombs might have been looked at in a different light, rather than from its purely military significance. However, there was at the time, no other measure to cause it to be considered. It was just another weapon in the arsenals of war. That is what Truman called it when he stated something to the effect, "This is a weapon of war. Of course we will use it."[4]

In the fall of 1995, two articles recounting the Hiroshima and Nagasaki attacks centered on the command pilots, Colonel Tibbets and Colonel Sweeney, relating their recollections.[5] Their accounts agree very closely with the narration by Dick Ashworth. It is remarkable that fifty years after the dropping of the atom bombs, the principals still had similar recollections. It is obvious that the events were deeply ingrained in their memories.

Ashworth left Tinian about the tenth of September and returned to Los Alamos. There were many loose ends to be handled at the laboratory that required continuing Navy input. Comdr. Tom Walker was nominated by Ashworth as his relief, and Capt. Dick Larkin relieved Parsons. Parsons and Ashworth were ordered to Washington to organize the Atomic Energy Division in the Office of the Chief of Naval Operations, which, after some fits and starts, ultimately became OP-36.

Naval aviation had entered the field of nuclear warfare with a bright young aviator as its first participant. He was tutored and mentored by a brilliant naval captain, "Deak" Parsons, an outstanding ordnance specialist. That tutoring, coupled with Ashworth's professional competence, provided naval aviation with a sound foundation for its future role in nuclear warfare. The worth of Ashworth's role in the Manhattan Project was well expressed by Lieutenant General Groves in an official letter he wrote to Ashworth, dated 29 February 1948. At that time, Groves was head of the Armed Forces Special Weapons Project.

I wish to express my appreciation for the part you played in our success. When I approved of your selection as the weaponeer for the Nagasaki bombing mission I did so with confidence that you would ensure the success of that operation no matter what difficulties were encountered. My confidence was not misplaced despite the fact that the difficulties proved to be far greater than any of us had anticipated. Knowing today the extent of the actual problems with which you were faced I am certain that there are few officers who would have been as wise a choice for the assignment. Your good judgment, determination, and courage were of the utmost value in bringing complete success out of what came so close to being disastrous failure.

The impact of the bomb on national and international security was immediately apparent to many. While some tried to pass it off as just another weapon, anyone cognizant of its tremendous destructive capabilities and what could be produced in the future knew that this bomb was not just another weapon by any means. The nation's leadership was forced to consider its impact on world affairs. A new national policy and strategy for implementing that policy had to be developed. The Soviet Union immediately became a critical factor in the policy discussions.

2. Policy and Strategy

The policy for the use of nuclear weapons had to be considered immediately after the Hiroshima and Nagasaki bombings. It was obvious that this new weapon would call for considerable modifications to, if not a complete overhaul of, our national security policy. President Truman was the first president forced to face the issue. For the United States and the Allies, World War II might have been over, but for the Soviets, the second phase was just beginning. Soviet plans for Communist domination of the free world led to the Cold War. As a consequence, national security policies and strategies were under constant study and revision.

Policy

The initial approach of the United States to the atomic issue centered on international control, a generous concept of sharing the mysteries of atomic energy with the world. It is hard to believe that in light of the thousands of nuclear weapons that have been produced since the attacks on Japan in 1945, the initial reaction in the United States was to establish some kind of international control including the banning of "the bomb." In October 1945, Gen. George C. Marshall, the chairman of the Joint Chiefs, discussed that issue with his colleagues, who agreed to present to the president a strong statement of military support for the position that, if adequate safeguards could be established, elimination of atomic weapons through negotiated settlement was in the national interest.[1] It is widely believed, particularly in U.S. Navy circles, that immediately following World War II, the Army Air Forces took the position that they should dominate the defense establishment of the United States, relying on the nuclear weapon as a mainstay. Joint Chiefs of Staff historical records do not support that view. On 29 March 1946, the Joint Chiefs of Staff approved a paper, JCS 1477/10, that stressed, "American security required a large force posture with considerable capabilities to conduct non-nuclear as well as nuclear operations." As the paper worked though its various versions, Gen. Carl A. Spaatz, then the Air Force chief of staff, asked for a change in wording to avoid suggesting, even indirectly, that the atomic bomb had been the decisive weapon in World War II.[2]

The Berlin crisis in 1948 made it clear that the attainment of international control or banning of the bomb was not realistic. The Soviets simply would not settle for the United States being the only nuclear power. They wanted a capability of their own and set about to gain one. Therefore, President Truman was forced to approve the development of a capability to produce nuclear materials and to authorize the production of atomic bombs as a counter to the Soviet threat. The race was on.

The rapid expansion of the Soviet empire throughout Eastern Europe was the major concern in developing a national security policy. In addition to their own conventional warfare capability, the Soviets acquired vast additional resources, particularly people, in their rapid territorial and political expansion. It would have been impossible for the United States and its allies to stem the Soviet tide without returning to an all-out wartime footing. There was no stomach in the allied camp for that kind of action. The trump card was the nuclear weapon, and the United States played it. The bomb would be the equalizer.

A "roll-back" policy was not realistic. Getting the Soviets to relinquish any of their territorial gains without full-scale warfare was out of the question. "Retarding" their expansion was considered essential, and overt action was taken to counter the Soviet efforts in Greece and overcome the blockade of Berlin with a massive airlift during the crisis of 1948. That was followed by the Korean War in the early 1950s. "Retarding" changed to "containment"—keeping the Soviet Union within its existing boundaries and prohibiting further expansion. The containment policy could be implemented only by the threat of the use of the bomb. As the Soviets developed their own nuclear weapons capability, the containment policy evolved into one of "deterrence"—deterring the Soviets from initiating any aggressive military action using the bomb, particularly against the allied powers. That deterrence became "mutual" rather rapidly with the escalating abilities of both superpowers to create massive destruction with nuclear weapons.

The policy for accommodating the atomic weapon was pursued vigorously by Gen. Dwight D. Eisenhower when he became president of the United States in January 1953. He inherited at least two major national security problems from his predecessor. The first was the Korean War, which he rapidly brought to a close. The second, which probably turned out to be more frustrating and more significant, was the emerging nuclear weapons issue.

One of the major accomplishments of the Eisenhower administration in its early days was the development and formalization of a long-range policy and strategy to accommodate the nuclear weapon. Building on the start made by the Truman administration, the policy of containment with an implementing strategy built around the bomb was endorsed and expanded. Later, as the Soviets acquired a significant nuclear capability of their own, the deterrence policy evolved, aimed at keeping the Soviet Union, or any nation, from using nuclear weapons. Truman's authorization of the use of the weapon in World War II and his approval of the production of atomic materials and weapons, coupled with Eisenhower's policies of containment and deterrence, set the stage for the buildup of a major nuclear weapons stockpile.

Eisenhower's basic philosophy in addressing the evolving Cold War conflict with the Soviet Union could be expressed as "strength with civility."[3] His experience with the Soviets during World War II would have prevented him from referring to them as "an evil empire," but he also understood that they respected strength. There was a need to be stronger than the Soviets, and the nuclear weapon provided a means for achieving that strength. He was going to have a superior capability but was not going to be bellicose with the Soviets about the issue. What strategy for using the bomb could be developed to implement the policy objectives of containment and deterrence?

Strategy

While there was relatively little argument among leaders in the United States concerning the acceptance of the containment policy, the development of the implementing strategy evoked probably the most emotional and vicious arguments that our armed forces have experienced. Who was to have the mission of delivering the bomb should such action be required? Arriving at an answer to that question took some time, and the episode provides perfect justification for civilian control over the military. Had the generals and admirals been left to themselves in answering the question of nuclear strategy, it is hard to predict the outcome. The United States had to have the civil authority to resolve such matters, and to their great credit, military leaders understood that principle—and still do.

In developing a strategy and associated military capability for implementing the containment policy, several factors had to be considered. The first was the availability of atomic weapons. The production of the Fat Man bomb used at Nagasaki was not an assembly line operation by any means. There was a very limited source of atomic materials and no capability of producing enough to implement a containment policy. Had the Japanese not surrendered after the Nagasaki bombing, the United States probably could have dropped two more bombs at most. Limited resources had an impact on the military forces to be assigned the nuclear mission, the implementers of the evolving strategy.

It made sense to assign the mission of delivering the bomb to the Air Force. They had proven the delivery capability of the B-29 bomber with the two raids on Japan. The plane could carry the 10,000-pound payload and accommodate the massive size of the weapon. That fact, coupled with the limited source of nuclear bomb materials, made it logical to concentrate the mission in a proven military force. Unfortunately, the Air Force chose not to settle for that mission alone.

For many years, the concept of a unified service had surfaced occasionally in the higher echelons of our national security. The Air Force essentially became a third service during World War II, occupying a seat at the Joint Chiefs of Staff meetings and being intimately involved in all campaigns. The Marine Corps was still an integral element of the Navy, but the Army coveted the Marine mission. Naval aviation was particularly vulnerable, and the Air Force contended that anything that flew should be assigned to the Air Force. Naval aviation could see the end of the road for all those aircraft carriers, despite their outstanding performance during World War II. Further, if the carriers were eliminated, it would not be long before the remainder of naval aviation would be eliminated or assigned to other services, most probably the Air Force.

Predictably, arguments surfaced calling for unification of the armed services, to which the Navy violently objected. It was a logical objection in that sea power is not easily integrated with other elements of warfare. The Army wanted to abolish or absorb the Marine Corps. The Air Force not only wanted to absorb all air operations but also would have placed major emphasis on the strategic bombing forces. The creation of the Strategic Air Command (SAC) was a major action, setting up a so-called specified command with the express mission of delivering nuclear weapons on any target anywhere in the world. That action alienated many members of the tactical air units in the Air Force. Naval aviation and the Tactical Air Command (TAC) of the Air Force found themselves with a common antagonist, the bombers of World War II. An interservice rivalry evolved with an ever-increasing intensity that was not pretty.

General Spaatz, a great leader of the Air Force during World War II, reflected the views of many in the Air Force when he said, "Why should we have a Navy at all? The Russians have little or no navy, the Japanese Navy has been sunk, the Germans never did have much of a navy. The only reason for us to have a Navy is because someone else has a navy and we certainly do not need to waste money on that."[4] Then spoke Gen. James Doolittle, the leader of the attack on Tokyo in 1942, who had flown a B-25 bomber from the flight deck of the carrier USS *Hornet:* "The [aircraft] carrier has reached, probably, its highest degree of development. I feel it has reached its highest usefulness now and that it is going into obsolescence. The carrier has two attributes. One attribute is that it can move about; the other is that it can be sunk. As soon as airplanes are developed with sufficient range so that they can go any place that we want them to go, or when we have bases that will permit us to go any place we want to go, there will be no further use for aircraft carriers."[5]

Here was a man who had been forced to use a carrier to get close enough to the target to make a one-way attack and, but a short time later, became one of the leaders attempting to eliminate the base that enabled him to make a major contribution to the war effort.

Others spoke up, as well. Brig. Gen. Frank Armstrong gave a speech in one of the centers of U.S. naval activity, Norfolk, Virginia:

You gentlemen had better understand that the Army Air Force is tired of being a subordinate outfit. It was a predominant force during the war, and it is going to be a predominant force during the peace, and you might as well make up your minds whether you like it or not, and we do not care whether you like it or not. The Army Air Force is going to run the show.

You, the Navy, are not going to have anything but a couple of carriers that are ineffective anyway, and they will probably be sunk in the first battle.

Now as for the Marines, you know what the Marines are, a small bitched-up army talking Navy lingo. We are going to put those Marines in the Regular Army and make efficient soldiers out of them.[6]

The Navy was greatly concerned—and for good cause. The emphasis on the bomb in national strategy and the assignment of the operational mission to the Air Force created an attitude of desperation. Visions of the end of naval aviation and even the Navy itself surfaced. The Navy position is well summed up by one student of the Cold War in discussing the intense interservice rivalry that existed at the end of World War II.

Finally, there was the unconscious smugness of the U.S. Navy itself. The Navy assumed that the American people understood that World War II could not possibly have been won by the United States and its allies without mastery of the sea: that they understood the long and bitter struggle against the German U-boats; that the so-called "strategic" bombing campaign against Germany conducted by the Army Air Force and the Royal Air Force would literally have not gotten off the ground without victory at sea on the North Atlantic; and that the long-range bombing campaign against Japan was possible only as a result of the Navy–Marine Corps amphibious team seizing islands for bases and as a result of ships delivering the bombs, fuel, and the multitude of logistics support required by the B-29s.

The Navy assumed that all this was understood; but it was an assumption in which the Navy was wrong.[7]

In time, the Navy organized its opposition to the exclusive assignment of the nuclear mission to the Air Force. Some of the more rational arguments were traditional treatises on the need for sea power, but those that received the most attention were the attacks on the evolving massive B-36 intercontinental bomber, which pitted the approved new carrier, the USS *United States* (CVA-58), against the bomber.

Adm. Arthur Radford headed the opposition, and Capts. (then) Arleigh Burke, Don Griffin, and John Crommelin supported him. Crommelin's tactics involved leaks to the press, resulting in the termination of his career. Burke was removed from the promotion list to the rank of rear admiral but later reinstated by President Truman. Some of the tactics employed were not becoming officers and gentlemen. One Navy team member fabricated a fictitious charge of fraud in the production of the B-36.

The Navy finally was able to obtain hearings on the issue with the Armed Services Committee in the House of Representatives. The Honorable Carl Vinson, presiding, said, "You need not have a Navy if you haven't any aviation. You might just as well scrap your ships if you don't have a strong aviation branch in the naval service, because the day is past when you can maintain a Navy without sufficient aviation."[8] During the hearings held by the House of Representatives, Gen. Omar Bradley, U.S. Army, testified in his position as the chairman of the Joint Chiefs of Staff. He let the Navy and the public know where he stood on the subject of the Navy, Marines, and carrier aviation. In his closing argument against the Navy's new carrier, he emphasized that the United States would carry the war to the enemy by means of strategic bombing and large-scale land operations, that the sea-going Navy was vulnerable to atomic attack, and that amphibious operations would be of questionable value in the future. In his final statements, he remarked, "I have participated in the two largest amphibious assaults ever made in history [and] in neither case were any Marines present. And in neither case were any Navy carriers present."[9]

He was referring to the amphibious operations at Sicily and Normandy. Carriers had not been involved, for there were land bases available for tactical air support. Literally thousands of aircraft were involved in the D-Day landings alone. On the other hand, the battles for Saipan, Iwo Jima, and Okinawa in the Pacific were fought to obtain bases for the operation of shore-based bombing aircraft. Carriers had to provide the supporting tactical air strikes in all of those campaigns. In the Pacific, the carriers were essential, but not so in the

European campaign. Bradley made a lot out of the necessity for teamwork, but he was certainly questioning the usefulness of one key member of the team—and he was the top man in our armed forces. Obviously, Bradley did not like the Navy, referring to its admirals as "fancy Dans" and claiming that their vigorous opposition to the total concentration on strategic bombing was a disservice to the country.

It was not a happy time and not a very good example of harmony among the leaders of our armed forces. How fast the bomb changed military unity! The strong cohesive force of World War II, with leaders from West Point, Annapolis, and other major military officer programs, had worked closely together for the ultimate victory. These same leaders were now displaying the worst in military arrogance and a paranoid dedication to their own particular fraternity, largely because of the bomb. It was despicable, a demonstration that hopefully will never be repeated again.[10]

It would be difficult to identify the specific individual or group of individuals who originated the idea of merging the aircraft carrier with the atomic bomb. Not many could have been involved, for very few knew anything about the bomb, much less the possibilities for future development. However, World War II proved early on that carrier aircraft of the future would have to be able to travel farther and carry heavier loads, because the targets under attack would not be limited to ships alone. In World War II, ships were the primary targets during the early years. Then military shore installations and industrial facilities became part of the system of targets. People, per se, were never the prime targets. Reaching land-based facilities generated a requirement for more range and bigger payloads. That realization could have started with the Doolittle raid on Japan in the spring of 1942. The sixteen twin-engine B-25 Army Air Forces bomber aircraft used in that raid, flying from the USS *Hornet,* were not carrier aircraft, but they demonstrated that an aircraft with their range and payload capability had to be in the cards for naval aviation in the future.

Vice Adm. Dick Ashworth recalls that during their days together at Los Alamos, Deak Parsons talked a lot about nuclear power for ships and submarines, visualizing also the use of a missile from the atomic-powered submersible. This was long before Hyman Rickover began to surface as an atomic energy guru.

Parsons expressed his views on the future of atomic energy for the Navy in a memorandum to his superior, the deputy chief of naval operations for plans and policy, in late March 1946. He gives evidence of his farsighted vision on the subject—its capabilities and some of the problems to be encountered.

As far as uranium and plutonium fission bombs are concerned, nuclear physics research is completed except to search for more efficient tampers, which would permit reduction in the amount of active material required per bomb. Carrying fission bombs in smaller airplanes than the B-29 or as the warhead of a guided missile will require engineering development not in the field of nuclear physics.

For the present (1946–1949) it is highly unlikely that the fission bomb can be engineered for delivery technique differing radically from that used at Hiroshima and Nagasaki. Thus as a weapon of the present and the immediate future the fission bomb is of primary interest to the AAF (Army Air Forces). In the late 1940s and early 1950s, it is probable that engineering of the bomb and progress in guided missiles will permit launching a fission bomb in the warhead of a guided missile of moderate range (300 to 500 miles). This launching could well be from a submarine or surface vessel. There is thus a definite primary naval application in sight even if the 1950 fission bomb could not be effectively delivered by any airplane smaller than a 4-engine bomber.[11]

Parsons goes on in his memo to address atomic power for ship propulsion, stating, "It is the obvious first feasible use of this phenomenon." He was predicting the future very accurately.

The weapons for the smaller aircraft, including those operating from carriers, came about in the early 1950s, just as Parsons had predicted. In the late 1950s the Navy had a very credible cruise missile called the Regulus, which was launched from a surfaced submarine, range about 400 nautical miles. It carried a small nuclear warhead, just as Parsons had predicted. Parsons has to be credited as one of the best thinkers the United States had at the time concerning the uses of atomic energy. He played a major role in getting the military services headed down the nuclear energy road.

In June 1946, Parsons's boss, Rear Adm. (then) Jerauld Wright, wrote a memo to the Operations Directorate of the Navy staff stating that "atomic weapons are the most logical justification for construction of a large carrier and twin engine carrier planes for the 1948 building program."[12] Those who had not known much about atomic energy were becoming educated by Parsons—and wheels began to spin.

In early August 1946, Wright sent a letter to Vice Admiral Blandy, who was in the Pacific conducting the atomic bomb tests called Crossroads. Wright reported that the secretary of the Navy had addressed the subject of atomic weapons for carriers to the president and that the president's reply was favorable. He then related that the chief of naval operations had met with General Groves, who was still heading the Manhattan Project. However, since the president had approved the establishment of the Atomic Energy Commission, Groves's status as the head of the Manhattan Project would shortly be terminated. Therefore, it was decided that the Navy should take immediate action while Groves was still in office to gain his clearance for the people necessary to enable the Bureau of Aeronautics to design an aircraft for the bomb and the Bureau of Ships to modify carriers and, if necessary, to assemble and prepare the bomb for use.[13] Support for the concept was strong in the proper circles of the executive branch.

Dick Ashworth believed that Chick Hayward might have been one of the first to consider aircraft carriers as a base for the delivery of nuclear weapons. Hayward had been flying some B-29 test flights from the Naval Ordnance Test Station in China Lake, where he was the experimental officer, testing various components of the bomb. He may have known more about the bomb than others, for he had occasional meetings with Deak Parsons and was involved in the actual testing of components other than the atomic material. Hayward recalls discussions with Parsons about the need to reduce the size and weight of the bomb and gives Parsons credit for foreseeing that tactical aircraft could eventually employ such weapons. That meant aircraft carriers for the Navy.[14]

Dick Ashworth started thinking about mixing carrier aircraft and the atomic bomb not long after he concluded his duties with the wartime operations of the atomic weapon program. During World War II, the maximum weight for most bombs was 2,000 pounds. Toward the end of the war, a requirement from the forward area was placed on the Navy Bureau of Aeronautics in Washington for an aircraft that could carry a bomb of 8,000 pounds and operate from a carrier. When Ashworth heard that, it was apparent to him that any aircraft that was fitted for an 8,000-pound bomb might be modified to carry a Fat Man–type weapon of 10,000 pounds and operate from an aircraft carrier. Interest began to rise in bringing the Navy into an atomic bomb capability from the carriers.[15]

In December 1947, Rear Adm. Daniel V. Gallery wrote a top-secret memorandum to the Navy military hierarchy laying out his views on the issue. The memo was leaked to the leading gossipmonger of the press at that time, Drew Pearson, who published the entire memo in his column over three days. The publicity made Gallery a "controversial" figure, but anyone who has studied the delivery systems and strategies that have evolved over the years can see that Gallery was obviously well ahead of his time. His memorandum is representative of the strategic thinking that was emerging in the Navy and is evidence of how military officers can become "controversial," often choosing to risk their careers rather than abandon a principle they feel very strongly about. The serious nature of his message and the fact that it flew in the face of an approved strategy was evidence of his personal courage.

Gallery contended that the major mission of the Navy should be the delivery of an atomic attack on the capital and industrial centers of the enemy. Its secondary mission should be control of the seas. For the Air Force, the mission should be the defense of the United States against air attack, including atomic bombs. A secondary mission would be the delivery of atomic attacks against the enemy from overseas bases. One can imagine the impact his concept had on the Air Force and the civil authority that was content with the atomic mission being assigned to the Air Force. The debates and interservice rivalry over the issue mounted in intensity and added to the building "revolt of the admirals."

Gallery's reasoning about the strategic mission for atomic weapons was logical—at least to him. He argued that it made more sense to build a carrier aircraft that could go 1,000 miles with a decent payload from a forward-deployed carrier than to build a long-range bomber that would have to travel the entire route to the target from some distant shore base, a base that might first have to be wrested from the enemy. His objective was a 1,000-mile carrier aircraft instead of a 5,000-mile bomber.

One of the major objections to his concept was the idea that the naval delivery of the atomic weapon would be essentially a one-time mission for the delivery aircraft. The plane would not require landing gear for returning to the carrier, and following delivery, it would proceed to land in the water at the location of a rescue submarine. He considered that the significance of the atomic bomb mission was such that it justified the loss of an aircraft: "one bomb, one city."[16] The rescue of the crew was all that mattered after delivery of the bomb. His one-way-mission concept turned aside many people, and yet it was not as far fetched as it sounded. Consider the Doolittle raid launched from the USS *Hornet* in 1942. The B-25 aircraft used in that raid could not land aboard a carrier, and the planned landings on friendly fields in China or the Soviet Union did not enjoy a high probability of success. Suppose those aircraft had been equipped for landing at sea near a rescue submarine. Would we have had more success with the rescue of the crew members?

How about the expenditure of the aircraft? Our leaders must have considered that the risk and the loss of the B-25 aircraft were well worth the impact on the morale of both the United States and Japanese citizenry. Should not the targets of an atomic attack enjoy the same trade-off values? One bomb, one city, one aircraft? It was the crews that presented the return problem, and Gallery's ideas in that regard were not unreasonable in light of the warfare potential of one atomic bomb.

Had Gallery and the nation's leaders had any idea that in the near future, atomic bombs would be lighter, smaller, and possess a much greater explosive yield, his carrier delivery concept surely would have had a greater chance for acceptance. What Gallery did not envision, evidently, was the full capability of the emerging ballistic missile. Its eventual development eclipsed the nuclear weapons aircraft delivery systems of both the Air Force and the Navy.

Of some interest is the treatment afforded Gallery by the civil authority following the unauthorized publication of his classified memorandum. He was in hot water, and the impact on his future career must have been significant. However, in the correspondence forwarding the memo to the secretary of the Navy on 8 April 1948, the chief of naval operations, Adm. Louis Denfeld, called the memo "commendable" and a demonstration of the "type of constructive thinking which the Navy at all times tries to encourage."[17] But the civil authority did not agree.

Later, Gallery wrote an article for the old *Collier's* magazine, including an account of his disagreements with the secretary of defense and the secretary of the Navy. That got him into more hot water. Eventually the matter was referred to the new chief of naval operations, Adm. Forrest Sherman. Sherman issued a letter of admonition to Gallery, who considered it comparable to a commendation, considering that he initially believed he was going to be court-martialed.[18]

In a speech in 1949, Gallery made some prophetic remarks concerning the direction the strategy was taking. "A strategy based on the sole objective of preventing defeat in war is an unworthy one for a country of our strength. . . . It is a strategy of desperation and weakness. . . . I believe we should abandon the idea of destroying enemy cities one after another until he gives up and find some better way of gaining our objective."[19] In any event, Gallery's strategy did not sell. His later assignment in guided missile programs put him in the forefront of the development of the submarine-launched ballistic missile, but further promotions in rank were not to be.

Another old "sea dog" who had some great thoughts about strategy for the use of nuclear weapons was Rear Adm. George Miller.[20] Miller's thoughts on nuclear weapons strategy were sound and, to some degree, have come to fruition. He insisted that basing our nuclear forces ashore merely provided targets on our land for the opposition to attack. As the enemy attempted to destroy our ability to destroy him, he would place high priority on attacking our nuclear capability. The collateral damage from such counterforce attacks would be tremendous, and millions would die.

Miller reasoned that if we based our nuclear forces at sea, they would be more difficult targets for the enemy to detect and destroy. Further, the weapons aimed at our military forces would not bring our populace under attack. Of course, if the priority of the enemy were the destruction of our urban industrial base (which was the initial priority of the U.S. strategy against the Soviets), many people were going to be killed anyway. But his reasoning made a lot of sense. Basing our nuclear forces at sea would most likely reduce the attacks on our own people.

Consider for example the decision to use the long-range bomber as the primary nuclear weapon delivery vehicle. Initially those aircraft had to be based overseas in order to be close enough to reach the intended targets. However, with the introduction of the B-36 and the B-52 bombers with in-flight refueling, the basing became more concentrated in the United States. As studies were developed and war games played, it became obvious that the first targets of the enemy, particularly of his missile-equipped submarine force, would be the air bases of the Strategic Air Command. The vulnerability of those bases was acknowledged, and great efforts and assets were expended to reduce that vulnerability. Major dispersal programs scattered bombers throughout the airfields of the nation. Special alert facilities were developed, and major readiness exercises were conducted with the objective of getting the force off the ground before it was destroyed by the enemy attack.

Included in the plan was the airborne alert tactic—keeping a certain number of bombers in the air continuously so that in times of high tension, some would already be airborne and ready to head for their targets. They could not be destroyed in the initial counterforce attack by the enemy. Exercises testing this tactic were conducted with some revealing results. An airborne alert flight in 1959 from Westover Air Force Base in the northeast United States took about twenty-five hours to complete. Seven men, a mattress, stacks of box lunches, and two Mark 39 nuclear weapons were on board. Flights were conducted in two-plane "cells," and the bombing wing kept three cells airborne constantly for about one month—a total of six aircraft constantly airborne. The airborne alert operation was feasible. SAC could keep some B-52s in the air around the clock, and there was no question that they could make it to their targets as far as range and payload were concerned. But the cost was tremendous. It took an entire wing of B-52s to keep six continuously airborne. In addition, it required the services of a large number of tanker aircraft, for two air-to-air refuelings were conducted during each twenty-four-hour flight. Further, the consumption of aviation fuel placed a strain on the supply in the northeast United States.[21] Had those weapons and their delivery systems been based at sea, there would have been no requirement for the airborne alert capability or base dispersal.

As intercontinental ballistic missiles came into the inventory of delivery vehicles, basing ashore became the accepted program. Again, studies proved that the silos for launching the missiles were vulnerable. That meant large expenditures of effort and funds to harden the sites, including the design and partial installation of a vast antimissile defense system to protect the siloed missiles. Putting the missiles in sea-based silos (submarines) was George Miller's idea of how to do the job.

During the years of the Reagan presidency, major studies came up with more survivable land-based missile systems. Mobile bases and deceptive basing were part of the effort. Even an idea of the early 1960s was revived. The Strategic Air Command had considered the "mobile Minuteman"—an intercontinental ballistic missile (ICBM) loaded on a special railroad train so that it could be moved about the country, defying the enemy to locate and destroy. Mobility at sea would have been easier to achieve.

George Miller's idea of sea basing was not intended for carriers alone. As the cruise and ballistic missile capabilities of the future became more evident, he started pushing for such weapons to be based in maritime ship hulls, ships that looked like any other merchant ship but contained nuclear weapons and their associated delivery systems as the cargo. George Miller was a maritime strategist of the first order. Adm. Thomas Moorer often referred to him as the Alfred Thayer Mahan of the twentieth century.[22]

Miller's concept of basing at sea was eventually implemented in several ways, although not necessarily because of his efforts to educate and persuade. By the late 1960s, over one-half of our strategic weapon force was based in submarines using ballistic missiles as the ultimate delivery vehicle. By that time, the term "triad" had come into popular use as a description of our strategic nuclear forces. It consisted of the bomber force, the ICBM force, and the submarine-based ballistic missiles. The sea-based leg of our sacred triad came into being strictly based on its tremendous capability to do the job, and most particularly the ability to survive a nuclear conflict. The difficulty of detecting and pinpointing the location of those submarines still guarantees a high probability of success for the mission. One has to question why we continue to base two legs of the triad on land. Perhaps the time has come to capitalize on the new cruise missiles and the older ballistic missiles, housed in survivable submarines or other vehicles at sea. Are the days of the shore-based bomber and the ICBM numbered?

George Miller participated in talk shows and other forums, educating the public and explaining maritime strategy. He always covered the theory, while others concentrated on the specifics of the weapons involved. Miller was never pleased with the results of his efforts. He felt that the Air Force and to some extent the Army had done a better job of selling their concepts of nuclear strategy than he and the Navy had done explaining theirs.

Following World War II, as Parsons and Ashworth joined Vice Admiral Blandy in the formation of the Navy's organization for the atomic program, the idea of the carrier and the nuclear weapon took hold in more positive terms. It was obvious that there was going to be intense interest among the services over the Navy's involvement in atomic warfare. Following Parsons's direction, Ashworth prepared a letter to the president from the secretary of the Navy, James Forrestal, seeking authority to proceed with the project. After some delay, the letter was returned from Secretary Forrestal's office with a note saying that presidential approval would not be required.[23]

The uniformed Navy was cleared to proceed with the program for merging the bomb and the aircraft carrier. The problem for the Navy was the lack of any realistic capability to deliver an atomic weapon. Those weapons were big and heavy, characteristics not compatible with aircraft carrier operations of the time.

3. Weapons

In the late 1930s, a collection of physicists with prominent backgrounds, people such as Lise Meitner and Fritz Strassman, came up with the theory that a derivative of uranium ore could be made to cause a chain reaction—an atomic reaction. If it were a controlled reaction in a reactor, it could be turned into power. If uncontrolled, it could become a bomb. The theory became widely known, and a race began, particularly between Germany and the United States, to produce a useful product. Because of World War II, the bomb—the uncontrolled reaction—became the priority. The United States established the Manhattan Project under Maj. Gen. Leslie Groves and won the race.

Of particular significance to the Navy was the fact that the two bombs developed at Los Alamos were different from each other. The first, known as Little Boy, was relatively simple, based on the straightforward engineering problem of creating a critical mass and a detonation at the same time. The task was to drive two pieces of uranium (U-235) together in some sort of chamber such as a gun barrel. If the assembly were completed under the proper conditions, the resulting mass would go critical and create a chain reaction, and a tremendous amount of energy would be released—an explosion. There was little question that the concept could be engineered and a useful bomb produced that could be dropped on a target from an airplane. That was the weapon dropped on Hiroshima. Its structure was relatively simple compared to the Nagasaki bomb, but it was less efficient.

The second bomb, Fat Man, was more complicated and required a much longer and far more difficult gestation period than Little Boy. For one thing, it used plutonium rather than uranium as the nuclear material. Unlike uranium, plutonium did not exist in a natural state. In order to produce plutonium in useful amounts, it had to be chemically separated from the products of the radiation that took place in a uranium-fueled reactor. In short, Little Boy developed from a mechanical means of making a derivative of uranium into a critical mass. Fat Man required the manufacture of the scarce plutonium and the invention of an entirely different method of creating the critical mass, a feat very difficult to accomplish.

Whereas the uranium derivative in Little Boy could be made to go critical in a simple gun chamber, the same process did not apply for the plutonium weapon. Many hours of frustrating theorizing and experiments were expended before a complicated system of "squeezing" the plutonium could be conceived and engineered to create an explosive critical mass in the plutonium. That process resulted in a massive weapon, about five feet in diameter and weighing about ten thousand pounds. It is interesting to note that the initial size of the system was limited and established by the physical dimensions of the bomb bay of the B-29 aircraft. Anything that size and weight was not welcome on aircraft carriers. The Navy had no vehicle that could carry such a weapon from an aircraft carrier, not to mention the handling, storage, and safety aspects that would be involved.

The plutonium bomb proved to be the weapon of choice for future development because it was far more efficient, and there was a good chance of making it smaller. Consequently, the Navy had to start thinking about large, carrier-compatible aircraft and suitable installations in the carriers for handling such weapons. None of these existed in the Navy, while the Army Air Forces had already proved they had

Fat Man and Little Boy. Photo courtesy of National Atomic Museum.

a realistic capability with the B-29 bomber in dropping the bombs on Japan. It was obvious to the leaders of the Navy that nuclear energy was going to play a major role in future programs and that it was necessary to begin taking action.

As mentioned earlier, one of the first actions by the Navy following World War II was the establishment of an office in Washington, D.C., in the Office of the Chief of Naval Operations. The leader of the office, finally designated OP-36 (deputy chief of naval operations, special weapons), was Vice Admiral Blandy. The assignment of an officer of his rank and ability as the head of the Navy's new "special weapons" office indicated the importance the Navy was placing on this new field of warfare.

With Blandy came Deak Parsons and Dick Ashworth. A fourth member was Capt. Tom B. Hill, who had been operations officer for Admiral Nimitz in the Pacific during the war and who had been responsible for the support given the Manhattan Project for its wartime operations in the Pacific theater. He had been Deak Parsons's roommate while they were midshipmen at the Naval Academy. The fifth member added to the team was Comdr. (then) Horacio Rivero. During the latter part of the war, Rivero served as the executive officer of the new cruiser USS *Pittsburgh*. He was decorated for being instrumental in saving the ship after it lost a large part of its bow during a hurricane in the western Pacific.

Surveying the Damage

One of the first questions to be answered had to do with the yield of the bombs that were dropped on Japan. What was the magnitude of the explosions in terms of blast and heat? General Groves gave priority to this question and asked the Navy to loan Rivets Rivero to him to help find the answers.

Rivero was ordered to proceed to London with British scientist (later Sir) William Penney, who had been at Los Alamos during the development of the bomb and was one of the first to visit the target cities at the conclusion of the war. Penney had obtained some residue from the bomb sites and was prepared to use that material in determining the extent of the damage the atomic bomb could produce. Rivero's role was to assist Penney as necessary, although he thought his main role was to put pressure on Penney to come up with some answers as soon as possible.[1]

Penney was a professor at the University of London, Imperial College, where he had the college laboratory at his disposal. From his tour of Japan, he had brought back some samples of damage, which were the basis for his tests. Penney knew exactly where his samples had come from at the bomb sites. He had road maps of Hiroshima and Nagasaki and had marked the spots where he had found the samples.

One sample was part of an oil drum that had collapsed from the pressure of the atomic bomb. In London, Penney and Rivero procured some oil drums similar to the type damaged in Japan. They subjected these drums to vacuum tests, evacuating them and recording the pressure at which they collapsed. That enabled them to determine the pressure that was created by the bomb blasts at a specific distance from ground zero.

Penney's samples also included some pieces of rice paper that had been burned at the bomb sites. He and Rivero subjected similar pieces of paper to heat to find out how many calories per square centimeter would be required to produce the same degree of burn found on the samples from Japan. With that knowledge and the number of pounds per square inch of pressure required to create the collapse of the oil drum, all from specific distances from the point of the bomb explosion, they were able to produce some points for a damage-effects curve, one for pressure and one for heat. The time was December of 1945. To Rivero's knowledge, these were the first curves developed on the effects of the weapons. "It was a fascinating project. It was just Penney and I, nobody else! I would crank up this hand pump for evacuation of the drums and do all these experiments with Penney. We worked out the details. I pressured Penney into sending the curves to Groves as early as possible. I helped him draw up the curves on rough cross-section paper, which I took back to General Groves in the United States. They provided the first determination of the yield of both the Hiroshima and Nagasaki bombs. They were exactly what Groves wanted."[2]

In reviewing Rivero's story of the Penney experience, Dick Ashworth stated that it was in complete accordance with his understanding of how the yields were determined. He pointed out that although Rivero had had little exposure to the atomic program at that time, he was a good choice to help Penney "purely from his technical reputation and just plain intelligence." Ashworth was quite sure that Penney's calculations were the first estimates of the yield of the bombs. Blast gauges, dropped from the planes accompanying the bomb carriers, had measured the intensity of the shock wave, which in turn gave an indication of the yield, but Ashworth suspected that processing that data took a bit of time.

Ashworth also said that Penney used the same basic technique at the Crossroads weapons tests in late 1946, when he used beer cans and other such containers. He also used pieces of pipe of varying lengths, known as "Penny's Harps," welded to the decks of the target ships.[3] The distance they were deflected by the shock wave gave him data on the yield of the weapons being tested.

Ashworth had some additional comments concerning the yield of those first weapons.

> The letter from King to Nimitz that I delivered personally earlier in 1945 stated that the estimated yield of the bomb would be about eight thousand tons of TNT equivalent. That figure is somewhat different than the later published figures of twenty thousand tons for the Nagasaki Fat Man. That may seem to be a contradiction, but when you consider the state of the bomb development by February of 1945, it is not surprising that any estimate of the yield would be an educated guess. Twenty thousand tons, as I understand it, was picked out of the air by Truman when he was at sea returning from Potsdam and announced to the world that the bombs had been used against Japan. I suppose that someone advised him on this, but I don't think that there was anyone on board (the ship) who had any real idea what the yield had been or had enough experience with the program to guess at it. The figure probably came from the contents of the message that must have been sent by General Groves to the President. That figure would have been based upon the observed effects of the two bombs and the experiment at Alamogordo (the Trinity Test).[4]

In addition to the yield of the bombs, there was considerable interest in the nature and extent of the damage that they created. In that regard, an organization was already in existence that could readily be deployed to Japan to find answers to the questions at hand.

One of the most significant aspects of World War II in Europe was the aerial bombing of Germany from England by both the U.S. and British air forces. The term "strategic bombing" came into prominence, and there was keen interest in the effectiveness of this bombing. Accordingly, the secretary of war established a formal group on 3 November 1944, pursuant to a directive from President Franklin Delano Roosevelt. Labeled the Strategic Bombing Survey, its mission was "to conduct an impartial and expert study of the effects of our aerial attack on Germany, to be used in connection with air attacks on Japan and to establish a basis for evaluating the importance and potentialities of air power as an instrument of military strategy, for planning the future development of the United States armed forces, and for determining future economic policies with respect to the national defense." The survey's complement provided for 300 civilians, 350 commissioned officers, and 500 enlisted men to carry out the mission. About 60 percent of the military segment came from the Army, the other 40 percent from the Navy. Initially it concentrated on the bombing in Europe and produced some two hundred reports assessing the damage and the effectiveness of the bombing campaign in that theater of operations.[5]

After the dropping of the atomic bombs on Japan and the surrender of the Japanese, President Truman promptly requested that the survey team conduct a similar study of the effects of all types of air attack in the war against Japan. One of the cochairmen of that phase was Paul Nitze, who later became the secretary of the Navy, the deputy secretary of defense, and eventually a key negotiator for the Strategic Arms Limitations Talks (SALT).

Among the military personnel placed in Japan by the survey was Comdr. (then) Thomas H. Moorer. In his discussion of the survey of damage in Hiroshima and Nagasaki, Moorer stated that both places were "still smoking" when they arrived. The survey provided graphic evidence of the magnitude of damage by heat, fire, and blast. The effects of radiation were noted as well. The team returned to the States in December 1945 to write its report.

In summing up his impressions of the experience, Admiral Moorer pointed out that at the time of their visit, they found that many of the Japanese industrial plants had already been shut down for lack of raw materials. Conventional bombing had certainly contributed to the shutdown, but the destruction of the supply pipelines for raw materials, whether within Japan or on the sea-lanes, had tremendously limited the Japanese industrial capability. The most significant aspect of the atomic bombing had been its impact on enemy morale, of such magnitude that it would have to be considered a major factor in future warfare. Bombing with conventional weapons could be tolerated and compensated for to some degree, as became evident in the Vietnam War. Atomic weapons, however, brought a destructive dimension that was devastating to morale, which meant the destruction of the will to continue, the hardest target to destroy with any kind of weapon.[6]

The results of the bombing survey brought up questions about the future use of atomic weapons. Who was going to conduct this "long-range" bombing mission using atomic weapons? Would it be the Army Air Forces, using long-range bombers, or naval aviation, using the long-range aircraft carrier and its relatively short-range aircraft, or a combination of the two?

Crossroads: Testing Atomic Weapons

As one might imagine, intense curiosity developed concerning the capability of atomic weapons. For example, what would be the effect on naval ships? The Manhattan Project addressed this question as early as 1944, and serious consideration was given to the idea of "testing" an atomic bomb against the Japanese navy at Truk.[7] The Navy urgently needed answers. What damage would occur from an airburst? From subsurface bursts? Against hulls? Against armor and armament? Against superstructure? Against crew members? Answers would affect not only ship design and construction for the future, but also the tactics for operating ships in combat under threat of atomic weapons attack.

At this time the Navy staff (Blandy, Parsons, Rivero, Hill, and Ashworth) was involved with getting the Navy into the atomic business. Again, Ashworth was in an excellent position to know what was going on. Although there were many legitimate questions that called for tests against ships, Ashworth contends that much of the impetus for a test against ships came from the Army Air Forces; that Gen. Billy Mitchell, who had long contended that aircraft could sink ships, had risen from the past; that a weapon now existed that would realize his dreams, a weapon that could destroy the mightiest of ships.

Vice Adm. Chick Hayward, who was now beginning to appear more prominently on the atomic weapons scene, felt very strongly about the Air Force role. He set forth his views in writing in 1981, following his retirement from active duty.

> The dust had hardly settled in Hiroshima and Nagasaki and the ink was barely dry on the surrender document signed aboard Missouri when the struggle for control of this new weapon began. The Army Air Forces, battling for its independence as the United States Air Force, and joined with the Army in the fight for the unification of the Armed Forces, began the greatest propaganda struggle of all. Hadn't their aircraft delivered the bomb? Wasn't it their role as the Strategic Air Force to control it? Weren't all navies and armies obsolete? Wouldn't they be the only ones involved in future wars? Navies were to be relegated to a purely transport and logistics force. Armies were just to occupy lands after the Air Force won the war! They were to be the elite offensive force of the nation. [Gen. Giulio] Douhet was right! Billy Mitchell was redeemed by the work on the mesa in New Mexico. A continual barrage went out day and night all over the country in what is now termed a "media blitz."[8]

The Joint Chiefs of Staff addressed the testing issue and determined that tests would cover the effects of the weapons on equipment of all the services, not just the Navy; that the testing program would be "joint" in its design and implementation. Accordingly, they recommended the creation of Joint Task Force One to carry out what became known as the Crossroads tests.

Approval by the president came on 10 January 1946. The mission was "to carry out the atomic bombing of a target array of naval ships."

Operations Crossroads Baker (underwater shot), Bikini Atoll, 25 July 1946. U.S. Navy photo.

More than 200 ships, 150 aircraft, and 42,000 men were involved, including representatives from the Army and Navy, and civilian scientists.[9] Vice Admiral Blandy was designated as the commander of the task force. He was the logical choice. At that time, he was the unofficial guru of the Navy's gun club. Parsons was in charge of the scientific aspects of the tests, and Rivero represented the Joint Chiefs of Staff to ensure that their objectives were met. Ashworth was involved with the assembly of the weapons at Kwajalein Atoll, their delivery to the target at Bikini, and subsequently with the assessment of the damage to the ships.

One of the first tasks of Joint Task Force One was the selection of a location for the tests. Ashworth, who had found a suitable site in the Pacific for launching the atomic bomb attacks against Japan, was also assigned the task of locating a suitable test site to learn more about such weapons. After much consideration, assisted by Rivero, he came up with Bikini Atoll. His recommendation was accepted.[10]

Two tests were ordered. More than twenty ships were in the target group, all within one thousand yards of the bull's-eye ship—an artificial formation for naval operations. The group included eight submarines, some of the most modern.[11] The special formation was needed to meet the Joint Chiefs of Staff requirement "of securing graded damage on all principal types of vessels, graded damage meaning damage ranging from negligible, as in the case of ships at a considerable distance from the explosion to lethal, in the case of ships close in."[12]

Test Able, the first, was conducted on 1 July 1946. The bomb was exploded in the air at low altitude above the targets and subjected everything in the vicinity to intense blast and radioactivity. The latter dissipated rapidly in the upper atmosphere in the mushroom cloud.

Test Baker, the second, was conducted on 25 July 1946. This underwater shot utilized the bomb's tremendous energy release in a different way. The huge pressure built up by the bomb, transmitted to the underwater portions of the neighboring ships, forced ship hulls inward on all sides at once. Furthermore, since the bomb was submerged in the lagoon, its radioactivity was prevented from passing instantly into the upper atmosphere. Intense and lasting radioactivity was produced in the water of the lagoon. The ships, drenched by tons of water thrown up by the explosion, became similarly contaminated. The extent of such contamination proved to be a matter of great interest.[13]

The nature of the damage is shown in photos of the thirty-four-year-old battleship *Arkansas,* the oldest ship in the fleet. She was one of three major combatant ships within one-half mile of the explosion point. Although little damage was done to her hull and turrets, her wrecked superstructure showed the hammerlike effect of the bomb. Amidships she was a shambles. When the lagoon was first reentered after Test Able, the *Arkansas* was still sending up clouds of smoke from smoldering fires on her decks. She was definitely put out of action and would have required extensive repairs at a principal naval base. In Test Baker she was near the bomb detonation point, took brief but terrific punishment, and sank almost instantly.[14]

Blandy's assessment of the tests was prophetic:

> These photographs no more than hint at the tremendous amount of data obtained concerning the effect of the bombs upon ships and material. They necessarily slight the technical and scientific lessons learned at Bikini. They do, however, evidence an incontestable truth. The Atomic Age is here. It is no myth. Nor is the atomic bomb "just another weapon." It is the most lethal destructive agent yet devised by man. Its energy release is staggering; its radioactivity is slow-killing poison.
>
> The purpose of these tests was to determine the effect of the atom bomb against various types of naval vessels. With the information secure, we can improve our ship design, tactics, and strategy, to minimize our losses in the unfortunate event of war waged with atomic weapons. A reliable and continuously effective plan to avoid competition in atomic armaments is the best possible defense against surprise attacks. With such a plan, atomic energy can in time become the controlled slave of man's peacetime pursuits. In the face of this new knowledge, these recently discovered truths concerning the atom, so suddenly thrust upon an already chaotic world, not only warfare but also civilization itself literally stands at the Crossroads. Hence the name of this operation.[15]

Blandy pleaded for an effective plan to keep the atomic bomb under control. Unfortunately, his plea was never heeded, particularly by the Soviet Union. When he wrote those words, a total of five atomic weapons had been exploded: the Trinity test in New Mexico, the two at Hiroshima and Nagasaki, and the two at Bikini. Blandy realized that the future use of atomic weapons for any purpose, under any circumstances, was a highly questionable action for any nation to take.

The Crossroads tests provided a tremendous amount of data that gave analysts the means to answer many questions. The damage is well summarized in a quote from the foreword of the pictorial report of the tests:

But an atomic bomb defies scrutiny. It shuns publicity. It shields its intense life span in a flash of light many times the brilliance of the sun. It dazzles human eyes. It limits its life to a matter of millionths of a second. It enshrouds itself in a cloud. And then it dies, mushrooming grotesquely to high altitudes as if for a better view of the havoc it has produced. Even if pent up beneath the surface of a lagoon it resists observation. Where before it blinded the eye here it succeeds in blinding the mind. In a matter of seconds it tosses up a column of tons of water higher than the Empire State Building. It sinks ships in a moment and crushes others into the deformed, stepped on shape of a child's bathtub toy. Itself the result of man's intellect, the bomb defies examination by its creator.[16]

Dick Ashworth pointed out that the radiation levels that developed in the tests exceeded expectations. Although several of the ships, including the *New York, Arkansas, Pennsylvania,* and *Saratoga,* sank to the bottom of the lagoon, the task force was still left with quite a number of highly contaminated ships. Radiation problems were particularly significant in the future design of protective measures required for ships that had any possibility of operating in a nuclear environment.

More Testing

It has become obvious after more than fifty years of living with the bomb that the lifeblood of a nuclear weapons program is testing of the various components in the bombs, their delivery systems, and their explosive characteristics. Because nuclear weapons deteriorate to some degree while in storage, testing has become essential to determining the reliability of weapons in the stockpile.

The Crossroads tests whetted the appetite of scientists and engineers for exploring the real parameters of what they had created. Naturally, the military became intrigued with the possibilities of this new weapon. What could it do? What were its limitations? What were its dangers to friendly forces? How much bang? At what weight and size? And what means of delivery? How many could be produced and at what rate? The stage was set for much more testing.

The constraint on initial testing was the lack of bombs. The impression received by many, probably including the Japanese, was that if the United States could drop two atomic bombs in a matter of days, they could probably continue with the effort. As Ashworth pointed out, this had been the original thinking when the facilities at Tinian were established. But the rapid surrender by the Japanese kept the knowledge of the scarcity of atomic bombs and materials from everyone except those intimately involved with their production and use. "By November 1947, the national stockpile of atomic bombs was composed entirely of inadequate and deficient components of a rapidly obsolescing design. Had the war continued for six more months, all of these items would have been scrapped and replaced by better-engineered components."[17]

There had to be extensive development and engineering work at the laboratory in Los Alamos between Crossroads and the next test. The logical objectives were increasing the number of weapons (a faster production rate), efficiency of the individual weapon (more bang for the amount of nuclear material used), and improvements in deliverability (getting the weapon to the target more easily).

Of great significance to the Navy was the efficiency of the atomic bomb. Harold Agnew, who was an early member of the Los Alamos lab and later its director, pointed out that the bigger the bomb, the better from an efficiency point of view because the bigger weapon could contain a greater proportion of high explosives and less of the costly fissionable material, while producing an equivalent or greater destructive yield. That was not particularly good news for the Navy, but it made the B-36 and B-52 aircraft delivery systems appealing and undoubtedly contributed to the view that atomic weapons would be huge and require big airplanes for delivery to a target. This had an impact on naval aviation's early approach to the size problem. "Big" and "heavy" continued to be adjectives associated with atomic weapons, with talk of bombs weighing 50,000 pounds, 25 feet long, and 5 feet in diameter. At a meeting on 14 June 1951, scientists at Los Alamos talked about a super bomb that could be carried in conventional Air Force aircraft, weighing 35,000 to 80,000 pounds, 120 feet long, and

9 feet in diameter.[18] By comparison, Fat Man weighed 10,000 pounds and was 5 feet in diameter. Predictions for future weapons were counter to what carrier aviation could accommodate with its delivery vehicles. The Navy needed a small, lightweight bomb with a respectable yield. Patience was required and eventually rewarded. The nation's scientific and engineering communities, given high priority and almost unlimited funding, were able to produce what the Navy needed, which incidentally also put the Air Force tactical air arm in the nuclear weapons business.

To conduct the large testing program, another atoll in the Pacific, Eniwetok, was prepared. A test site was also developed in the Nevada desert. Many tests, categorized by "series," with several "shots" or tests in each series, produced some significant milestones. In 1948 the Sandstone series was conducted at Eniwetok to investigate the fundamentals of the bomb.

The following year was significant for testing, but it was the Soviet test program that attracted the attention. Keeping track of Soviet activity in the race to become nuclear capable had started early in the incubation stage of nuclear weapons development. Early in World War II, President Roosevelt and General Groves learned the value of what is now called technical intelligence. The Soviets were mounting a massive intelligence effort in the United States, Canada, and England to acquire detailed technical knowledge on how to make atom bombs and the status of the U.S. effort—and the United States knew it. The use of trained mining engineers to make estimates from aerial photography of the uranium output of the Joachimistal mines in Czechoslovakia had impressive results. Later records showed they had been off by only 15 percent. Postwar efforts by trained physicists and chemists had proven that proper use of scientific experts produced solid results.

The decision was made to develop a technical intelligence unit under Col. (then) L. E. Seeman, initially in the Manhattan Project and later in the newly formed Central Intelligence Agency (CIA). Col. Frank A. Valente, former professor of nuclear physics at Columbia

University, represented the unit at a series of joint meetings involving nuclear scientists, weather experts from the fledgling Air Corps, and experts from the Bureau of Standards, the Army, the Navy, and the State Department. Their objective was to recommend measures to develop the long-range detection of nuclear detonations. They chose five methods, of which the use of aircraft carrying filters to collect radioactive debris was the first to be implemented.

Under General Eisenhower, the State Department, the Army, and the new Atomic Energy Commission (AEC) agreed that the Air Force was to manage the effort under a special new organization, AFOAT-1. The CIA was to spearhead the collection of foreign information, including the use of technical collection equipment. The AEC was to back up this effort through technical developments and would spearhead the efforts to develop new collection tools for both the CIA and AFOAT-1.

A major effort was mounted in the AEC to determine what radioactive effluents were inadvertently dispersed from its own facilities. Analysis tools hundreds of times more sensitive than those in general health-physics use were developed. From this came the CIA covert environmental sampling effort against foreign nuclear facilities as well as its civilian counterpart, the Environmental Protection Agency.

Many top-flight nuclear physicists and chemists at Los Alamos National Laboratory and Argonne Laboratory contributed their expertise to the mission. Willard F. Libby, later chairman of the AEC, developed methods for measuring exceedingly low concentrations of the inert radioactive rare gases, such as xenon 135 and krypton 85, gaseous fission products of nuclear reactor operation and atomic bomb detonation. Later, he applied these techniques to the measurement of radiocarbon 14, obtaining a Nobel Prize for the important development.[19]

The mission of carrying filters to collect radioactive debris was assigned to the new U.S. Air Force, in addition to the mission of getting atomic bombs to the targets. The intelligence mission was called Long Range Detection (LRD)—determining the progress of the Soviets in producing their own atomic bomb. The degree of preparation and effort the U.S. Air Force devoted to fulfilling that mission was impressive, especially considering the lack of budgetary support or enthusiasm for the effort. For about two years, the Air Force flew many missions to take air samples from the atmosphere over particular parts of the globe. A total of 111 missions were flown with zero detections of nuclear activity. Finally, on mission number 112, they hit paydirt. Coupled with other information from the intelligence community, their findings established beyond a doubt that the Soviets had set off an atomic explosion. Labeled "Joe 1," it had occurred at Semipalatinsk in the Soviet Union. It took place at 1:00 A.M. Greenwich Meridian Time on 29 August 1949 and used plutonium. The yield was about twenty kilotons.[20]

The development of this detection capability had a major impact on at least one facet of the intelligence mission. It enabled the Air Force, specifically the Strategic Air Command, to develop an outstanding intelligence capability related to the nuclear weapons issue. That capability grew and contributed greatly to the success of our overall ability to implement the containment/deterrent policy and the evolving strategies and tactics.[21]

U.S. testing continued. In 1952 came the Greenhouse series, involving several shots, some aimed at gaining more information on the "super" weapon—the thermonuclear or hydrogen bomb. Also came the Tumbler-Snapper and Upshot-Knothole series at the Nevada test site, the objective of which was to improve the efficiency of the bomb. It was a banner testing year for the United States as scientists sought more information on the possibilities of the thermonuclear bomb. It was also the year of the Ivy series, including the Mike shot on 1 November, which fulfilled Edward Teller's dream of a thermonuclear weapon. The yield was reported as 10.4 megatons, over five hundred times the yield of the bombs dropped on Japan in 1945. From kilotons (KT) to megatons (MT) was a massive increase in the destructive capabilities of humankind—and a new measuring scale for nuclear weaponeers.

Even before the Mike test, the Air Force had believed that with intensive effort, the United States could produce a relatively inexpensive and easily deliverable thermonuclear weapon that could be used against any potential target. Ten such weapons, it was thought, could destroy the urban centers of the Soviet Union, or if used by the Soviets, the great cities of the United States. It was therefore imperative for the United States to develop this capability before the Soviet Union.[22]

In 1955, the Teapot series of tests were conducted at the Nevada test site. Data were obtained on "clean" (low-radiation) and "dirty" (high-radiation) weapons. Also these tests showed that a substantial volume and weight reduction could be achieved without loss in primary yield.[23] Small devices appeared to be a reality, and naval aviation was investing heavily in the development of a nuclear delivery capability for its carrier-based aircraft.

These tests marked the end of the period of "emergency capability" for nuclear weapons and the beginning of "normal deployment." They were a departure from the so-called doctrine of scarcity, which had dictated U.S. Air Force strategic war planning and, indirectly, the entire foreign policy of the United States, defining when, where, and under what circumstances the government would be prepared to wage nuclear war.[24] This policy worked in favor of the Air Force for a while, for a scarcity of nuclear weapons meant that only established, proven systems should be in the war plans. With nuclear weapons in abundance, planning for the method of delivery was unbridled by numbers. More weapons meant that more delivery systems could be utilized, which opened the door for Army and Navy systems. Further, more weapons meant more targets could be taken under attack. The targeting strategy became very simply one of using the additional weapons, whether they were needed or not, to implement the containment/deterrence policy. There seemed to be no limit to how many could be used.

In 1956 the United States conducted the Redwing series of tests at Eniwetok Atoll to develop a variety of atomic weapons to meet a wide range of military needs, provide defense against air attack, and perfect devices with reduced fallout hazards. The Redwing series also better defined the atomic weapons delivery capabilities and limitations of late-model Air Force and Navy aircraft and marked the beginning of tests of the upcoming intercontinental ballistic missiles. Further, the tests proved that a B-52 aircraft could safely free-drop a weapon of one-megaton yield.

In 1957 the Soviets successfully tested a multistage thermonuclear superbomb. A new threshold in worldwide security had now been crossed. The race was on in full stride. As for the ten weapons envisioned before the Ivy test, by 1960 the fever of competition found the United States planning to launch at least 3,500 weapons of varying yields and accuracies at targets in or surrounding the Soviet empire. Concern about "overkill" began to surface in various communities, including the Navy.

In 1958 the Hardtack series at Eniwetok consisted of twenty-eight shots, including one (Umbrella) with the weapon submerged 180 feet on the bottom of the lagoon. Teak and Orange were detonated at high altitude (250,000 feet), which tested effects on the communication spectrum and resulted in a nine-hour disruption of short-wave, high-frequency communications in Australia.

Following a briefing on test results to President Eisenhower by leading nuclear scientists Edward Teller and Norris Bradbury, the president noted "that while the new thermonuclear weapons were tremendously powerful, they were not, in many ways, as powerful as world opinion at the time that obliged the United States to follow certain lines of policy regarding nuclear testing."[25]

An idea of the nature of nuclear weapons testing can be gleaned from the experience of Capt. Georges "Frenchy" LeBlanc Jr., USN (Ret.), who reported to the weapons facility at Kirtland Air Force Base in Albuquerque in May 1956 to become a nuclear weapons test pilot. From May 1956 until September 1957, LeBlanc flew 235 project sorties in the Vought F7U-3 Cutlass in support of nuclear weapons development projects for the AEC. The AEC project engineers em-

The Chance Vought F7U Cutlass. Smithsonian National Air and Space Museum (NASM) collection.

ployed by the Sandia Corporation loved the F7U-3. No matter what the size or the shape of their research vehicle, it would fit beneath the aircraft, one of the few advantages of the stork-like landing gear on the Cutlass.

Eventually, the F7Us were retired from service, and LeBlanc was assigned to weapons-effects testing. His specific assignment was to test the in-flight response of a sweptwing aircraft to a thermonuclear detonation. The flights were to be made during the Hardtack series of atomic tests, conducted at the Eniwetok Proving Ground in the summer of 1958. The Navy employed four highly instrumented aircraft: two FJ-4 Furies and two A4D-1 Skyhawks (hereafter referred to as the A-4). Both were Navy sweptwing, carrier-based aircraft of the late 1950s. Comdr. Francis Buchner headed the detachment. The Furies were configured and instrumented by North American Aviation at their Columbus, Ohio, plant, and a team of North American engineers was assigned to the project. They helped determine the position of the test aircraft in relation to the detonation of the nuclear device to gather and subsequently analyze the data.

For aircraft positioning purposes, a land-based radar operator was dedicated to the control of each test aircraft. For positioning, the test aircraft was flown in an elliptical pattern, the final leg of which traversed the point of detonation (ground zero) at a predetermined time before detonation. The timing was critical. At T-zero (time of explosion) minus twenty seconds, the test aircraft was to be within two seconds of the desired position, or the run was aborted. Altitude was to be maintained within one hundred feet of that prescribed.

From 6 May to 15 June 1958, each of the four Navy project aircraft participated in seven live shots. LeBlanc flew in six of them in the FJ-4. On each test, one A-4 and one FJ-4 were positioned to optimize measurement of overpressure occurring at the altitude of flight. The other two aircraft were to measure thermal energy and gust loading. LeBlanc was assigned to the FJ-4 to gather information on the latter.

For protection, each pilot wore the standard Navy flight gear and light-restrictive filter goggles, which looked like one-way mirrors. Other special pilot equipment included dosimeters and film badges placed at various locations on the pilot's body to measure radiation. For thermal protection, the cockpit was configured with a thermal shield, an asbestos hood that was manually closed by the pilot after takeoff. When tightly secured, there was no visible daylight in the cockpit, even at high noon. With the light-restrictive filter goggles in place and the hood closed, it was necessary to illuminate the instrument console with a floodlight.

All of the test shots in which LeBlanc participated were scheduled to be detonated at first light. At the moment of detonation, the entire cockpit would illuminate. The larger the yield, the longer this light endured. It was a rather eerie sensation to move in an instant from complete darkness to brilliant light. It gave LeBlanc a feeling of being buoyed upwards, although the aircraft instruments remained steady.

At time of shock arrival, however, the story was very different. When hit by the shock wave, those flying at the higher elevations experienced high gust loads, which slammed the aircraft about. To make matters worse, the overpressure engulfing the pilot's static instruments caused the cockpit altimeter to unwind rapidly and the air speed indicator to show a rapid increase in velocity.

On one test, LeBlanc was positioned so that the aircraft was heading directly toward ground zero at time of detonation. He was directly over ground zero when the shock arrived, flying at 12,000 feet. It was particularly violent, causing every accelerometer in the aircraft to register maximum positive and negative Gs. The wings of the FJ-4 flexed considerably in the vertical plane. Given his instrument readings, there were some anxious moments until LeBlanc could be certain that the aircraft was not falling into the rapidly building mushroom cloud. Later, as confidence was gained in the ability to predict weapons effects accurately, the test aircraft were moved in closer to the detonation.

The first shot in which Navy pilots participated in Hardtack involved the detonation of a relatively low-yield device to test the adequacy of their positioning methodology for timing and data gathering. The data to be collected were really not much different from those already available from the Nevada tests. The aircraft in which LeBlanc was flying was far enough from the detonation to create no real concern about pilot safety or aircraft damage. However, following T-zero, his curiosity overcame his good judgment, and he quickly removed the thermal hood and turned toward ground zero to observe the rapidly developing mushroom cloud. The colors and turbulence within it were spectacular. He maintained what he felt was a comfortable distance, but apparently, the radioactive fallout particles extended well beyond the cloud itself. He was shocked to learn that the skin of the aircraft was sufficiently contaminated to be parked in a remote area, where LeBlanc was removed from the cockpit via forklift. He did not know the level of radiation recorded on the film badge worn on his chest, but one of the dosimeters on a leg registered in excess of eight REM. Since the test limit had been established at five REM, LeBlanc received a stern lecture from the officer-in-charge about sightseeing. He did not need to deliver it a second time.

On LeBlanc's final shot, which was to be the Navy's last in-flight participation in Operation Hardtack, the light from the detonation was particularly intense and lasted for many seconds. It was clear that this one was much larger than anything that he had previously experienced. As LeBlanc taxied into the flight line, he observed an unusual display of activity in the group that had gathered to welcome him back. The cause of the excitement was the visible damage to the aircraft. The metal on the underside of the wing had buckled in the areas that were painted blue. The anticollision light on the other side of the fuselage was completely glazed. Much of the insulating material in the instrumentation pod was melted, as was some of the binding material used on the aircraft control surfaces. It was clear to LeBlanc that he was going home, a particularly wonderful prospect for him, since his wife had delivered their second son in his absence. LeBlanc believes that few if any aviators have flown aircraft any closer to a thermonuclear detonation than did the four Navy pilots flying in Operation Hardtack.[26]

Both the United States and the Soviets were determined to increase the yield of the weapons. Stockpiled versions could yield twenty to twenty-five megatons, and in 1961, the Soviets set off a three-stage weapon that yielded fifty-eight megatons. It seems that the power of militarily useful warheads was limited only by the lifting capabilities of their delivery vehicles.[27] Later, however, the targeteers found that getting weapons with massive yields to the target successfully and with high damage expectancy was very difficult. Those difficulties essentially ruled out their usefulness. The requirement for massive-yield weapons disappeared, but testing remained a big part of the operation, and much controversy surrounded the issue of whether to test or not. At the time that the fifty-megaton weapon was tested, the Soviets "exploded fifty bombs in almost as many days."[28]

Testing covered other areas of military warfare. In 1962 tests measured the effect of nuclear weapons against submarines and involved an anti–submarine warfare rocket called ASROC. Eventually there were nuclear depth charges and antisubmarine rockets to be fired from patrol aircraft and helicopters. Tests of low-yield weapons suitable for artillery and battlefield use by the Army were conducted. Retardation of the bomb after release by parachute emerged as a means of increasing safety for the delivery aircraft and crew. Most significant for the Navy were the development and testing of warheads for cruise missiles, as well as intercontinental and submarine-launched ballistic missiles.

The many tests conducted provided information to meet the evolving needs of the military services, although the traditional method of determining military requirements based on an enemy threat was not followed at all times. Does a needed capability become a requirement—or does the requirement evolve from a capability? Ashworth had some interesting comments on this issue.

It is useful to see how some of these smaller bombs came to be introduced into the fleet. In the early 1950s when I was assigned to the Military Applications Division of the Atomic Energy Commission, Norris Bradbury, then the Director of the Los Alamos Laboratory where most of the bomb development was going on, would come to Washington and inform us that they thought at the laboratory that a small bomb of about thirty-five inches in diameter and maybe to weigh around five thousand pounds and with a pretty good "bang" could now be designed. Could the service use such a bomb? The answer was, "Of course," because the sooner that we would have weapons of this dimension the sooner we could get the more conventional carrier aircraft into the act. One particular capability that he addressed turned out to be the Mark V weapon.

Soon Bradbury would come to town and tell us that a bomb of about twenty-two inches in diameter with a yield of maybe ten kilotons was now possible. Could we use it? This turned out to be the Mark VII. So now we were getting down to bomb sizes that could be used by the current family of carrier-based fighter and attack aircraft. It was this experience that used

The Mark VII nuclear weapon. Photo courtesy of National Atomic Museum.

to prompt me to say in those early days when no one knew much about atomic weapons that Bradbury was in effect setting military requirements for atomic weapons because he was the only one in a responsible position who knew the territory intimately.[29]

The Stockpile

From the tests, it became very clear that the bomb was now the major factor in planning for national security. It was something one could see, feel, deploy, and analyze forever. As the scientists made their improvements, the requirements increased. More people became fascinated with the weapon, and more scenarios were developed for its employment. The Soviet capability spurred the activity for more weapons, and the producers met the demand. Quality improved constantly, with more bang for the buck and the amount of nuclear material used in each bomb—and the stockpile continued to grow.

One report claims that the number of strategic offensive force loadings in 1945 numbered six warheads and fifteen nuclear-capable bombers. By 1959, that number had risen to over 2,500 warheads and over 1,500 launching systems. With the introduction of the ICBM and submarine-launched ballistic missile (SLBM) systems in 1960, the number of warheads rose rapidly, to over 6,000 in 1970 and peaking at almost 14,000 in 1987.[30] As the number of weapons was increasing, the total explosive yields were undergoing changes. According to one report, the total rose from about 75 megatons in 1950 to a peak of 19,000 in 1960. As the weapons became more efficient and the accuracy of the delivery systems improved, the yields were reduced, replacing yield with accuracy. By 1984 the total megatonnage of the U.S. nuclear weapons stockpile had dropped to less than 5,000.[31] That is considerably more than Alain Enthoven, Secretary Robert McNamara's number one "whiz kid," felt the nation needed when he and his coauthor wrote their book, *How Much Is Enough?*[32] Four hundred megatons was the figure they calculated. Obviously, there were going to be disagreements on the size and quality of the required stockpile.

Proliferation accompanied the increases in number and yield. Chuck Hansen says that by 1963, weapons were dispersed worldwide and that many were lightweight, highly efficient thermonuclear bombs and missile warheads that could be stored in a "ready" condition for a long time. He points out that because of the testing, a lot of money, and innovative energy, thermonuclear weapons had gone from a "theoretical abstraction" to a significant fraction of the U.S. nuclear weapons stockpile in just twenty years. He claims that by 1962, "12,000 to 21,000 hydrogen warheads were in existence, with another 5,000 to 9,000 in production."[33]

There could be many versions of the actual size of the stockpile, but the bottom line was that there were plenty of weapons in the arsenals of major powers. But for all its destructive power, was the nuclear weapon really of military value? Would it ever be used? Or would it eventually be eliminated from national security arsenals? Hadn't it become a purely political weapon, a series of bargaining chips for the arms control community? Did we really need that many weapons and that much destructive power to contain or deter the Soviets?

Gen. Andrew Goodpaster is a fountain of knowledge for historians trying to piece together the details of the nuclear weapons story. He is an established military authority, and his views must be considered seriously in any discussion of matters nuclear. Joining with other authorities on the issue, he has publicly expressed concern about the existence of the nuclear weapon and its usefulness. "With Russia, with China and with our Allies our task is to build and sustain relationships aimed at assuring that the possibility of armed conflict does not again arise among us, and for the nuclear threat, taking action to reduce existing arsenals over time to the lowest verifiable level consistent with stable security. *I myself believe this can be as few as 100 to 200 weapons for each of the nuclear weapons nations* [emphasis added]. We must concurrently prevent the spread of such weapons to other nations now non-nuclear."[34]

Other experienced military commanders have expressed similar views. Adm. Noel Gayler, USN (Ret.), former deputy director of the Joint Strategic Target Planning Staff (JSTPS), director of the National Security Agency (NSA), and finally commander-in-chief, U.S. Forces, Pacific, frequently—while still on active duty—advocated the removal of nuclear weapons from overseas bases and ships.[35] Gen. George Lee Butler, USAF (Ret.), was commander of the Strategic Air Command and director of JSTPS, the agency putting together the detailed Single Integrated Operational Plan (SIOP) for U.S. strategic nuclear forces. Following retirement, he joined with General Goodpaster and many others, calling publicly for the "abolition of nuclear weapons."[36] When such highly qualified leaders have views that differ dramatically from those commonly accepted, one has to question the nature of our stockpile of nuclear weapons.

Testing gave us answers to many questions. The Air Force knew that if they were going to sink a ship with an atomic bomb, they would have to be quite accurate or have a bomb with a much bigger yield than twenty kilotons. They could damage the superstructure of a ship, but unless the weapon exploded close to or beneath it, an armored ship would probably survive. The Navy learned that it was going to have to greatly modify its tactics when employing ships in an atomic environment; that the ships would have to be dispersed, and, although one or two in a formation might be sunk or at least put out of action, most would survive. To improve the chances of survival, some major design modifications in hull structure and armor protection would have to be incorporated.

Of major significance, however, was the lesson that all learned about radiation, both "prompt," from the detonation, and "residual." Whether on a military or civilian target, any atomic explosion was going to create a residual radiation hazard of immense proportions. For the Navy that meant developing means of decontaminating ships subjected to atomic attacks. For all, it meant learning protective measures to neutralize or eradicate the effects of exposure to both prompt and residual radiation. That meant bomb shelters, protective clothing, and water wash-down (decontamination) procedures. The Navy had to get organized to deal with the potential of atomic energy and the problems it would bring for the defense of naval forces.

Getting Organized

As mentioned earlier, Vice Admiral Blandy was established as the head of the new organization in the Office of the Chief of Naval Operations, which would deal with atomic energy. It started as a separate "directorate"—OP-06—a high place in the staff structure. In time, Blandy departed the scene, and his prophetic words about the bomb following the Crossroads tests were forgotten. The staffing for this new energy capability was then established as a "division"— OP-36—in the operations directorate of the staff under Vice Adm. Jerauld Wright. Parsons was promoted to the rank of commodore and then to rear admiral. Under Wright, Parsons headed the small organization that was responsible for atomic energy matters for the Navy. Staffing consisted of Parsons, Tom Hill, Rivets Rivero, and Dick Ashworth. They were charged with leading the Navy into the nuclear energy field.

In the command structure, this action put Admiral Wright between Admiral Parsons and the chief of naval operations (CNO), Admiral Nimitz. Admiral Wright was uneducated in atomic matters. Unfortunately, he was also very jealous of his position as Parsons's superior and expected that all relations with the CNO would go through his office and vice versa. The net result of Wright's unfamiliarity with atomic matters was that Nimitz would invariably go directly to Parsons. This situation generated a bit of bad blood between Parsons and his boss, Admiral Wright. Relations could have been better.

In his inimitable style, Parsons immersed himself immediately in generating Navy policy for the future of nuclear weapons and the possibility of the new field of nuclear power. He had many sessions with members of the newly established Stanford Research Institute. He had already concluded that the possibility of nuclear power made it possible to build the true submarine, that is, one that could stay submerged and operate for long periods of time. Later, he was sure that these submarines could take on a missile capability and make a major contribution to the strategic defense of the country as an invulnerable part of the nuclear triad.

As things settled down a bit, Tom Hill was selected for rear admiral and assumed Parsons's duties as head of OP-36. Parsons finally realized his goal of commanding a division of cruisers on sea duty.[37]

Control

With such a massive new destructive capability and with the probability of a new and revolutionary potential power source, arguments arose as to who would have control of the new atomic energy program in the United States, particularly as it related to atomic bombs. An early proposal called the Acheson-Lilenthal Plan would have placed all atomic programs under international control. The Soviets were opposed to any such plan because it might preclude their independent development of the bomb, which was well on its way as a result of spying at Los Alamos during World War II.

As early as the summer of 1944, James B. Conant and Vannevar Bush, key scientific advisers to the government, pushed for the establishment of a "commission on atomic energy." In May 1945, the secretary of war established an interim committee "to survey and make recommendations on postwar research, development, and controls, as well as legislation necessary to effectuate them."[38]

Properly exercising its authority and responsibility, the Congress created a Joint Atomic Energy Committee, held hearings, and on 1 August 1946 passed the Atomic Energy Act, creating the Atomic Energy Commission. All phases of nuclear energy research and production came under the control of the AEC on 1 January 1947, including atomic power and weapons.[39]

The Military Liaison Committee (MLC) was established to be the legal and formal conduit for the exchange of all atomic energy plans and information between the AEC and the military, which were to keep each other informed of all atomic energy activity that related directly to the other. The Navy's Dick Ashworth was assigned the task of organizing the MLC and was its first executive secretary. One incident stands out clearly in his memory concerning Doctor Oppenheimer and the hydrogen bomb.

The Committee was discussing the matter of the development of the "super" bomb, as it was known then, which became the hydrogen bomb or thermonuclear bomb. I remember that Oppenheimer stated his opposition to the development of that bomb at the time. It was his opinion that we needed to build up the stockpile of plutonium bombs before undertaking anything like the "super." It was his opinion that the reactors at Hanford should continue making plutonium and not use the neutrons in the reactors to manufacture tritium, an important ingredient of the "super." We should be making plutonium and building up the stockpile.

I recall that sometime later Oppenheimer objected to the development of the super bomb presumably for moral reasons. This, of course, started the feud between Oppenheimer and Teller that lasted until Oppenheimer's security clearance was revoked by the Atomic Energy Commission under Lewis Strauss. It could be that the objections he posed were misinterpreted. I don't know. My guess is he probably did have moral concerns about it later and decided that the super bomb shouldn't be in anybody's stockpile. Unfortunately, this didn't deter the Russians from going ahead with it, as we did also.[40]

The struggle for control of the atomic energy program continued for many years. There was an aura of mystery surrounding nuclear energy, kept that way by the excessive secrecy that was attached to the subject. How could one make intelligent decisions about the control of the weapons if so few knew of their capabilities and dangers?

Custody

The Manhattan Project continued for a few months after the war with responsibilities set forth in the Atomic Energy Act of 1946. On 31 December 1946, a joint Army-Navy organization, the Armed Forces Special Weapons Project (AFSWP), was created to assume the military function of the Manhattan Project. General Groves was placed at the head of that organization.[41]

The Manhattan Project had been under the control of Major General Groves, assisted ably by a myriad of military personnel including two naval officers, Parsons and Ashworth. However, there was no way that the custody and use of the weapons in response to threats to the United States were going to be placed in the hands of the military. Even though the armed services would be expected to deliver atomic weapons in time of hostilities, as at Hiroshima and Nagasaki, control and custody of the weapons were to be denied the military for many years.

The custody struggle between the newly created Atomic Energy Commission and the Department of Defense (DOD) created some strong feelings on the issue in the leaders of the two factions, starting with Secretary of Defense James Forrestal and the chairman of the AEC, David E. Lilienthal, an appointee of President Truman. The struggle continued with their successors.[42]

The split between the AEC and the DOD made it difficult for the people storing and handling the weapons, particularly aboard ship. Partial relief came in the form of an edict by President Eisenhower in 1959 directing the "transfer of custody to the DOD of all weapons dispersed to the DOD."[43] This meant the transfer of more than 80 percent of the existing stockpile.

Final transfer of the custody of all nuclear weapons was effected in 1967 following an agreement signed by the late Glenn Seaborg of the AEC and Secretary of Defense Cyrus Vance.[44] Thus, what had begun as a bitter clash between titans almost twenty-one years earlier ended in a whimper of administrative harmony. In retrospect, many factors contributed to this evolution, the most significant of which was the belief that the prescribed procedures for transferring custody of warheads for missiles and aircraft from the AEC to alert units of the DOD would seriously degrade our deterrent and defensive capabilities. The realities of modern intercontinental warfare had reduced the time for operational decisions from hours to minutes. However, it should be noted that AEC's participation with the DOD in safety, security, command and control, and dispersal (physical placement) procedures had immeasurably assisted in easing the transition of custody. Thus, the MLC's quest for military custody of finished nuclear weapons was completed.[45]

The custody struggle was later replaced by arguments over the authority to use the weapons, with continuing distrust of the military by civilian authorities. The scientific community developed devices called permissive action links (PALs), which were placed on many weapons and prevented their use until the insertion of a proper code. PALs were principally for weapons stored in shore-based sites. The security of weapons in Navy custody was disputed but reluctantly accepted by many. Scary scenarios were developed in which the weapons in ships and submarines were taken over by adversaries of many sorts, with a resulting threat to the nation's security. One solution to the problem caused by this distrust between the civil and military communities was the production of more weapons, a highly questionable solution, particularly to many who were intimately involved in planning for the use of the weapons.

Although the custody problem existed, it really had little effect on personnel working with the weapons aboard ship. As usually happens, the troops in the field can find ways to work around or live with the restrictions and often ridiculous constraints imposed by higher authority in their attempt to keep things under control.

Assembly, Storage, and Handling

The assembly of weapons continued to require special attention. In his customary fashion, General Groves called for top-quality people to conduct this phase of the business. Some of the best and brightest in the armed forces were assigned to the task of putting weapons together in New Mexico. Lt. Gen. Ernest Graves, USA (Ret.), was a young graduate of West Point when the bomb-assembly tasks developed. He was ordered to report to Los Alamos in 1946.

The weapons that had been assembled up to that point had been assembled by teams of scientists and engineers from Los Alamos and Sandia Base in Albuquerque. At that stage, nuclear weapons were not being mass-produced as they are today or as other weapons were then. They were not being produced in a factory. All the components were made separately. Then a special team put them together.

The fusing, the batteries, and other components had to be monitored constantly. The plan did not call for assembling a lot of weapons and having them in storage. Assembly was part of the operation. If you were going to use them, then you would assemble them. There were about sixty of us.[46]

As nuclear weapons became more numerous and easier to assemble, a whole cadre of support personnel developed. These were essentially technical personnel, usually in the higher ranks of noncommissioned officers, who became experts on preparing weapons for delivery on targets. This included handling in storage sites such as ships, submarines, or wherever a nuclear weapon was stored or to be mounted on a delivery vehicle. Some Navy veterans of these programs formed the Navy Nuclear Weapons Association. They have periodic conventions, as most veterans groups do. They are a fraternity of individuals that were and continue to be very significant in the nuclear weapons arena. Without their expertise, there would not have been a viable nuclear weapons force.[47]

Further Development

By 1952 nuclear weapons had evolved from the Little Boy and Fat Man (designated Mark IV) of World War II into the Mark VII, an implosion weapon considered the first true tactical nuclear weapon the United States ever developed. It existed in several modifications, was capable of being used by tactical aircraft, including those on carriers, and was one of the first weapons aerodynamically optimized for external carriage by small aircraft such as the Air Force Republic F-84. It was of the "capsule bomb design," which meant that the nuclear fission elements were stored outside the bomb casing in a special container until ready for use. The Mark VII was over 15 feet long and over 30 inches in diameter, and weighed about 1,700 pounds with the nuclear core installed. The explosive yield was twenty kilotons. It had three tail fins, one of which retracted. The retracting tail fin was essential for carrier aircraft when catapult launched, which depressed the landing struts of the plane; without it, one fin of the bomb would have dragged on the flight deck had it not been retractable. It was deployed longer than any other U.S. free-fall bomb, for more than fifteen years, and was instrumental in putting the light-attack carrier aircraft into the nuclear weapons delivery business.[48]

The Mark 28 series of weapons, capable of low-level delivery and designed for both internal and external carriage, was introduced in

The Mark 28 (external) nuclear weapon. Photo courtesy of National Atomic Museum.

1958. There were several variants and several yields.[49] Weighing about 2,000 pounds, with an explosive equivalent yield of one megaton, and capable of being delivered by any tactical aircraft configured for nuclear weapons delivery, the Mark 28 became the workhorse of carrier aviation. The first nuclear weapon designed as a complete weapon, it was a standard for strategic and tactical aircraft of both the Air Force and the Navy, including those operating from aircraft carriers, until it was retired in 1990. Approximately 4,500 were produced between 1958 and 1966.

Improvements continued in weapons efficiency and design. By 1963, sealed-pit weapons constituted the major portion of the stockpile and were dispersed worldwide. In these weapons, the nuclear components were integral, and there was no longer a need to insert a nuclear capsule before use. Most of them were lightweight, highly efficient thermonuclear bombs and missile warheads that could be stored in a "ready" condition for a long time.[50]

People

One significant aspect of the postwar development of nuclear weapons is the role played by military officers, particularly those from the Navy. For example, Capt. Dennett Keith "Deke" Ela was an outstanding naval engineer and ship architect who later became heavily involved in the design, modification, and construction of carriers for the nuclear weapons delivery mission. However, in 1953 he was at the Sandia weapons laboratory in New Mexico, assigned as the deputy chief of development. Following are some comments he made about the Sandia experience.

I should add a note here in reference to the impact of the Navy on weapons development. After World War II, weapons development labs experienced a mass exodus of brains and management. The Sandia laboratory operation became notably inefficient or incompetent, resulting in the Armed Forces Special Weapons Project headed up by General Groves and manned with a lot of military personnel. Among naval personnel assigned were Dick Mandelkorn and Red McQuilken, outstanding naval engineers who went into the business of nuclear weapons with a drive and determination to make things better. They are credited with being in the forefront, causing a major shakeup in some of the Sandia operations. Just as Parsons and Ashworth played an invaluable early role in bomb design pragmatism (aerodynamics and ejection dynamics) with the physicists, Navy personnel continued to work both sides of the AEC/Navy interface to ensure program success. For example, I had some of my officers actually staffing design desks in Sandia Corporation. Furthermore, the development office at AFSWP worked without interservice rivalry to support all service applications; mission rivalries were left to higher headquarters. While I was there, I had about equal numbers (about fifty total) of Air Force, Army,

Navy, and Marine officer specialists working harmoniously. All of us were dedicated to advancing the nuclear capabilities of our country.[51]

The Trinity test, the two bombs dropped on Japan, and the Crossroads and subsequent testing led to technological achievements by our scientists and engineers that enabled them to produce thousands of weapons of varying capabilities. By 1974, the nation's Single Integrated Operational Plan alone programmed more than eight thousand such weapons for attacks on the Soviet Union and her satellites. Did we really need that many to implement the containment/deterrence policy? President Truman would not use the weapon after World War II. Much of the impetus for the buildup occurred during President Eisenhower's administration, yet he would not use the weapon and expressed considerable concern about the magnitude of the stockpile.[52] The Johnson/McNamara administration went as far as proclaiming there were too many weapons, but the size of the stockpile kept rising.

4. Heavy Attack

Whether or not nuclear weapons would ever be used was of little concern to most people in the military forces during the late 1940s, 1950s, and 1960s. Nor were many concerned about the size and composition of the stockpile. The goal was to develop a delivery capability. Whether it was to be used or not, the bomb was the key to implementing the national containment/deterrence policy. Any of the services simply had to have a nuclear weapons delivery capability to be a player. The consequences of no capability were no dollars in the budget and no membership in the fraternity. It was that simple, such was the impact of the bomb on national security thinking—at least in the armed forces.

As a result, everyone wanted to be in the nuclear act. The Navy had already fought its battles for a piece of the action, which was granted by the Congress of the United States. Now, developing a realistic delivery capability was the task at hand. The main problem facing the Navy was finding a vehicle that could make it to a target from an aircraft carrier.

In the late 1940s, there was no question that for any issue in the military relating to atomic energy, Deak Parsons was the key. He did not have the senior rank of others, but he had something more important, namely knowledge of the subject and the respect of all, particularly the civilian scientists. He was "the man," be the issue atomic energy for the propulsion of surface ships and submarines, the delivery of atomic bombs, or educating the public on the subject through speeches and articles.[1] The scientists and engineers were producing atomic weapons. Parsons was the atomic admiral as far as knowledge of the subject was concerned, and his views were being supported by the Navy hierarchy. It was time to move forward. The political pressure was mounting, and action was needed.

A major problem facing Parsons was the exuberant enthusiasm and impatience emanating from those who wanted to get moving yet knew relatively little about nuclear energy. With only a smattering of knowledge, some Navy leaders wanted to charge full speed ahead. They started developing various plans of action, which became a problem for Parsons. He felt that these plans lacked realism and that few, if any, of the planners of senior and intermediate rank in the Pentagon had firsthand knowledge based on actual participation in operations for delivery of atomic bombs. "Lack of realism in atomic bomb delivery plans can be more serious than in other war plans involving more conventional operations, primarily because there would be less cushion of time in the case of atomic weapon delivery."[2]

One great mark of Parsons was his ability to keep things in order, to avoid charging blindly into areas where major mistakes could be made. He insisted on an orderly approach to the Navy's aircraft delivery problem. That meant educating both aircraft and ship people. The bomb could not be treated like any other weapon going aboard a carrier.[3]

Early on, Parsons told Dick Ashworth that when time came to organize a squadron of aircraft with the capability of delivering atomic weapons, he, Ashworth, should take command of the squadron. Ashworth's response was typical of the man, who always put the good of the service before his personal career. He demurred on the idea and told Parsons that only one naval aviator could pull this off—Chick Hayward. Ashworth reasoned that there would be political and technical aviation problems and that he lacked the experience to solve them. He felt that Hayward had forgotten more about naval aviation than he ever knew, and further, Hayward was a good politician, a necessary attribute in selling the program along the way to the Navy Department and the government. Hayward would also be able to offer his broad experience in aviation and his technical competence.

Parsons accepted Ashworth's position. Hayward was to be the leader, and Ashworth would be the executive officer of the first squadron. If and when a second squadron was formed, Ashworth would command that unit. Hayward became the commanding officer of Composite Squadron 5 (VC-5). The Navy traditionally used the letter "V" to denote "heavier-than-air" aviation. The "C" stood for "composite," indicating that the squadron would be composed of more than one type of aircraft. The "5" was used because there were already four composite squadrons in existence. Further, it was felt that the "composite" designation would help camouflage the mission of the squadron. Rightly or wrongly, security was an important factor. The security philosophy imposed by General Groves with the Manhattan Project carried over into subsequent developments in the nuclear weapon field. Later on, Ashworth did become the skipper of the second squadron, Composite Squadron 6 (VC-6).[4]

It is significant that the real authoritative power to get naval aviation into the atomic bomb business was in the hands of Parsons, a gun clubber, not an aviator. His specialty was ordnance and gunnery, but aviation was a means of getting "shots that counted"—the ancient adage of the gun clubber.

VC-5 was commissioned in September 1948 at the naval air station (NAS), Moffett Field, California, just south of San Francisco. Because the mission was going to involve the delivery of a "heavy" weapon, the aircraft also had to be big and "heavy." It did not take long for the program to be known as "heavy attack." The name represented a philosophy that was guarded closely. Actions aimed at getting the lighter, smaller, more conventional aircraft into the atomic bomb business were often viewed with alarm by the "heavy" protagonists, for it was felt that anything that tended to create a split in the Navy position and program would be detrimental to achieving the ultimate goal. Naval leaders were beginning to realize that obtaining the nuclear weapon delivery mission was going to be a key factor in the survival of the carrier.

The choice of people to be assigned was given a high priority. Hayward figured heavily in this aspect. It was decided that the pilots would be senior aviators, some with carrier experience, and others with a multiengine patrol plane background. He believed that the atomic bomb mission would require the ability to conduct operations day or night, in good or bad weather. At that time, carrier pilots were somewhat limited in night and all-weather operations. To compensate for that shortcoming, he wanted some multiengine patrol pilots.[5] He was criticized for this decision later because of some difficulties in operating the "heavy" aircraft from carriers, but at the time his reasoning made sense. It would be embarrassing, to say the least, to have an atomic bomb mission ordered and the carrier not able to fulfill the role because of a lack of night or all-weather experience. Therefore, Hayward started with senior aviators with varied flight backgrounds from their days in World War II.

For the technical side of the mission it was decided to have a bombardier in the crew, who would perform the role that Parsons and Ashworth had played in the Hiroshima and Nagasaki attacks. Qualifications for such a role meant a good flight record as an aviator and demonstrated academic excellence, often attained through postgraduate training. The commissioned officers selected for these assignments were outstanding.

The officer placed in charge of recruiting personnel for the program was Comdr. Joseph A. Jaap, later the commanding officer of the third heavy-attack squadron, VC-7, and eventually a rear admiral. The high priority placed on the program gave him a great charter for selecting people for the new venture. He reviewed records, conducted interviews, and made offers. Enlisted personnel were of a caliber equal to that of the commissioned officers.

The squadron was established initially in one of the old dirigible hangars at Moffett Field. Squadron spaces were surrounded with a security fence and guards to monitor the security, which was paramount. With a crew, a leader, and a high-priority mission, the squadron was ready for some flying. But in what?

The P2V Neptune

The Navy had one aircraft at the time that fulfilled some of the requirements for delivering an atomic bomb. The P2V Neptune, built by Lockheed Aircraft Corporation, was a superb aircraft for the mission it was designed for, namely, finding, identifying, and killing enemy submarines. Land-based and reliable, it could fly a long distance. In late September 1946, a stripped-down version of the aircraft, called the *Truculent Turtle,* flew from Perth, Australia, to Columbus, Ohio, in fifty-five hours, seventeen minutes and broke the world's record for distance without refueling—a flight of 11,235.6 miles.[6] It was piloted by Comdr. Thomas D. Davies, a bright young officer who later went on to be a key executive in the Arms Control and Disarmament Agency. That flight proved that the P2V had intercontinental range, at least (see table 1 for specifications).

The P2V was a very reliable aircraft, but not carrier capable in the true sense of the word. However, Hayward was convinced the P2V could be launched from the deck of a *Midway*-class carrier. He was right and proved the point many times. At the time, three such carriers existed: *Franklin D. Roosevelt* (CVA-41), *Midway* (CVA-42), and *Coral Sea* (CVA-43).

Twelve aircraft were specially configured for the atomic mission. They were identified as the P2V-3C, the "C" standing for "carrier." The plane would be loaded aboard the carrier by crane while at dockside. Then, after the carrier had sailed and arrived at the launch area, the planes would take off with a deck run. Jet-assisted takeoff (JATO) was required. JATO consisted of a pod of four small rockets fastened to each side of the fuselage. As the plane started to accelerate down

Table 1
Representative Aircraft Characteristics

Model	Empty Weight (lbs)	Wingspan (ft)	Length (ft)	Engines (number and type)	Power (hp, prop; lbs thrust, jet)	Maximum Speed (knots; clean)	Ceiling (ft)	Range (nautical miles)[1]	Weapons (bomb-lbs)[1]	Crew
P2V[2]	34,700	100	78	2 Wright R-3350	3,150 hp each	276	26,000	2,240	2,000	5+
AJ	30,800	75[3]	63	2 P&W R-2800 1 Allison J33	2,300 hp each 4,600 lbs	390	42,000	2,190	3,000	3
A-3	36,000	72.5	74.5	2 P&W J57	10,000 lbs each	545	42,000	2,325	2,000	3
A-5	32,800	53	76.6	2 GE J79	17,000 lbs each (AB)[4] 10,900 lbs each (non AB)	Mach 2.1 Mach .98	49,000 (AB)[4]	1,750	2,000	2

Source: Based on declassified standard aircraft characteristic (SAC) charts on file at the Naval Aviation History Center, Washington, D.C. Prepared by Harold Andrews, research associate, Smithsonian National Air and Space Museum.

Note: Characteristics are *generally* representative of the models listed. Some, such as range, may vary for the various versions of some models that were produced and with the payload placed on the aircraft. In-flight refueling also affected the range.

[1] Range and weapon data are typical for the heavy-attack mission, using only internal fuel tanks (except the AJ, which used full tip tanks).

[2] The P2V-3C version of the aircraft was stripped of defensive armament. A large fuel tank was installed internally. Some training and demonstration flights exceeded 4,000 nautical miles in range.

[3] The AJ wingspan includes tip tanks, which improved aerodynamic performance and were carried regularly.

[4] AB = after burner.

The Lockheed P2V Neptune. NASM collection.

the deck, the pilot ignited the rockets to provide the extra thrust needed to get the plane off the deck at its weight of about 70,000 pounds. Once airborne, the task was one of navigating to the target, day or night, fair weather or foul. Following delivery of the bomb, the plane would return to a friendly field or a ditching in the water, preferably near a carrier or friendly submarine. To facilitate the water landing, a flat plate about two feet square was installed on the underside of the nose section of the plane. It was actuated by a hydraulic system and intended to help hold the nose of the plane up during the water landing. No one was particularly enthusiastic about this prospect, but this was the intent.[7]

There was much interest in the new program, and Hayward was very active in selling the concept. As part of his effort, he took appropriate personnel for demonstration rides from the carrier deck to show that the plane could be launched and fly an atomic bomb mission. Hayward had a unique opportunity to demonstrate a P2V take-off from the USS *Midway* on 26 September 1949, at the conclusion

First launch of a P2V aircraft from a carrier (USS *Coral Sea*), mid-1948. Launch was aided by jet-assisted takeoff. The pilot was Comdr. (then) Tom Davies. Navy photo, NASM collection.

of an air show for Secretary of Defense Louis Johnson and the Joint Chiefs of Staff. The passengers going back to Washington National Airport on the P2V included Johnson, Chairman of the Joint Chiefs of Staff Gen. Omar Bradley, Secretary of the Air Force Stuart Symington, and William Randolph Hearst. At that time Johnson was in the process of canceling the carrier USS *United States,* which was to have been a flush-deck carrier. Hayward put the secretary of defense in the right seat of the cockpit for the takeoff. The wingspan of the P2V was so wide that the right wing of the plane would come very close to the island structure of the ship as the plane roared down the deck on takeoff. As Hayward strapped the secretary into the copilot seat, he remarked that if the starboard engine quit, the Navy would have a flush-deck carrier, and he would be in the middle of it!

Symington laughed and kidded Johnson about it. Bradley said nothing. Hayward fired the rockets, and off they went to Washington, where he left his passengers and immediately departed for Moffett Field. He landed early next morning, only to be greeted by the duty officer, who said that the chief of naval operations wanted him on the phone. It seems that Symington had told the *Washington Post* of his remarks to the secretary. Needless to say, the Navy was quite upset! It was just a part of the Navy's struggle to get an atomic capability to sea.[8]

Hayward also believed that the P2V-3C could be recovered aboard the carrier, using the normal carrier-arrested landing techniques. To validate his belief, the Navy conducted arrested-landing tests at its facility at Patuxent River, Maryland. A tailhook was installed in a Neptune, and Lt. Comdr. (then) E. L. "Whitey" Feightner, one of the Navy's most highly regarded test pilots, took on the testing project. An arresting-gear installation at Patuxent River is similar to that on board carriers. In testing, the plane is flown in a normal carrier approach pattern and lands, with the tailhook engaging one of the arresting wires laid across the runway.

Feightner and Don Runyan, another test pilot, made about fifty landings into the shore-based arresting gear. They thought that landing aboard ship was entirely feasible, and Feightner was ready to do so. They put Chick Hayward in the cockpit, and he made several successful landings at the test center. Eddie Outlaw, another senior carrier aviator and member of the squadron, made several landings with "no problem." Things were looking good.[9]

Then one of the more senior pilots in the squadron, not a carrier aviator, took over the controls. Sitting in the right seat of the cockpit in the copilot station was Lt. Comdr. (then) Raymond Herzberger. They made several practice landings with the tailhook in the "up" position to get a feel for the arrested landing. Everything went well, so the pilot dropped the hook and came around, intending to catch a wire for a full arrested landing. The hook engaged the wire properly. However, the pilot did not relax the controls after receiving the cut-engine signal from the landing-signal officer, in order to ease the plane down closer to the ground—a rather natural maneuver for most carrier pilots at that time. As a result, the aircraft was arrested in midair and came crashing to the runway. Feightner was standing at the side of the runway, observing the tests. He and Herzberger concur. "There were rivets everywhere!"[10]

Still another effort was made to develop a carrier-landing tactic. The P2V had the ability to reverse the pitch of the propellers. To ensure that the reversal occurred only after landing, a switch was installed on the landing gear so that if the weight of the plane was not on the gear after landing, the propellers would not reverse. However, the switch could be bypassed if desired. Vice Adm. Turner Caldwell was a young test pilot at the time. With the switch on the landing gear in the bypass position, he made some attempts at a landing. Just before touchdown, he would reverse the props, thereby stopping the plane after a short run, but on one landing he reversed the props a bit too soon, and the plane came crashing to the ground.[11] That was the end of attempts to land the P2V on a carrier. Although many takeoffs were made from carrier decks, the arrested landings never progressed beyond those flown at the test center at Patuxent River.

The P2V's inability to land on the carrier was a serious deficiency, which was to be corrected eventually with the introduction of the AJ aircraft. The AJ was designed specifically for a long-range, heavy-payload mission from an aircraft carrier, but the development of that aircraft was taking time. Hayward wanted a capability now—and the P2V was his only option.

Another problem with the P2V was accuracy. The bomb would have to be dropped from high altitude for the plane and its crew to survive the ensuing explosion, which would detract somewhat from the accuracy of the attack. Ashworth pointed out that the size of the bang would make up for a lot of inaccuracy of delivery. Unfortunately, the APA-5 bombing system in the airplane was designed for low-altitude delivery of a weapon against ships and submarines and had to be modified for high-altitude performance. The only system available at the time, it was carried over into early versions of the successor airplane, the AJ Savage. Eventually a better system was provided for the later AJ Savage and its successor, the Douglas A3D Skywarrior. That system, known as the ASB-1, was a significant improvement, adding considerably to the accuracy of delivery.[12]

Despite the deficiencies of the P2V aircraft for the mission, its use as an atomic bomb delivery aircraft was not as unrealistic as some might imagine. In late 1950, during the Korean War, the Marines were caught at the Chosin Reservoir area of North Korea as large numbers of Chinese forces came across the border and joined in the combat. Task Force 77, in the Sea of Japan, enjoyed good weather and kept fighter and attack aircraft over the withdrawal area for many days as the Marines fought their way back to the port of Hungman and evacuation to sea, along with about 100,000 Korean civilians. On 6 December 1950, after the Chinese had crossed the Yalu River in force, President Truman endorsed the Joint Chiefs' request that nonnuclear components of the bomb be stocked on board the aircraft carrier USS *Franklin D. Roosevelt,* stationed in the Mediterranean. Concerned about developments in Korea, he was obviously taking steps recommended by his advisors to use nuclear weapons if the occasion demanded. Two suggestions for exploiting that asset were made by the administration's best-known critic, Gen. Douglas MacArthur: dropping nuclear weapons in the Yalu River area to irradiate China and sowing radioactive waste to impede the Chinese advance down the Korean peninsula.[13] The nuclear weapon had some possibilities, but mounting the support to use it was another matter. As President Eisenhower mentioned later, public opinion was in some ways more powerful than the atomic bomb.

Training

The nuclear weapons delivery mission called for some of the most serious flying that the Navy had been involved with since the combat flights of World War II. There was no precedent for preparing for the mission, but Hayward was the leader, and he was the right man for the job. He had a good feeling for what would be required, and he set about getting a squadron ready to accomplish the assigned task. Much effort was directed toward bringing the pilots up to Hayward's stringent requirements for night and instrument flying. All pilots attended an instrument flying course at the naval air station in Corpus Christi, Texas, and were required to make long-range navigational training flights, many of them trans-Pacific flights to Honolulu and back, to practice over-water navigation. Flight crews navigated by celestial navigation, and the bombardier/navigators became very proficient in this art. Hayward stipulated that on any long flight, at least half the trip had to be made at night. Under no circumstances would the trip be canceled or delayed for adverse weather. As the night and instrument training was being conducted, the bombardier/navigators were learning the squadron-level maintenance and operational requirements for handling the bomb. Early on, it was evident that they simply were not ready for actual bombing, and they needed a lot of training.[14]

In early 1947, Lt. (then) Frank Ault was in the third class of naval aviators to receive the specialized weaponeer or bombardier training in Albuquerque, New Mexico. There were only four naval officers in the class, training to monitor the "go/no-go" status of an atomic weapon en route to the target, then complete the final assembly and arm the weapon just prior to drop. Chick Hayward was also at the facility in a top-level job, before taking over command of VC-5. He stressed to the class the seriousness of the training and emphasized that they would be in a weaponeer class with their contemporaries in the Air Force and that they were expected to stand 1-2-3-4 academically at the completion of the course. "While we didn't realize it at the time, Hayward's mandate was indicative of the fact that Navy leadership understood just how important it was that the Navy present authentic proof of its determination and readiness to become an accomplished performer in the nuclear warfare arena. Deak Parsons and Dick Ashworth had already set a precedent for high quality performance. We were expected to follow their example."[15]

The first six weeks of the weaponeer course were strictly academic.

During that period, students reviewed mathematics up through integral calculus, refreshed and added to their understanding of chemistry and physics, and built a workable nine-tube radio. They then turned to the details of the design and function of the implosion and gun-type atomic weapons.

A major consideration was the flight test box (FTB), which was connected to the bomb and provided indications of the "health" and status of the bomb while en route to the target. This box, about $2 \times 2 \times 1\frac{1}{2}$ feet, was as complicated as the bombs themselves and more likely than the bombs to malfunction in flight. Since an authentic no-go indication on the FTB required the mission to be aborted, it was very important that the source of the problem (i.e., bomb or FTB) be isolated and its consequences vis-à-vis mission completion thoughtfully evaluated. In the early days, troubleshooting of the FTB was a major enterprise and occupied a lot of training time. Weaponeers were trained and equipped not only to diagnose problems with the FTB, but also to repair it in flight. It was clear that there had to be a better way to reach a go/no-go decision, which would turn out to be an essential element in the development of a tactical nuclear weapon delivery capability in light attack and fighter aircraft.[16]

Upon graduation, Ault was retained as an instructor in the program. His duties involved instruction in bomb design and function for weaponeers, weapon-assembly teams, and bomb commanders. His first weaponeer class included Navy and Air Force students, including Maj. Jim Ferebee, who had been the bombardier on the Hiroshima mission with Deak Parsons. It became Ault's unpleasant task to wash Ferebee out of the weaponeer program for failure to meet the academic requirements. The decision was a delicate one, since interservice politics loomed in the background.[17] Ferebee's case drove home the point that being a bombardier did not necessarily qualify you to be a weaponeer.

Naval aviation was making a mighty effort to stay in the atomic warfare act. The inability of the P2V to land on a carrier was another reason for the Navy to speed the entry of its successor into the fleet.

Obviously, the P2V operation was a long way from being practical. But in the light of the political situation after World War II, when the Air Force was laying claim to all military aviation, including the carriers and particularly the atom bomb, it was imperative that the Navy demonstrate that it was not going to give up in the competition for a role in atomic bomb operations. The P2V represented a real capability, albeit not very efficient. The pressure was on Hayward to get the new AJ aircraft into the fleet operations as soon as possible.[18]

The AJ Savage

In the late months of World War II, Vice Adm. Marc A. Mitscher, the great leader of carriers during the early days of the war, was the head of naval aviation in Washington, D.C. Mitscher was relieved by Vice Adm. (then) Arthur W. Radford, a particularly strong personality.[19] During the Mitscher and Radford era, two significant weapons requirements were promulgated for naval aviation. One called for aircraft that could carry a ten-thousand-pound payload for a good distance. The need for such an aircraft was apparent well before the atomic bomb arrived on the scene. World War II had taught the admirals that they would be attacking more than ships in future campaigns. They would have to have more range and payload capability in the aircraft. That meant better aircraft and better carriers, part of the evolutionary improvement process that has gone on in naval aviation for over eighty years.

The other requirement was for an aircraft carrier from which this new, big, heavy-attack aircraft could operate. It became erroneously labeled a "super carrier," for there was nothing particularly "super" about it. It was a larger version of the *Midway* class, displacing about 85,000 tons. Its most unusual aspect was that it was to be a flush-deck ship, that is, there would be no island structure above the flight-deck level during flight operations.

So, with plans for a big airplane and a big ship from which it could operate, the Navy was on its way to attaining an atomic bomb delivery capability, with something better than the makeshift P2V-3C Neptune, to be matched with the *Midway*-class carrier and the Mark VII atomic weapon.

One of the ludicrous aspects of the program stemmed from the extreme security classifications that were imposed. Although the Navy issued a set of specifications for a new airplane, they would not tell the contractor the intended mission of the aircraft. That posed some questions for the designers. When Dick Ashworth was the secretary of the Military Liaison Committee, serving the Atomic Energy Commission, he learned of the contract with North American Aviation Corporation to produce the new heavy bomber for carrier aviation. Capt. J. N. Murphy headed the attack-aircraft desk in the Navy's Bureau of Aeronautics and had the necessary security clearances for atomic information. He and Ashworth went to the North American factory to ensure that the new bomber would, in fact, accept the Fat Man type of bomb. On first look, it seemed entirely feasible. There were some obvious conflicts in the bomb bay, such as the location of hydraulic lines and wiring, but these seemed to be solvable. It looked as if the large-box tail of the bomb would make it difficult to close the bomb bay doors. Ultimately, bulges were worked into the doors to accommodate the bomb tail.

Before Ashworth and Murphy could be sure that they were on the right track, they needed a full-scale model of the bomb to check the fit. However, because of security regulations, they needed permission to discuss various design aspects with the contractor, which was obtained from the chief of the Armed Forces Special Weapons Project in Albuquerque.

Murphy brought an actual bomb suspension lug and the dimensions of the sway braces that would stabilize the bomb in the bomb bay. From these he could determine where the braces would contact the bomb case. Ashworth knew that the bomb case was an ellipsoid, and he thought the North American draftsmen might be able to make a mockup of the bomb from the specifications. They asked the contractor representatives if they could come up with something like a mockup.

The North American AJ Savage. NASM collection.

About an hour later, the project engineer showed up with what appeared to be an exact wooden copy of the external Fat Man bomb shape, something that would have taken a lot longer to produce than the one hour they had waited. They attached the lug, hoisted the wooden mockup into the bomb bay, and checked it for clearances, all with the North American people restricted from the mockup room. It appeared that the design of the plane would accommodate the bomb. After it was all over, the North American people said that they did not understand what all the secrecy was about. They had just gone through the whole exercise with the Air Force, fitting their Fat Man model into an Air Force aircraft.[20]

According to George Spangenberg, a key official in the procurement of naval aircraft, the AJ was intended to be a "demonstration aircraft," that is, one meant to test and prove a concept. Many were skeptical about the ability of naval aviation to operate a large aircraft from carriers. The critics had valid questions, and the Navy had no proof that it could double the weight of its strike aircraft and still operate successfully. Therefore, the AJ had to become part of the aircraft inven-

USS *Midway* with twelve AJ Savage aircraft on board. U.S. Navy photo.

tory to convince many in naval aviation, as well as the civil authority and members of the other services, of the mission's viability. The real capability would come later, when the weight of the atomic bomb was decreased, when jet engines were improved, and when catapult and arresting gear on the carriers were built up to handle the increasing energy requirements that were emerging.[21] But the pressure was on to get a capability, and "demonstration" turned into real operations.

The atomic bomb delivery mission was a logical use for the AJ aircraft, but major problems developed because of the pressure to get it into the active inventory as soon as possible. That pressure forced the airplane out of the normal development/testing cycle. As a result, its entry into service was fraught with mishaps. Its few successes came from heroic efforts of individuals devoted to gaining an atomic weapons capability for the carriers.

Chick Hayward called the aircraft a "dog." It was not user friendly. It killed people. It was also "ugly," a label placed on it as it was rolled out of the hangar at North American for its first view by the general public (see table 1 for specifications).[22]

Because the AJ was big and the carrier for which it was destined had been canceled, the plane was forced to operate from the decks of the *Midway*-class carriers. Its presence on board ship was not welcome. It was so big and cumbersome that it complicated any other flight operations the ship was required to conduct. When the AJ showed up on board, it meant the ship was in an atomic mode. By the time the large *Forrestal*-class and subsequent 90,000-ton angled-deck carriers came into being, the AJ was out of date. It was used as a tanker for in-flight refueling for a time and then retired from service in the Navy. Eventually some models were used for fire fighting in commercial roles. By that time, it had become user friendly.

There was a lot of political pressure on Hayward to get the AJ into a nuclear-capable operating status, much of it generated by the admirals themselves. In order to expedite the introduction of the airplane into the fleet, Hayward chose to abandon the traditional method of having new aircraft tested thoroughly before introduction to operational fleet squadrons. Some AJ aircraft went into the test program, but many went directly to the squadrons, first at Moffett Field, and later at Patuxent River, Maryland, where VC-5 and VC-6 had been relocated from California. Hayward dealt directly with the North American factory, working out the bugs, getting spare parts, and solving the many problems that arose. The P2V-3Cs still assigned to the squadrons were often used to ferry parts and people to and from the North American factory.

Hayward received considerable criticism for taking this approach, but politics plays a big role in the ability of the services to remain viable, and this was a serious challenge to the Navy. It is difficult to predict what might have happened to naval aviation had Hayward not taken the short-cut approach. The nuclear mission was the only game in town, and the Navy had to get into it. Although pilots reported that the AJ had good flying qualities, the problems were many. It was capable of launching and landing on the carrier with considerable ease, always a factor of concern to carrier aviators. However, in sharp contrast to the P2V, the AJ was very unreliable, and that feature caused great concern. The inability to operate without some kind of an emergency occurring while in flight could be devastating to the success of any program. Nonetheless, the fact of the matter was that this program had to succeed. The future of the carrier was threatened.

Ashworth had some serious doubts about putting the aircraft into the fleet without the traditional testing. After he took command of VC-6, he recommended "that the aircraft be taken out of service and placed under the Service Test Division at the Test Center at Patuxent River." Further support for taking it out of service came from the head of the Test Center. Hayward absolutely refused to go along with the recommendation. He understood the reasoning behind Ashworth's recommendation, but he was under pressure that no one could really appreciate and fully understand. In reflecting on the issue in later years, Ashworth commented, "With the inside information that Chick had, I think that in the long run he was right. Certainly, we got the planes into the fleet quicker. This is not to say that it was a smooth operation."[23]

Because the AJ aircraft was so large and the carriers relatively small, the method of employing it was unique. Instead of being based aboard the ship and integrated with the embarked air group, the aircraft were deployed to Port Lyautey in Morocco and operated from a shore station. When needed for the atomic bomb mission, they were to proceed to the carriers and land aboard. While the carrier headed toward the target area, the aircraft were to be loaded with the atomic weapons that were already on the ship. This unorthodox tactic represented a viable carrier nuclear delivery capability, despite its impact on other carrier operations. The presence of the AJ on board made it quite unpopular with the other members of the embarked air group and personnel in the ship who were handling it. World War II operations were still prevalent in the minds of the traditional naval aviator—and the new mission did not fit the World War II mold by any means.

The deaths caused by the AJ started early, with the second experimental airplane. Two North American test pilots were conducting a rudder test off the California coast. During one maneuver, the tail came off the airplane, causing the death of both pilots. Other accidents followed during the test program with North American personnel. However, at least one test pilot reported that the early version of the AJ, with a stick instead of a wheel for control, super high control-boost ratios, and a dihedral horizontal stabilizer, "was a dream to fly." When everything was working properly, "it handled like a fighter." The problem was that everything was working properly only about 5 percent of the time; the rest of the time, the pilot was coping with everything from a minor annoyance to a struggle to stay alive. This early version of the aircraft had, to say the least, "some very peculiar characteristics during high-speed flight."[24]

One student of the program believes that accidents were caused by two major factors. The first was design deficiencies, brought about by drastic reductions in North American's workforce following World War II, which adversely affected the engineering design staff. Another factor was the pressure to get the aircraft into the operational forces as soon as possible. "Design deficiencies which surfaced during test and early operational flying were the source of accidents causing the loss of aircraft and a number of fatalities. Major problem areas included the hydraulic system, flight controls, turbosuperchargers, fuel systems, and the jet engine installation, particularly the fuel system. Many of the problems undoubtedly would have been detected and corrected during the early stages of a normal contractor and Navy flight test program."[25]

One accident in particular, resulting in the loss of Lt. Comdr. David Purdon and his crew in October 1950, created a great deal of concern. Purdon was a brilliant young officer with postgraduate training in aeronautical engineering. Before a catapult launching, he was observed to rotate his control stick throughout its range and bring it back to center, which was standard practice to check on the freedom of operation of the elevators and ailerons. During the launch, Purdon made a normal run down the catapult track, as recorded by motion pictures. Immediately off the bow of the ship, where he should have started his rotation to climb, the aircraft dove straight into the sea ahead of the carrier.

The investigation of this accident concluded that after Purdon checked his flight controls and brought them back to center position, they locked in that position. If so, there was no chance for recovery, and the crash was inevitable. What was worse, in checking all aircraft in the squadron, it was learned that the same thing could have happened with other planes. This was the sort of malfunction that could have been detected and probably solved in the Service Test Division at Patuxent River.[26]

Hayward's solution to the AJ problem was to bring a large group of North American engineers and repair people from California to Patuxent River and set up a modification line in one of the hangars on the station. Most of the problems were straightened out, but even after that, when the aircraft were deployed to the Mediterranean and Port Lyautey, they continued to have accidents in which aircraft and people were lost.

The fact that the AJ had no integral wing-folding system brought gray hair to flight deck crews on carriers in the Atlantic. Because of its size, if the AJ had problems and had to abort a scheduled launch, the flight schedule for the day became a shambles. It was difficult and time consuming to get the aircraft out of the way so that other planes could launch. To fold the outer wing panels, a crewman had to mount each wing, open an access plate, hook up a hand hydraulic pump, and pump up each wing panel separately. This was not a very speedy operation.

Further, the AJ had a bank of overheat lights on the left side of the cockpit, and alongside that, a smaller bank of fire-warning lights. Nothing could give a pilot a quicker squirt of adrenaline than to be on solid instruments at night and have those lights start winking at him. It happened so frequently that pilots became complacent, but fortunately, it was usually no cause for alarm.[27]

The training and tactics planned for the use of the AJ in the nuclear weapons delivery mission were also of great concern. In preparing for the attack on an assigned target, flight crews used stereo photos, analyses of building heights and construction in the target area, existing radar returns from rivers, bridges, and railroad marshaling yards, and so forth to prepare a picture of what would appear on the bombing radar during a specific approach. From these predictions, crews could select the target, the initial point (IP, a reference point that was a known distance and direction from the target) during the approach, and the release point. They tested these predictions with practice runs on the radar bomb-scoring site at Richmond, Virginia, which was operated by the U.S. Air Force. Bombing runs were usually made at an altitude between 25,000 and 35,000 feet. Training sessions lasted about an hour, and ten or twelve runs were made during each session.

When deployed overseas, in the event of an actual nuclear strike, squadrons operating from the shore base in Port Lyautey, Morocco, would fly onto a carrier in the Mediterranean to be loaded with a nuclear weapon and then launched from some location in the eastern Mediterranean. Tactics called for flying at low level through Bulgaria and Romania, avoiding briefed radar and antiaircraft areas. Nearing the target, the pilot was to climb at maximum power to drop altitude. Following the drop of the weapon, the pilot was to execute a hard wing-over and, with maximum power, dive for a low-altitude withdrawal, positioning the tail of the aircraft so that it was aimed directly at the bomb burst in order to avoid serious damage to the plane.[28] Targets on the periphery of the Soviet Union had to be taken out in order to provide for a reliable penetration of the air space surrounding the strategic objectives.

In retrospect, the AJ had a pretty spotty career. It was put into service faster than it should have been. It was the largest carrier-designed airplane that had been operated by the Navy up to that time. There was a learning curve to be mastered. The airplane was capable of conducting the delivery mission, if it encountered no serious maintenance problems in flight. It was probably a good example of the consequences of trying to bypass the traditional test program. But the roles and mission battle was raging between the services, and the Navy had to produce. Unfortunately, some good people paid a high price to gain that capability.[29]

The A3D Skywarrior

The Navy finally began to get the heavy-attack program under control in the mid-1950s. Two major events made it possible. The first was the introduction of the USS *Forrestal* (CVA-59), a large carrier with an angled deck and some of the modern features developed during the long hiatus in new carrier construction. The second was the introduction of the A3D Skywarrior (hereafter called the A-3), designed under the direction of master aeronautical engineer Edward Heinemann and built by the Douglas Aircraft Corporation. Contrary to the expectations of many naval aeronautical experts, Heinemann and his team were able to design an airplane that weighed about 68,000 pounds, the weight that the flight decks of the *Midway*-class carriers could withstand during carrier operations (see table 1 for specifications).

Douglas Aircraft Corporation's experience with nuclear weapons security during its design of the A-3 was similar to that encountered by North American Aviation in the design of the AJ. Heinemann, who figured so prominently in the design of many Douglas aircraft, faced a frustrating situation with the tight security associated with nuclear weapons production. Although deeply involved in the design of an aircraft that would meet the Navy's requirement of carrying a large nuclear weapon, he was not provided with the details of the payload the plane was to carry, though he tried in vain to obtain specifics on the atomic weapon.

Heinemann was convinced that state-of-the-art weapons technology could produce a much smaller weapon than what was laid out in the specifications for the new heavy bomber, but he could not get any information on the subject. During the design of the aircraft, he discussed the bomber with Col. Otto Glasser, a representative from the Sandia Corporation. Heinemann said that if a nuclear weapon con-

The Douglas A-3 Skywarrior heavy-attack aircraft. NASM collection.

siderably smaller than Fat Man could be produced, the design of the aircraft could be greatly improved. Considerable reduction in weight could be achieved, with a commensurate improvement in the capability of the plane. When Glasser asked Heinemann how much reduction he had in mind, he came up with the figure of thirty-two inches in diameter, as opposed to the five feet of Fat Man. Thirty-two inches just happened to be the diameter he had set on his compass as he worked on the features of a new fighter, the F4D Skyray.

This information alarmed Glasser, for the scientists at Sandia were at that time moving in the direction of a thirty-two-inch-diameter bomb. Heinemann's intuitive idea earned him a prompt visit from the government security hawks in Washington. It was a period in which nuclear weapons and aviation technology were making great strides, and security of all information was of high priority. As Heinemann commented in 1980, "Jet technology, high altitude flight, and the increasing speeds of aircraft were viewed as sensitive topics by government officials. We were on a new threshold of learning. The restrictions placed on us then would seem ludicrous today."[30]

Although the A-3 was a great airplane, its introduction as an integral part of the regular air wing on the carriers did not come about easily. Even though it went through the normal test program, which had been partially bypassed for the AJ aircraft, it encountered some difficulties in the fleet, much the same as any new aircraft entering service.

Many people were involved in the introduction of the A-3 into carrier operations, starting with the test pilots at Patuxent River, Maryland. Moving the plane from the test phase to an operational phase was critical. Great credit must be given to Capt. Paul Stevens, who worked with it at Patuxent and then was assigned to head up the unit that would take it to sea for the first time, one of the most critical and significant assignments any aviator can receive.[31] The squadron, designated Heavy Attack Squadron 1 (VAH-1), would be an integral part of the embarked air wing when operating at sea. The days of shore basing at Port Lyautey were over. The A-3 was to fit into normal carrier operating procedures.

The squadron selected for conversion to the A-3 was a patrol plane squadron. Manpower assignment authorities assumed that the patrol plane pilots and the enlisted maintenance element in the squadron would convert to the A-3 jet. Stevens spent many hours working on the personnel situation until he got some dedicated people who had in common "desire, motivation, and the will to excel as carrier pilots." Whether a pilot had carrier background or patrol plane experience seemed to make little difference in performance. Other characteristics were more important. Stevens was supported in his personnel efforts by the wing commander, Capt. Tom Blackburn, who was instrumental in making many things go right for the heavy-attack community in its early days. To Stevens, Blackburn represented aggressive competence in every instance. He was a pillar of strength, highly knowledgeable, and always in the right place at the right time.

The A-3 made significant demands on a pilot making an arrested landing on a carrier. It was neutral to unstable in pitch, and airspeed control was difficult in the landing configuration. The margin for error was substantially less than with any of the airplanes Stevens had flown aboard ship during his tour as a test pilot. One really had to work and pay close attention. A good scan of the instruments in the cockpit was essential, and still, the pilot never knew whether he would get a wire or bolt off the angled deck for another try at landing.[32]

The squadron received its last of twelve airplanes in August 1956 and deployed in November for the 1956 Suez crisis, with half of the squadron on the *Forrestal* and the other half on its new sister ship, the *Saratoga* (CVA-60). Since that relatively short deployment went well, the decision was made to deploy the entire squadron to the Mediterranean aboard the *Forrestal* in January 1957. Stevens must receive a great deal of the credit for that highly successful deployment, although his time had run out, and he was detached for another important assignment at the Test Center just prior to the deployment. Tom Blackburn had kept Stevens on board for an extra three months prior to the deployment, refusing to allow a change of command until all details had been completed.

Ed Heinemann viewed Stevens's role in heading the introduction of the A-3 into the fleet as critical and a great plus. He commented to Stevens that the introduction of an airplane into the fleet was always of great concern to him, since he knew from experience the importance of a good introduction and was well aware of the trials and problems that are encountered in making new equipment function properly. The A-3 was of special concern because it represented one of the most significant steps taken in recent years. With the introduction under Stevens's guidance and supervision, however, Heinemann soon had the feeling that the airplane was in the best possible hands and that if anyone could get if off to a good start, Stevens could, in spite of all the problems that were bound to occur.[33] Having the aircraft designer and the fleet operator on good terms was a good omen.

Stevens considered the A-3 one of the all-time great Navy airplanes. Because of its size, it was not exactly loved by the flight deck officers on the carriers. However, the higher levels of command appreciated its capabilities, particularly in the night and all-weather attack modes. It was a winner that excelled in the nuclear role until replaced by the magnificent A-6 Intruder aircraft.[34] Its introduction began to ease the fears of some leaders about the future of the carrier.

The officer assigned to relieve Stevens as the commanding officer of VAH-1 was Comdr. Joe Dorrington, whose carrier experience was negligible, but who was one of those multiengine pilots that Hayward was seeking, one with extensive night and instrument flying experience.[35] Unfortunately, prior to assuming command of the squadron, Dorrington was involved in a serious automobile accident and was hospitalized for two months. He was unable to qualify for night operations with the A-3 before deployment, a serious deficiency for the squadron commander. His injuries hampered his ability to perform the more challenging missions during the deployment. Fortunately, he had chosen as his executive officer Comdr. William Spiegel, who had an excellent background for the position in which he was placed.[36]

During the squadron deployment to the Mediterranean starting in January 1957, under the leadership of Dorrington and Spiegel, the squadron experienced several problems in the area of deck handling and catapult positioning, which one might expect with an airplane as large and unwieldy as the A-3. However, after a week or two of air operations, the flight deck crews and plane handlers got used to the idiosyncrasies of the thirty-ton jet. Round-the-clock, all-weather operations became routine. NATO leaders were impressed by the squadron's nuclear delivery capability under all conditions. The squadron also operated without accidents and won an award for operating safely. The deployment gave great confidence to Navy leadership regarding its nuclear weapons delivery capability: "The sight of the gigantic sweptwing jet bomber riding down the landing approach groove onto the broad flight deck of the *Forrestal* was seeing a dream of naval air power come true."[37] Along with Stevens, Spiegel deserves much credit for the success of the A-3 during this early deployment.

Some of the subsequent deployments did not measure up to the first. Shortly before Dorrington was succeeded by Spiegel as the commanding officer of VAH-1, a serious accident occurred during a short postdeployment exercise. Then, not long after Spiegel became the commanding officer, two serious accidents occurred within forty-eight hours, one involving a low-level escape from the aircraft.

One emerging problem was the proficiency in carrier operations exhibited by some of the "second generation" heavy-attack pilots. Paul Stevens had concentrated his diligent attention on getting people who were dedicated and motivated to become good carrier pilots, regardless of their aviation background. Whether pilots in succeeding squadrons may have been short on carrier experience in the first place or awed by the size and weight of the aircraft, some were not as positive or as comfortable in their approach to carrier duties as others thought they should be. Their operations elicited some adverse comments.

Of these, one of the most published came from Vice Adm. (then) Charles "Cat" Brown, who was the commander of the Sixth Fleet in the Mediterranean at the time. He was not impressed and sent a very thoughtful and critical message concerning the heavy-attack program, stating that he had "at last reached the conclusion that our whole approach to the training of our heavy attack squadrons has been based upon an erroneous premise, namely that we should start with multi-engine pilots and qualify them on carriers." While he was complimentary about the great accomplishments of the patrol plane community, there was no question that he felt the original concept started by Chick Hayward had serious flaws. His recommended solution was "to undo the mischief that has been a long time brewing. . . . [A]t an early date the senior officers in each heavy attack squadron [should] be former carrier pilots."

His message was not helpful to the morale of the heavy-attack community. Whereas Paul Stevens had concentrated on getting motivated pilots for the first A-3 squadron, regardless of their flying background, Cat Brown was recommending a major change in policy—carrier pilots only as the leaders. His message, which was widely publicized,[38] at least got the attention of the A-3 aircraft community. The Navy had recognized the problem. They knew they finally had a good airplane, but some pilots were flying the airplane as if it were a large patrol plane, not a high-performance carrier aircraft.

Subsequent to the infamous Cat Brown message, Capt. (then) James D. "Jig" Ramage was again brought into the nuclear business. He was chosen to take command of the Atlantic Fleet wing of heavy-attack squadrons and get the pilots properly oriented toward carrier operations. The Cat Brown message gave him a perfect incentive to convince his charges that they had some work to do.[39] Ramage had previously studied the command structure of the heavy-attack pilot community and had some reservations, which he submitted in a report to the deputy chief of naval operations for air warfare. He was familiar with some of the problems that were surfacing. As he commenced his new assignment, he delved deeply into the personnel situation. Within a month, he ascertained that among other things, there was a severe morale problem among the bombardier/navigators who were also rated pilots; further, that there was a number of senior pilots who were in no way qualified to operate the A-3 from carriers. On the plus side, he was tremendously impressed with the caliber of the maintenance personnel and found that several enlisted personnel were the best-qualified bombardier/navigators.

Finally, although he felt that the A-3 was a remarkable carrier-based aircraft, the A-3 community was suffering from an inferiority complex. Flight crews needed to establish a new image as competent carrier aviators, and this could only occur if they demonstrated their ability around the carrier. Ramage pointed out that although operations near the carrier were only about 5 percent of the mission, it was the first 5 percent and the one on which a lot of their reputation would be based. His first problem was producing quality pilots, and second, the withdrawal of rated pilots from the bombardier/navigator role. With some help from higher authority, new rules for induction of pilots into the heavy-attack wing training program were established. Pilots would come from four categories. The first would be jet pilots on a current tour of flying duty. The second would be carrier-qualified jet pilots returning to sea duty. The third would be carrier-qualified propeller pilots. And the fourth would be young, motivated pilots from any source, including the bombardier/navigators moving out of the right-hand seats in the A-3.

Ramage was very concerned about some of the older pilots who had not demonstrated the required degree of carrier expertise and would have to leave. He blamed personnel assignment policies, not the individuals themselves. He was supported completely by higher authority in his plan to accept a limited number of motivated junior and middle-grade officers from the patrol plane community, but he did not want Navy officers in the grade of commander without previous carrier experience. There had been fatalities in this group, and Ramage felt it was a basic reason for the problems in A-3 operations.

Ramage was also concerned about morale. Nicknamed "The Whale," the A-3 was not welcomed aboard ship. Its great size and the previous operating problems had set the fleet against the now-improving squadrons. To emphasize that they were part of the carrier Navy, Ramage hung a tailhook over his office door. New pilots were given the famous Cat Brown dispatch to read upon reporting aboard for duty. In addition, Ramage introduced several morale-boosting events. He had the pilots working on the new low-level delivery approach, which stimulated a lot of interest. He instituted bombing competitions between heavy-attack squadrons, between squadrons in the emerging light-attack community, and against units of the Strategic Air Command. The impact of his actions, coupled with the capabilities of the airplane, seemed to bring the heavy-attack program into the carrier Navy as a full-fledged partner, a key instrument in the offensive armament of the Navy.[40]

The success of the Ramage approach was reflected in a subsequent message from Adm. Cat Brown wherein he said that he was glad to "eat crow" in this case; that he very much wanted the A-3 in his fleet. Many joined in the admiration and respect given to Ramage for taking a good airplane and a good program, and creating a truly professional carrier operation. In the words of Dick Ashworth: "I say thanks to Jig Ramage, a first class carrier aviator, for bringing carrier people into the program and putting it on its feet. Much of the later success of the program should be credited to Ramage. The famous dispatch that Admiral Brown sent to Washington to the effect "Get this gang of unqualified people out of my fleet" was followed later by a follow-up message, "This is a capability I want in the Sixth Fleet." That was quite an accomplishment on the part of Ramage."[41]

The A-3 was highly successful on the *Forrestal,* but there was more to come. The plane was so capable that it was decided to use it on the smaller, converted, *Essex*-class carriers, not with full twelve-plane squadrons, but with small detachments. In the late 1950s, Heavy Attack Squadron 4 (VAH-4), based in Whidbey Island, Washington, provided six-plane A-3 detachments to the converted *Essex*-class carriers in the Pacific Fleet. Detachment size was cut down to four planes when it was found that the A-3 took up too much deck space for efficient operations. VAH-4 was quite large, with up to twenty-two A-3 aircraft assigned at one time or another. The commissioned officer rank structure was heavy. Pilot background was varied, with a mix of multiengine and carrier pilots. Some had many hours of jet time, and some only jet transitional training. There were even a handful of former lighter-than-air (LTA) pilots on board. Pilot assignment was at best haphazard and did not seem to take into account the demanding requirements that could be placed on A-3 pilots flying from the smaller-class carriers in all weather conditions.

There was always a detachment leaving for deployment or arriving home from deployment. Assignment to a detachment was uncertain, and lots of politicking went on. Much depended on whether a pilot wanted to deploy or whether he wanted to join the "stump ranchers" and stay at home. Some people didn't worry or care about their careers and made no bones about wanting to remain at home. Others fought to get on the deployment assignments as soon as possible.

New and significant improvements continued to be made to the A-3 by the Douglas Corporation, including an aerial refueling tanker configuration that became a four-letter word to many. Regardless, the tanker configuration added a lot to the overall capability of the air wing embarked in the carrier. A VAH-4 deployment to the western Pacific is illustrative of the fact that the A-3 could do many things and do them well. For example, VAH-4 pilots were tasked to provide some high-altitude flights in the Formosa Strait to give the Chinese the impression that they could operate above 45,000 feet at night. They took the A-3 to 52,000 feet, with a bit of flap extended, but it was not easy. The plane was on the edge of a stall and at the same time on the edge of limiting Mach. Descending from that high altitude was a tricky proposition. However, intercepts at that altitude by our own fighters were very difficult and impossible for other types of fighters.

It was routine at the beginning of the cruise to keep an A-3 on the flight deck, loaded with a nuclear weapon parked aft of the carrier island structure. On one occasion, one of the A-3s came aboard when the ship was making all the wind required for landing. The aircraft drifted from left to right, and the pilot made a slight dive for the deck. Any nose wheel–first landing in the A-3 caused a bad bounce. The starboard wing of the landing aircraft actually went over the nose of the ready A-3 sitting on deck, and the landing aircraft came to rest just short of the island structure. There was no damage, but shortly thereafter, the VAH-4 Detachment was no longer required to keep a nuclear weapon in the ready A-3.[42]

Operating the A-3 on the *Essex*-class carriers was always a reason for concern. The relatively small size of the *Essex* compared to the *Forrestal* and later 90,000-ton nuclear-powered carriers greatly reduced the margin for error and operational efficiency. Great credit must go to those who flew missions from those decks. Some influential high-ranking naval and civil authorities have argued for carriers smaller than the 90,000-ton ships so prevalent in the current inventory. The A-3 experience with the 45,000-ton converted *Essex* class was typical of problems associated with ships not large enough to continuously provide a stable landing platform, particularly when the direction of the wind is not the same as that of the heavy seas, a phenomenon that occurs occasionally.

With the A-3 Skywarrior and the *Forrestal*-class carrier, the Navy finally achieved a realistic, highly reliable, and very credible nuclear weapons delivery capability. One could make a good case that the first deployment of the A-3 in 1957 was a critical and significant event in the Navy's efforts to develop a realistic delivery capability. The plane had the range, accuracy, and ability to put a weapon with a high yield on the target—and it gained considerable respect.

The A-5 Vigilante

There lingers a strong suspicion in the minds of many that the requirement to improve on the capability of the A-3 aircraft was generated by continuing competition with the Air Force over the atomic bomb mission. The Air Force wanted to counter the increasing threat of surface-to-air missiles. Flying high and fast was one solution. As a consequence, they came up with the concept of the B-70 aircraft, a high-flying supersonic strategic bomber, which would provide a greater probability of mission success. Some feared that the entry of such an airplane into the Air Force inventory would result in charges that the naval aviation heavy-attack program was vulnerable; that its aircraft would be shot down because they didn't fly high enough or fast enough. The Navy responded with the North American A3J Vigilante (hereafter referred to as the A-5).

The A-5 was never much of a success as a strategic carrier-based bomber. Its opportunity to serve was cut short by a reduction in emphasis on aircraft-delivered weapons in favor of intercontinental and submarine-launched ballistic missiles. The airplane looked sleek, with beautiful, graceful lines, and a certain menacing quality. It was the only supersonic bomber in the Navy inventory (see table 1 for specifications).

The A-5 was designed to carry a 1,500-pound nuclear "store," or weapon, called the Bedfellow. The Bedfellow was to be ejected rearward from the internal bomb bay, which was situated between the two

The North American A-5 Vigilante. NASM collection.

J79 engines. Bedfellow was equipped with a parachute to retard flight after release and had inflatable bladders to cushion impact with the ground when a ground burst was intended. It was found to be unsatisfactory for a number of reasons. First, the combination of aircraft and bomb was aeronautically unstable, and the chances of a successful drop were less than acceptable. Second, the mechanical complexity and sequencing requirements for extraction, retardation, and cushioning of the bomb resulted in a very low probability of end-to-end success. Third, the size of the bomb bay and the bomb-release procedures would seriously inhibit the design of future weapons since they would have to conform to the carriage and release criteria of the A-5.[43]

Although the A-5 was designed to carry weapons internally to be capable of supersonic flight, it could also carry them externally at subsonic speeds. That gave it an acknowledged nuclear weapons delivery capability, and it was included in the nation's nuclear warfare

The A-3 Skywarrior, serving as tanker for the A-5 Vigilante. Dick Ashworth collection.

plans for a short period of time, possibly favoring naval aviation, an advantage gratuitously granted by the Air Force.

In 1962, Comdr. (then) Kent Lee became commander of an air wing that included a squadron of A-5s. Lee tagged the A-5 a "political" airplane, one that was procured because of pressure from Congress trying to get business for the constituency or because of internal armed services politics. He thought the Navy was trying to get a supersonic nuclear weapons bomber to compensate for similar actions by the Air Force and labeled the A-5 a colossal dog. Though it had two good engines, it was not a very good carrier airplane, requiring very precise flying to get it on board. From an aircraft-maintenance point of view, even the later reconnaissance version, the RA-5C, was a "hopeless cause." During the Cuban missile crisis, when the air wing went to the Caribbean aboard the USS *Enterprise,* the A-5 was left behind. Later, the squadron did go to the Mediterranean for its first overseas deployment, but Lee was not impressed with the A-5.⁴⁴

The A-5 was not successful in its mission of supersonic weapons delivery because the very concept was flawed. The supersonic speed alone was not enough to counter developing supersonic missiles. Supersonic weapons delivery also imposed many design penalties. A better way to go would have been some combination of low-altitude penetration, electronic countermeasures, standoff smart weapons, and tactics designed for the particular environment.⁴⁵

Chuck Chute was an experienced heavy-attack pilot with flying time in the AJ and the A-3. He also had experience with the A-5 and formed some definite opinions about its capabilities. By 1964, the A-5 had been modified to perform the reconnaissance mission in addition to bomb delivery and was designated the RA-5C. Although the original concept called for the plane to carry its weapons internally in a bomb bay between the two J79 engines, experience on deployments with the Sixth Fleet in the Mediterranean led to changes in operational concepts and aircraft configuration. Loading of weapons was difficult, and monitoring the weapons during the loading and postloading checks was even more so. The decision was made to put extra fuel tanks in the internal bomb bay and carry the weapons externally on wing racks. This arrangement was satisfactory, but the aircraft flew like a Mack truck with weapons and external tanks.⁴⁶

When operating with the fleet, RA-5Cs were assigned targets mostly in Eastern Europe, launching from the Bay of Biscay. Consequently, everything that could hold fuel was hung on the aircraft. The flight profile for a bombing mission called for the fuel tanks to be dropped as fuel was expended, so that by the time the bomb run to the target began, the aircraft would be clean. Contrary to targeting strategy in the 1950s, targets were more military in nature, less likely to be population centers. Delivery of the weapons was from pure loft maneuvers in contrast to the modified loft used by the A-3. The hard wing of the RA-5C was a plus factor in the delivery tactic.⁴⁷

The A-5 was the last of the so-called heavy-attack aircraft. Technology brought other more capable aircraft into the nuclear delivery mission.

The Bombardier/Navigator

The training program for bombardier/navigators was conducted at the Heavy Attack Training Unit, Atlantic, in Norfolk, Virginia. The training was conducted by World War II and Korean War veterans who put the fear of God into the hearts of many nonbelievers. They were very serious about the nuclear weapons delivery mission. Ground school covered nuclear weapons familiarization, celestial and dead reckoning navigation, aircraft flight systems, and even the Morse code for emergency communications. Delivery pilots were required to pass examinations on the weapons they were cleared to deliver. These exams required production of a detailed schematic of the weapon, including all operating components. It was an interesting course of instruction that required serious concentration. Failure of the course resulted in dismissal from the nuclear program. It did not happen often, but an occasional failure did occur.

The flight phase for the bombardier/navigator was a "walk-before-run" building-block approach, commencing with several navigation flights in the P2V Neptune aircraft over the Gulf of Mexico, using dead reckoning and celestial navigation procedures. Finding the Mississippi River Delta on the outbound leg and Tampa Bay when inbound, without any outside assistance such as a radio beacon, was a significant achievement for the fledgling bombardier/navigators. Practice bombing runs were made on an old World War II landing ship tank moored in Lake George, north of Deland, Florida.

The real training of the young bombardier/navigators began after they reported to their fleet squadrons, where they were assigned to an A-3 crew. The crew for the aircraft consisted of a pilot, bombardier/navigator, and third crewman, each performing specific duties. The pilot was responsible for the overall mission, which included delivery of the weapon on the target and landing his 60,000-pound aircraft on an aircraft carrier at sea, in fair weather or foul. The bombardier/navigator's primary function was to plan the flight, navigate to the target area, operate the ASB-1 bombing system during the run-in to the target, release the weapon, navigate back to the ship, and assist the pilot as required. The third crewman was usually a senior petty officer from the enlisted ranks. He served as assistant navigator, utilized the sextant for celestial navigation, and acted as an airborne troubleshooter, ready to assist the pilot or bombardier/navigator as required. He also operated the remotely controlled machine gun in the stern of the A-3 before that gun was removed from the plane's configuration.

The crew planned and flew three-hour training missions over major cities in the United States and Puerto Rico. The Air Force had established a series of radar bombing scoring sites in several cities protected by the Nike antiaircraft missiles. When cleared for a bombing run-in, the Nike sites of the Air Defense Command would track the plane inbound and calculate the flight of the imaginary weapon, based on weather conditions and point of weapon release. The flight crew would receive a coded set of numbers from the Nike site via radio. When deciphered, they revealed the theoretical location of bomb impact, giving the score in bearing and feet from the intended target. Each city presented a unique challenge: radar target identification, aim-point selection, and wind were among the factors that had to be addressed. The missions were conducted at altitudes above 35,000 feet and at speeds above 450 knots.

Flight crew skills were constantly being honed to a fine edge by internal squadron bombing competitions, which were expanded to competitions with other squadrons in the wing. Ultimately, competitions were arranged with U.S. Air Force Strategic Air Command crews. The intraservice and interservice rivalry produced by these competitions led to great results for the competitors and the nuclear weapons capability overall. Winning a competition with SAC was no small achievement.

The ASB-1 bombing system had been installed in the later AJ aircraft and was standard equipment for the A-3. It was a quantum improvement over prior systems, utilizing the latest state-of-the-art analog computer, a new air data computer, and significantly improved radar. The typical bombing run from initial point to weapon release was a blur in the mind of the bombardier/navigator: spinning dials; cranking control knobs; delicate tuning of the radar scope; intensive study of the radar picture to determine the correct aim point; and, the most important factor in achieving a good score, the demanding "wind solution." The accuracy of the wind solution was critical in hitting the intended target or receiving a "gross error," the most dreaded score in all of aviation, regardless of the service.[48]

The Naval Flight Officer

One significant problem facing naval aviation emerged to some degree from the experience of the bombardier/navigators assigned to the heavy-attack program. As indicated earlier, the initial cadre of bombardier/navigators was composed of young, high-caliber aviators. The restrictions on their opportunities to fly as pilots became a problem, causing some to have second thoughts about a naval career.[49] By the mid-1950s, naval aviation was shifting from pilots to other commissioned officers for these duties. Some enlisted personnel also were qualified for the role.

As weapons-delivery systems in all aircraft became more capable, they also became more complex to operate. The concept of a pilot performing all operating functions in the cockpit was being questioned. The use of young pilots as bombardier/navigators in the heavy-attack program was a departure from past operational manning in naval aviation. It focused the attention of naval aviation leaders on the potential of commissioned officers to operate the weapons systems in other types of aircraft.

When it entered service in 1961, the F-4 Phantom II fighter had a radar intercept officer riding in the back seat operating the weapons system of the airplane. The A-6 Intruder had a side-by-side arrangement in the cockpit for the pilot and bombardier/navigator. Anti-submarine warfare aircraft had several officers operating the complex systems used for the detection, identification, and kill of submarines. Electronic warfare aircraft required officers who were specialists in the operation of the very useful systems employed in early warning, air control, countermeasures, and so forth.

A cadre of new professionals was developing in the naval aviation community. Labeled naval aviation observers, they were a holdover from the early days of naval aviation, when aircraft were used principally for scouting purposes, detecting the presence and location of the enemy fleets. These men rode in the rear cockpits of scouting aircraft and "observed." The modern cadre was doing a lot more than observing. In most instances, they were the keys to the success of a mission. However, they faced one significant problem. Although they were legally empowered to command aircraft carriers, the law of the land prohibited anyone but an aviator from commanding an aviation squadron. In reality, if a flight officer did not command an aviation squadron during his career, his future was quite limited. There was no way he was going to advance in rank and command a carrier. This created an inequity in command opportunity for a group of fine young men. Many had wanted to be pilots but could not pass the required eye examination and settled for the observer category just to be in naval aviation.

The issue came to a head during the Vietnam War. Commanding officers of squadrons in carriers were burdened with this problem. They were having a hard time facing these young men, many of whom could obviously be great leaders. Having to tell them that there was no realistic way in which they could expect a full career with high rank was tough. It was the senior aviators in the squadrons—the designated leaders—who were asking that something be done. "The frustrations of not being able to compete for the cherished assignments leading to command gnawed at the very fiber of the individual, but the hope and belief that naval aviation leadership would recognize the talent exhibited by these individuals kept the desire to serve alive."[50]

In 1969, Vice Adm. Thomas Connolly, the deputy chief of naval operations for air, gave approval to start action to have the law changed. Congress was sympathetic, and shortly thereafter, members of the cadre were designated as naval flight officers (NFO), eligible to command aircraft squadrons. They started moving up the chain of command with more rank and authority, many becoming squadron commanders and then commanding officers of ships, including carriers. Next came flag rank. Indeed, some day a naval flight officer will probably become the chief of naval operations.

Vietnam was really the catalyst that enabled the NFO to rise to the challenge and compete alongside his pilot brethren for the coveted goal of command at sea. In each of these "tailhook" communities, the NFO proved himself an equal member of a cohesive, combat-ready flight crew. Operating sophisticated, complex weapon systems requiring intellect, physical dexterity, and moral and physical courage, these flight crews proved their worth in combat innumerable times in the skies over North Vietnam. "The door was opened, the opportunity to excel was offered, the NFO community accepted the challenge, and the rest is history."[51]

Priorities

In retrospect, the caliber of people in the heavy-attack program and the concept of their assignment and utilization were unique in the history of U.S. naval aviation. A key factor in the early days was the selection of only the "best and the brightest" as pilots and weaponeers/bombardiers. Keeping people in this program for long periods of time compounded this excellence. Ten years in heavy attack was not uncommon. There is no question that the individuals chosen were outstanding. Some of the more senior had already proven themselves during World War II. There were many, however, in the junior ranks who were just getting started in their flying careers—one tour in a carrier or patrol squadron and then postgraduate school—expecting to return to an active pilot seat for at least one more tour of duty before heading into the technical world. It was a great kudo to be a member of that initial heavy-attack group, but was it the best policy for the overall good of the Navy? Did the program shunt some of the individuals out of the normal career path so much that it curtailed their potential for the future? Many of these people were from the Naval Academy classes of the early 1940s. How did their futures compare to those of their contemporaries who where not chosen for the program?

For one thing, this group missed aviation combat, specifically the Korean War. For example, the class of 1942 from the Naval Academy produced many aviators, yet only about a dozen actually went to air combat in Korea. That experience compensated to some degree for their lack of aviation combat in World War II. It kept them in the running for future contributions. At least one-quarter of them were subsequently selected for flag rank, but not so their contemporaries in the heavy-attack program, who had been the front-runners when the heavy-attack program started.

It is hard to overemphasize the priority that was placed on the atomic bomb delivery mission, particularly the heavy-attack program. Getting that capability was so significant that the Korean War was treated in some ways like a sideshow. As Jig Ramage often commented, the Korean War "was fought by the Reserves." The early days of that war found many reserve squadrons being recalled to active duty, checked out in jets, and deployed in ninety days to combat. After one tour, most returned to their civilian careers, which was to be expected.

Meanwhile, with the emphasis on atomic bomb delivery, the people in that program were kept out of combat experience. Keeping the best and the brightest from opportunities to exercise combat leadership must have had some subsequent impact on their futures.

During the Korean War, gaining experience in atomic war capability, rather than in the more conventional combat role, was the priority mission of naval aviation. When atomic war never materialized, the nation was faced with a situation where the most talented were missing a key check mark on the career advancement list. Had some form of nuclear conflict occurred involving the actual use of nuclear weapons, those with that kind of combat experience would have been the future leaders. Their Korean contemporaries would have fallen by the wayside. Fortunately for the world, it did not happen that way.

Capt. Frank Ault, a member of the Naval Academy class of 1943, with no aviation combat duty in World War II, is a good example. He was an outstanding candidate for the heavy-attack program, so good that he became an instructor of juniors and tutor for seniors (including General Eisenhower) in the basic elements of the bomb and its handling. His contributions were many, and he later became a member of the light-attack community, but he was missing a key check-off box, combat in aviation.

As for the initial personnel policy requiring a mix of carrier and multiengine patrol plane pilots, some, such as Vice Adm. Cat Brown, appeared to believe that the policy was in error. Paul Stevens, and many others in the heavy-attack community, seemed to have proven that one's flying background had little to do with success in heavy attack. The prime quality was the dedicated desire to be a good carrier aviator, the concept that Stevens so aptly applied as he built the first highly successful A-3 operational squadron. It is hard to imagine that concept ever failing.

The heavy-attack program covered a period of less than twenty years in naval aviation history, eventually providing a realistic, reliable, nuclear weapons delivery capability. It consumed a tremendous amount of energy and money, in addition to some people, as the Navy went all out to become highly competent in this new form of warfare. A good case can be made that the effort and sacrifices expended by so many in achieving the approval of the mission and the development of the delivery capability saved carrier aviation.

5. Light Attack

Naval aviation's entry into the nuclear weapons delivery mission was necessarily oriented to the word "heavy": the bombs were big, and they were heavy. Initially, there was no route to mission success other than the building of big airplanes. As the program developed, the heavy-attack concept took a firm hold on Navy strategy. Efforts to divert attention from that direction were not met with much favor. The Navy was dedicated to gaining a nuclear delivery capability as soon as possible, in which big airplanes operated from *Midway*-class carriers until an improved ship could be constructed.

The Navy's light-attack capability came into being despite initial internal opposition. Perhaps the lesson is that it is difficult to keep a good idea from coming into fruition, particularly with the advances provided by the scientific and engineering communities. It did not take long before light attack became the Navy's only carrier-based nuclear attack capability, taking over the role of heavy and medium attack. That forty-year period, from 1950 to 1990, is now just a part of naval aviation history, but during its heyday, light attack played a key role in the nation's nuclear deterrence capability.

Some aviators did not rule out the possibilities of the smaller, more traditional carrier aircraft playing a role in the total mission. One of these individuals was Rear Adm. James D. Ramage, who, ironically, was so effective later in helping to orient the A-3 heavy-attack program to the carrier Navy.

As mentioned in chapter 2, while a student at the Naval War College in 1946–47, Ramage wrote a thesis proposing the introduction of atomic bombs for operational use on aircraft carriers. Because of the high security around the subject, he had few facts at his disposal. Security was so tight that students at the college knew nothing of the requirements for the new AJ aircraft, much less anything about the characteristics of the atomic weapon and its potential. However, it was obvious to Ramage that if the Navy was to save the carriers, it needed to get into the A-bomb business.

In a subsequent assignment at the headquarters of the commander, Naval Air Forces, Pacific Fleet, Ramage listened to a briefing by Chick Hayward in which he told the audience of the program involving the P2V and the upcoming AJ aircraft. Ramage was not impressed, believing that horizontal bombing was not for the Navy. This view was not surprising since his glory days had been as a dive-bomber pilot in World War II. In the spring of 1950, Ramage attended an orientation course at Sandia Base and gained more insight into what was happening in weapons development. He learned of the Mark VII weapon, which was to weigh about 1,700 pounds and would fit externally on either the Navy AD Skyraider or the F2H Banshee. The Skyraider was a propeller-driven airplane that could carry a lot of weight a reasonable distance. The F2H Banshee, on the other hand, was a twin-engine jet, one of the first introduced into carrier aviation capable of carrying a good load for a respectable distance. The Air Force already had the F-84 Thunderjet, which could carry the weapon and put the Air Force Tactical Air Command in the nuclear delivery business. Ramage and others began to visualize a nuclear weapons mission for the more conventional aircraft, operating from the several *Essex*-class carriers that were the mainstay of the carrier Navy, particularly in the Pacific Fleet. Ramage also felt that the Strategic Air Command could perceive the nuclear-capable carrier as a threat to their control of the bomb.

Ramage did not feel that the Navy was pushing for this new

weapon very aggressively, which was undoubtedly so, since commitment had been made to the "heavy" concept, and nothing was to interfere with that objective, lest the big game be lost. In June 1950, Ramage managed to get a duty assignment to the Armed Forces Special Weapons Project in Albuquerque, the successor to the Manhattan Project. It was a joint staff assignment, wherein he served with officers from the other military services, which gave him some leeway to operate outside of Navy circles. Ramage traveled to various Navy commands, extolling the Mark VII bomb, so much so that he gained the enmity of the Special Weapons Division in the Office of the Chief of Naval Operations. However, Vice Adm. T. L. Sprague, the commander of the Naval Air Force, Pacific Fleet, at the time, was particularly receptive to Ramage's ideas, since at that time the only carriers capable of carrying nuclear weapons were in the Atlantic Fleet.

Ramage's job permitted him to associate with many top-notch people and to sit in on the Special Weapons Development Board meetings. Not only did he learn a great deal, he was able to emphasize an interest in the light weapons, in spite of Navy priorities. He attended the Bomb Commander Course for Air Force B-36 aircrews, which qualified crewmen to arm the bomb in the air. When a similar course became available for the tactical weapons (Mark VII), he was in the first class.

Comdr. (then) Tom Walker was also in the command. On one of their first selling trips together, they called on Rear Adm. F. I. Entwistle, who commanded the Navy's Operational Development Force. Although the admiral was not an aviator, he perceived immediately what small atomic weapons would do for the Navy and decided to establish a squadron to develop tactics for fleet squadrons. That squadron was Air Development Squadron 5 (VX-5), and Walker was assigned as its first commanding officer.

Ramage was able to obtain the services of a bomb-assembly team to "ring out" a weapon on an unmodified carrier aircraft. A weapon-assembly team and a complete Mark VII training bomb, less the nuclear capsule, were flown to NAS, San Diego, where the team successfully assembled the weapon, tested it, and loaded it on an AD aircraft in the USS *Philippine Sea*. Washington was informed of the new emergency capability, which did not sit well with the staff of the chief of naval operations. Ramage had exceeded his authority, but because he was on a joint staff, his status was protected.

Ramage was dedicated to expediting the introduction of the smaller nuclear weapons into the fleet, though strict security in the nuclear program kept most Navy people in the dark concerning the tremendous breakthrough in the production of small, high-yield weapons. On one visit to the commander, Naval Air Force, Atlantic Fleet, the chief of staff told Ramage that he should get the message directly to the chief of naval operations, Adm. W. M. Fechteler. Failing that, the chief of staff would come to Washington to see that the mission was accomplished. That opportunity came much sooner than expected and quite by accident.

In 1951 Ramage was working with two key academics in the Sandia Corporation on problems with the Mark VII. From that discussion, Ramage became aware of the relationship between accuracy and yield of the weapon—the key was accuracy, not yield. Therefore, if the Mark VII were more accurate in its delivery than the earlier, larger, and more efficient implosion weapons, the improved accuracy would compensate for the lower efficiency.

The Sandia academics were Comdr. Jack Sloatman, a naval aviator and mathematician, and Ted Youngs, on loan from the University of Indiana, where he held a chair in mathematics. This three-man team went on the road with their story about "yield versus accuracy." At a briefing in Washington to a group of about forty officers, the carrier people in the audience could see immediately what this study meant to them. The next audience for the team was with the secretary of the Navy, Dan Kimball. He listened to the pitch and liked it so much that he set up an appointment for the chief of naval operations to hear the briefing the next morning.

The CNO was impressed. Apparently, he had been unaware that the smaller weapons could be made available. He asked that Youngs have copies of the study made as soon as possible. Youngs said he would get the paper in proper form and forward it to him the following Monday.

Ramage knew right away that he should inform the head of the special weapons staff, Rear Adm. F. S. Withington, to avoid having the latter blindsided. Ramage told one of Withington's staff captains what had happened and cautioned that the CNO would definitely be calling for his admiral soon. Apparently, the captain did not think the message was important. When Withington returned, he went into the CNO's office, apparently unaware of the situation. He was accused of not keeping the CNO advised on an important development in weaponry and was admonished for not making the smaller bomb the Navy's highest priority. Withington was not happy, and Ramage was in trouble.

Attempts were made to have Ramage and Youngs fired from their jobs for allegedly using their positions "to set Navy policy." Fortunately, the deputy commander at AFSWP was Rear Adm. Fred Trapnell, who interceded and got Ramage off the hook. Ramage gained a few enemies, particularly in the heavy-attack community, but he also impressed many people with the feasibility of a "light-attack" program. Further, his immediate superior in the Navy, Trapnell, knew that they were on the right track.

Shortly after the Korean War, Ramage was ordered to command Carrier Air Group 19, soon to deploy to the western Pacific in the USS *Oriskany*, one of the first ships in the Pacific Fleet to be equipped with a nuclear weapons storage and handling capability. Ramage wanted to have the most nuclear-capable air group in the fleet. He had fifty pilots in the air group who were qualified and ready to go. The deployment of the *Oriskany* could be considered a milestone in the Navy's nuclear weapons delivery capability.

When the *Oriskany* arrived at Yokosuka, Japan, in the fall of 1953, she had to carrier-qualify the aircrews in her AJ heavy-attack detachment. It was a terrible performance, and Capt. C. D. Griffin, the commanding officer of the *Oriskany*, threw the unit off his ship. Ramage advised the captain not to worry; that if an occasion should arise, his attack aircraft, the propeller ADs and the jet F2Hs, would be ready.

Such an occasion occurred soon, when the ship was in the Sea of Japan. Captain Griffin and Ramage were called to the cabin of Rear Adm. J. D. Whitney, commander, Carrier Division 5. Whitney ordered them to prepare for a nuclear strike on North Korea. As far as they knew, this was no drill, even though the Korean War was over. Only general direction was given; a few military targets were specified, most of which were in and around the North Korean capital of Pyongyang. Comdr. William Elliott, the commanding officer of Attack Squadron 195 (VA-195), was considered by Ramage to be the most capable nuclear weapons planner in the fleet. He was pressed into targeting service immediately. Inexplicably, however, the operation was canceled. Admiral Griffin later discovered that it had been a drill ordered at the highest level, the reason for which he was never able to ascertain. In any event, the *Oriskany* was ready. The Navy had a nuclear readiness of sorts with its light-attack aircraft.[1]

The efforts by Ramage and his cohorts did not meet with favor in the ruling heavy-attack contingent in the Pentagon. However, it was obvious to many that as the nuclear weapons became smaller, lighter, and more accurate, the conventional carrier aircraft would be able to play a major role in the mission. Traditionally, the accuracies were generally better for the smaller aircraft, which did not employ high-altitude, horizontal-delivery tactics.

This possibility was also evident to the Air Force. As mentioned earlier, the F-84 Thunderjet, which performed so well as a light-attack aircraft in Korea, could handle the nuclear mission. The F-105 Thunderchief was also an excellent aircraft, designed specifically for the nuclear weapons mission. Ironically, it evolved into a very effective conventional attack aircraft, its primary combat role during the Vietnam War.

The advent of the thermonuclear weapon—the H bomb—was a great asset in establishing the light-attack program for the Navy.

Vastly increased yield came in a much smaller package. The scientists and engineers were now providing the armed services with a 1,000- to 2,000-pound package that could be mounted externally on an airplane. It could produce an explosive yield in the one-megaton range. Further, these new weapons began to be produced in greater quantity, offsetting the weapon-shortage aspect that had favored the Air Force with a dominant role. Light attack had arrived in the Navy and the Air Force, although in some ways, it flew in the face of the established heavy-attack, big horizontal bomber philosophy.

The Douglas A-1 Skyraider

An essential element in the success of the light-attack program were the aircraft that could be adapted to the mission. A cornerstone of the program in the early days was the piston-engine Douglas AD Skyraider (hereafter referred to as the A-1) aircraft, affectionately known as the "Able Dog." Designed under Edward Heinemann's direction, it was a truly great accomplishment in the annals of aviation. It arrived on the scene too late for World War II, but it did great service in both the Korean and Vietnam Wars. The Skyraider was maneuverable, easy to fly, and one of the most carrier-suitable aircraft of all time. Further, it could take heavy damage and still return to home base. It played a role in the nuclear weapons delivery mission for several years, including the initial single integrated operational plan (SIOP), placed in effect in the spring of 1961. The SIOP was the nuclear war plan of the United States. If you were in that plan, you were on the first team.

The Skyraider could go a long distance with a heavy load, but at a relatively slow speed, and it took forever to get to the target (see table 2 for specifications). Like all aircraft of its time, it was readily detectable by radar, which meant that to have any chance of reaching the target, it had to stay low, under the surveillance umbrella of enemy radar. Therefore, training involved long flights called "butt busters."

The Douglas A-1 Skyraider. NASM collection.

Stories of training for the nuclear mission in the A-1 are some of the most fascinating in naval aviation history.

Although the A-1 was replaced in the nuclear role in the early 1960s by more capable jet aircraft, it had served a useful role. It could proceed over water at low level for a long distance and attack defensive military installations such as radar sites on the periphery of the target area. These capabilities led to a highly successful probability of creating the desired damage, a key factor in the targeting process.

The McDonnell F2H Banshee

In the late 1940s, the McDonnell F2H Banshee began to appear in operational squadrons. In its day, the Banshee, particularly the F2H-2, had a unique capability to operate at a high altitude. The Banshee went through much of the same nuclear weapons mission testing and training evolution as the A-1. It could be considered the first jet aircraft in the Navy capable of delivering a nuclear weapon (see table 2 for specifications).

Table 2
Representative Aircraft Characteristics

Model	Empty Weight (lbs)	Wingspan (ft)[1]	Length (ft)	Engines (number and type)	Power (hp, prop; lbs thrust, jet)	Maximum Speed (knots; clean)	Ceiling (ft)	Range (nautical miles)[2]	Crew
A-1	12,100	50	39	1 Wright 3350	2,700 hp	295	31,900	2,050	1
F2H	11,270	41.6	40.2	2 Westinghouse J34	3,250 lbs each	503	49,100	1,050	1
F9F-8	12,800	34.5	48.5	1 P&W J48	7,250 lbs	553	40,400	845	1
A-4	8,600	27.5	39	1 Wright J65	7,000 lbs	577	43,000	1,365	1
FJ-4B	13,780	39	36.3	1 Wright J65	7,700 lbs	590	46,200	1,700	1
A-6	25,300	53	54.8	2 P&W J52	8,500 lbs each	560	42,000	2,600	2
A-7	18,500	38.7	46.1	1 Allison TF41	15,000 lbs	602	46,500	2,000	1
F/A-18A	23,100	40.4	56	2 GEF404	16,000 lbs each (AB)[3] 10,600 lbs each (non AB)	Mach 1.7 Mach 1.0	52,500	1,300	1

Source: Based on declassified standard aircraft characteristic (SAC) charts on file at the Naval Aviation History Center, Washington, D.C. Prepared by Harold Andrews, research associate, Smithsonian National Air and Space Museum.

Note: Characteristics are *generally* representative of the models listed. Some, such as range, may vary for the various versions of some models that were produced and with the payload placed on the aircraft.

[1] For the F2H, wingspan includes tip tanks; for the F/A-18A, tip-mounted AIM-9 Sidewinder missiles. Both are typical operational configurations.

[2] For a bomb load equivalent to 2,000 pounds, using typical external fuel tank(s). In-flight refueling extended the range.

[3] AB = after burner.

The McDonnell F2H Banshee. NASM collection.

In the historic Navy vs. Air Force arguments concerning the vulnerability of the Air Force B-36 intercontinental bomber, the Banshee was the aircraft the Navy touted as one able to shoot down the B-36. The Navy and the Air Force were at each other's throats, the Navy saying the B-36 was no good, that the F2H could easily intercept and shoot it down. The Air Force contended otherwise. Since the advertised service ceiling of the B-36 was above 45,000 feet, the Navy had to be able to demonstrate an intercept capability above that altitude.

As part of the effort to prove its point, the Navy specially configured six airplanes at the Naval Air Test Center at Patuxent River, Maryland. Previous efforts to conduct such high-altitude intercepts had encountered engine flameouts above 45,000 feet, high engine tailpipe temperatures, and lack of oxygen capacity for the pilots, since they were breathing 100 percent oxygen during the flight.

On 27 August 1949, an attempt to demonstrate the ability of one F2H to intercept another above 50,000 feet was conducted. Comdr. William Leonard and Lt. John Iler were the test pilots involved, flying two F2H aircraft. Before the flight, the pilots sat in their airplanes for some time breathing 100-percent oxygen from a portable bottle. They were then towed to the end of the runway so that after starting engines, they could hand out the portable oxygen bottle, go on 100-percent aircraft oxygen, and take off. From that point on, they were under the control of ground-controlled intercept radar.

The pilots were able to reach an altitude of 51,000 feet. At that altitude, indicated airspeed reduced to 195 knots, and the engines began to experience the onset of compressor stalls, which sounded to the pilot like sand being thrown into the engine. At 197 knots, the aircraft hit its limiting Mach of 0.85 and began shaking. Therefore, the pilots had about a 2-knots margin of error to work with, or they would experience engine flameout and be unable to complete the mission. Fortunately, the intercept was a success.

Immediately after the intercept, both of the engines in Lieutenant Iler's airplane quit, while one engine flamed out in Commander Leonard's Banshee. The pilots had been riding on a cockpit pressure altitude of 43,000 feet, the maximum allowable without a pressure suit. When the engines quit, Lieutenant Iler lost all cockpit pressure. Immediately, oxygen began to flow into his mask at greatly increased pressure, so much so that he had to hold the mask close to his face. He extended the Banshee's speed brakes, and, holding the mask tightly, headed down as rapidly as possible. As he approached 35,000 feet, he attempted an air restart, and both engines fired off, giving him cockpit pressure—and a great sense of relief. Since this emergency consumed only a few seconds of time, he never lost consciousness. Leonard had a similar experience but lost only one engine. The rest of the flight was uneventful as they returned to base, having demonstrated that, in theory at least, the F2H-2 could intercept the B-36.[2]

Capt. Robert Hunt was another aviator in the early light-attack programs. Hunt's first involvement with the carrier-based nuclear weapons capability was with the F2H-2B aircraft in March 1952, during his tour of duty with Composite Squadron 4 (VC-4) at the Naval Air Station in Atlantic City, New Jersey. VC-4 had experience in fielding detachments of aircraft for carriers, and the pilots had the jet instrument experience needed to provide a higher expectation of success with the nuclear mission. Hunt deployed in August 1952 aboard the carrier USS *Franklin D. Roosevelt* with a detachment of four F2H-2Bs for the nuclear mission. Also assigned on the same deployment were four F3D Skyknight jet night-fighter aircraft from VC-4. The deployment was part of a major NATO exercise and was followed by a cruise to the Mediterranean.

Before deployment, the Banshee pilots conducted one or two nuclear weapons loading drills with the Mark 12, a very heavy, gun-type weapon, and the Mark VII, an implosion type with a relatively large diameter and consequent drag penalty on the delivery aircraft. About all those drills accomplished was proof that the weapons would fit the aircraft and that the control wiring circuits were satisfactory. Each pilot was checked out on the switching sequence to ready the weapon for release. During the work-up period, Hunt conducted one catapult shot carrying a Mark VII shape, taking the weapon to the shore station in Norfolk. However, during the deployment, none of the detachment pilots ever performed a catapult takeoff with a training version of either the Mark 12 or the Mark VII weapon. They were operating on a lot of theory, without much realistic practice.

The landing gear struts of the F2H-2B were over-inflated to obtain the necessary ground or flight-deck clearance while an external store was attached. The airplane had a stringent recovery-weight restriction, so that bringing a store back aboard would have required the pilot to burn his fuel down to a low level before attempting to land on board. There was little margin for error if that maneuver were required.

The tactic to be used in the delivery of a nuclear weapon consisted of a simple dive or glide bombing attack with speed brakes extended, with a release at about 12,000 feet, followed by a 135-degree turn away from the target, retiring at high speed, close to the ground. Some thought that prayer would also have been appropriate.

While deployed, the pilots flew whenever they could and bent the routine assignments to their mission requirements, as they understood them. This was early in the nuclear weapons business, and not many of the controlling brass or members of their staffs understood much about the mission. VC-4 pilots had to convince them that their aircraft were not equipped with radar, did not have a computer bombing system like the heavy-attack AJ aircraft, and that they were not night fighters. Things got better later on, but understanding the nuclear mission took some time for the leaders of naval aviation.[3] After all, the nuclear bomb was not a World War II weapon.

Another deployment of the F2H in the early 1950s involved the aforementioned Whitey Feightner. After being deeply involved in developing the low-level flight profile for penetration to the target, Feightner was ordered to take a select group of VX-3 pilots and form a squadron of twelve nuclear-configured F2H-3/4 aircraft. All aircraft were equipped with the latest in night and all-weather intercept gear, because the all-weather fighter intercept mission had been assigned, as well as that calling for nuclear weapons delivery.

Feightner took the squadron to sea in the USS *Coral Sea* in 1954 and deployed to the Mediterranean Sea in 1956. While in the Mediterranean, all squadron pilots were assigned real, specific targets in case a nuclear attack was ordered. Target assignments and the weapons to go on them were very carefully controlled by a small select team of nuclear weapons specialists on the staff of the commander-in-chief, Atlantic Fleet, in Norfolk, Virginia. Feightner recalls that one of his targets was a fighter airfield in Hungary. "It would be a one-way mission as far as I was concerned. There were no tankers to bring the pilots home. That 'one-way mission' thought seemed to be a general view among squadron pilots. We spent a lot of time updating our target folders and studying our penetration routes."[4] Feightner felt that even with the reliability difficulties that the heavy AJ aircraft was facing at the time, it represented a more realistic nuclear weapons delivery capability, mainly because of its long-range capability.[5]

That was 1956. A specialized jet squadron had deployed on one of the Navy's biggest carriers. There were nuclear weapons on board,

The Grumman F9F-8 Cougar. NASM collection.

coupled with a proven capability to fly long distances at low level to a target area. Getting home was another matter.

The Grumman F9F-8 Cougar

A short-lived workhorse in the light-attack business was the Grumman F9F-8 Cougar. A two-seat version was used extensively for teaching delivery maneuvers. A contemporary of the F2H series, it lacked some of the performance characteristics of the Banshee, such as service ceiling. However, it was rugged and able to stand the relatively high-G maneuvers that were developed during the weapon delivery maneuver (see table 2 for specifications). The Cougar was assigned a role in the nuclear mission for a short time, although its relatively short range hindered its mission performance. Further, it was about to be replaced by an exceptionally good light-attack nuclear bomber, the Douglas A-4 Skyhawk, one of designer Ed Heinemann's premier accomplishments in the field of carrier aircraft design.

The Douglas A-4 Skyhawk

Initially designated the A4D, the A-4 Skyhawk was specifically designed to accommodate the nuclear weapon. The length of the landing gear kept the airplane relatively high off the ground, a feature that would accommodate the tail fins of a nuclear bomb attached to the belly of the aircraft as it launched from the carrier. The airplane was the best in the current state of the art and was a great joy for all carrier aviators who manned its cockpits. Many of the later versions of the aircraft were deployed to combat during the Vietnam War, where it proved to be highly effective in the delivery of conventional weapons in the ground-attack role.

The aforementioned Comdr. Bob Hunt was fortunate enough to command the first A-4 operational unit. The squadron, Attack Squadron 72 (VA-72), acquired its aircraft in August 1956 and was based at Quonset Point, Rhode Island, a base that was dedicated to the anti–submarine warfare mission. Training for the nuclear delivery role in that area was a challenge. Because of the dense population and lack of open areas, low-level flights were difficult to schedule. There were no suitable targets for practicing the new delivery maneuvers that had been developed and were being perfected. The best training came about when the squadron deployed to the Caribbean. An excellent target range existed at the training base in Guantanamo Bay, Cuba, where the pilots had the field and targets to themselves for intensive training. As they flew the various bomb delivery profiles, they learned how to maintain and use the new Low-Altitude Bombing System (LABS) gear that was installed in the aircraft. It was a great disappointment to the squadron and air group when the authorities chose not to deploy the early versions of the A-4, apparently because of aircraft support problems.

The A-4 was limited to a maximum strike radius of about five hundred miles because it had no in-flight refueling provisions. Incorporating that capability was one of the priority changes that went into the subsequent models of the A-4 aircraft. Perhaps because the A-4 had such high performance characteristics when there were no

The Douglas A-4 Skyhawk. NASM collection.

weapons or fuel tanks hung under the wing, it seemed to flight crews that the drag increments acquired when shapes and fuel tanks were added penalized the performance significantly. However, that was part of the mission. At least, pilots had the comforting thought that on departing a target without any external baggage, they would be exiting at high speed (see table 2 for specifications).

The carrier suitability of the A-4 was superb. VA-72's first group of pilots was brought along very quickly for carrier-landing qualifications. It was a jewel to bring aboard the carrier and steady as a rock in the landing configuration. At high speed, during bombing runs of any type, the airplane tracked well and could be flown into highly accurate bombing and rocket attacks. At maximum range cruise speeds, the plane had close to neutral stability and was therefore very maneuverable. A pilot could just about wish it through turns, but one had to fly it all of the time. As the Navy increased its all-weather flying capabilities, a basic automatic pilot was installed in later A-4s.

There was very little training support or special weapons delivery doctrine available to the jet light-attack squadrons in the mid 1950s. Air Development Squadron 3 (VX-3) developed the most useful special weapons delivery information, but they had not had the time or the aircraft to develop information pertinent to the A-4. At the time, there was little experience in the light-attack, low-level delivery profile. Pilots developed some strip charts and tentative planning factors for a final low-level run-in to a loft delivery. The centerline stores station was a great aid to carrying the shapes that were fitted to the aircraft. The delivery maneuvers required symmetrical flight evolutions, and good accuracy was achieved.[6]

The North American FJ-4B Fury

The North American FJ-4B Fury, a successor to the very successful FJ-3 fighter, possessed excellent capabilities for the delivery of nuclear weapons (see table 2 for specifications). Operating from converted *Essex-* and *Midway*-class carriers and using in-flight refueling, it gave the Navy a capability to deliver nuclear weapons one thousand miles from the carrier. The plane was pilot friendly, easy to handle on the carrier decks, and easy to maintain.

Comdr. Richard "Ace" King, who was slated to take command of the first A-4 aircraft squadron in the Pacific, actually commanded the first FJ-4B squadron, because a decision to expedite the deployment of this latest in the Fury series resulted in his squadron being equipped with the FJ-4B. After a suitable training period, the squadron made the first deployment of the FJ-4B on board the USS *Hornet* in early 1958. The ship's commanding officer was Capt. (then) Thomas Connolly, formerly a skipper of one of the early AJ heavy-attack squadrons.

Practice missions during the *Hornet* deployment in the western Pacific included delivery tactics of 70-degree dives from high altitude with a standard 4-G pullout after release of the weapon, as well as the standard loft/toss and over-the-shoulder delivery maneuvers (see chapter 6). The squadron also conducted an operational suitability test

The North American FJ-4 Fury. NASM collection.

(OST) flight that called for the delivery of a Mark 12 nuclear weapon without the nuclear core in a realistic training mission. The flight was successful in all respects, convincing the authorities that the FJ-4B was a viable vehicle for delivering the nuclear weapon.[7]

During a later deployment of the FJ-4B to the western Pacific on board the USS *Midway,* the squadrons came equipped with the gear needed to implement the "buddy tanker" concept, which called for an FJ-4B to launch with a refueling package hung on a rack under the wing. The package consisted of a full tank of fuel with a hose that could be extended behind the aircraft from the tank. On the end of the hose was a basket arrangement, called a drogue. When airborne, the tanking aircraft would deploy the hose upon call. Another squadron aircraft would then approach from astern, plug its refueling probe into the basket, and take on whatever fuel was needed before proceeding on its assigned mission. The buddy tanker concept significantly extended the strike range and flight endurance of the aircraft.[8]

In-flight refueling came into its own with the first buddy tankers. With a refueling capability within the squadron itself, flexibility, dependability, and combat radius increased by an order of magnitude. It was no longer necessary to rendezvous with an itinerant AJ aircraft tanker at a lower altitude and a lower airspeed—assuming there was a reasonable probability that the undependable AJ could get into the air on any given day.

One of the first things pilots learned about the FJ-4B buddy tanker was that plugging in was not the piece of cake it had been with a nose probe on the F9F or the large basket hanging behind the AJ aircraft, as it poked along at 20,000 feet altitude. The buddy tanker drogue was a much smaller basket, traveling faster and on a shorter tether. The probe was somewhere behind the pilot's left shoulder. Trying to stick it into a drogue that went into a nervous random orbit as soon as the probe came near was no easy task, no matter how carefully one made the approach. Closing the drogue with a higher-than-normal relative airspeed put an awkward bend into the hose dragging the drogue but resulted in a successful engagement. Easing off a bit of power made the kink in the hose disappear.[9]

The FJ-4B Fury was almost an order of magnitude better than the F9F-8 Cougar. It had longer range, higher service ceiling, higher speed, and better maneuverability. It could carry any one of a variety of nuclear weapons plus three droppable wing tanks of external fuel. The near Mach-1.0 speed capability at high altitude gave it a formidable air-to-air capability. With four available bomb stations on the wings in the days before multiple-carriage bomb racks, it possessed an excellent capability with conventional ordnance.

The FJ-4B's problem was that its design took the airplane to the limits of a safe operating envelope in almost every maneuver. Some limitations, like the landing weight, were peculiarly critical. Further, although the plane was cleared for dive-bombing from 35,000 feet with a nuclear weapon, if the pilot did not drop the weapon (or training shape) during the dive, he would be well outside the allowable G limit for pullout and recovery with the store still on the airplane.

During a deployment to the western Pacific on board the USS *Midway* in 1958, the FJ-4B's in-flight refueling capability gave the fleet a new dimension in nuclear weapons delivery. There was some doubt, however, that the high-level ranks of authority really understood the magnitude of the new capability. For example, the *Midway* would occasionally get a random "special weapons alert." Someone would plot the combat radius of the heavy-attack A-3s, and the Air Operations Department in the ship or embarked staff would establish a launch point and a prospective launch time based on the A-3 capability. The heavy-attack strategy was deeply ingrained in the thinking of many. The light attackers would then diplomatically suggest that the FJ-4Bs could get four planes off with four buddy tankers some two hundred miles sooner than the A-3s—and six to eight hours earlier in the extreme case, where the carrier might have to make up the two hundred miles with all boilers on the line.[10]

A great deal of emphasis was placed on the nuclear weapons delivery mission during that deployment of the USS *Midway* to the Pacific in 1958. Capt. Tom Blackburn, who had been so helpful in getting the heavy-attack wing started in the Atlantic, was the commanding officer of the ship. His support and emphasis on the nuclear mission made for some impressive advancements. One was an OST flight using a Mark 28 nuclear training weapon, a device that contained high explosives but no nuclear core. The flight was to demonstrate a realistic delivery capability.

With the OST weapon came a host of important people from Washington, Oak Ridge, Albuquerque, Columbus, and other places—military and civilian. The planners had an exercise in mind. The *Midway* would steam to within a hundred miles of Okinawa, and the FJ-4B would be launched to proceed directly to the target, a small island forty miles west of Okinawa. Upon arrival at the target, the pilot would execute an over-the-shoulder delivery maneuver (see chapter 6). Observers in a propeller-driven aircraft would orbit the target to observe and report on the results. The entire operation raised a valid question in the minds of the FJ-4B squadron pilots. Did anyone really plan to sail carriers to within a hundred miles of Siberia or the China coast before launch? What real-world operation did the plan simulate?

The squadron proposed instead that they make a predawn launch under electronic silence conditions and fly the kind of track they had been practicing—six hundred miles southeast and then back to Okinawa, with a low-level run-in to the target. The exercise commenced at 4:00 A.M. on 4 December 1958, and the launch and flight went like clockwork.

We passed Okinawa inbound to the target at a hundred feet of altitude, on time and on course. West of Okinawa, a thin overcast had developed at about 1500 feet. Existing safety regulations prohibited pull-ups through an overcast for delivery of the weapon, although in the selected delivery maneuver, the pilot was totally on instruments from pull-up to release, and was oblivious to overcasts unless the tops were above a few thousand feet. To abort at this point just did not seem reasonable, so up we went into our standard delivery tactic. From all indications, there had been a successful release. As I completed my high-speed escape maneuver, the weapon exploded as programmed. I have seldom seen a prettier sight than the explosion of the test weapon a couple of thousand feet above the overcast—and, perhaps, over the target. With a one-megaton explosive yield, it did not have to be a bullseye to create great destruction.[11]

In the early 1960s, Comdr. Bob Hunt commanded an air group that included two FJ-4B aircraft squadrons. Both had operated the airplane for some time and were experienced. They did have an in-flight refueling capability and therefore were capable of a 1,000-mile combat radius. This was the apparent criterion in the competition for the nuclear mission and subsequent funding. The air group made a deployment to the western Pacific aboard the USS *Lexington* in 1961, just as nuclear weapons targeting was being transformed into the nation's SIOP.

In Hunt's opinion, the FJ-4B was a respectable aircraft, but by the time a fuel drop tank and a special-weapons store were hung underneath, it was slowed considerably. However, it had North American's solid handling characteristics and feel. The cockpit was comfortable, with room for the strip charts and target detail maps that pilots used to fly the en route and low-level parts of the nuclear delivery mission. The FJ-4B had the range advantage over the A-4 because of its in-flight refueling capability. However, by this time, the A-4B was entering the fleet, and it did have in-flight refueling.

The few "shapes" that the pilots got to train with or drop revealed that the 4-G loft bombing maneuver (to be described in chapter 6) with the weapon shape on the left wing was quite different from that of a symmetrically loaded FJ-4B. It required strong corrective aileron and rudder action on the part of the pilot to stay within a 100-foot circular error of probability (CEP). Because the training shapes were in short supply, not every assigned pilot had the opportunity to drop even one. However, with the equivalent explosive yields of the weapons for the assigned targets in the SIOP, the loss of accuracy probably did not matter all that much. Nevertheless, pilots all competed aggressively for better accuracy—a lower CEP.[12]

In a way, the FJ-4B/carrier combination represented what Rear Adm. Dan Gallery had envisioned fifteen years before: a carrier that could steam four thousand miles toward a target, with the delivery aircraft covering the last one thousand miles. Although the FJ-4B Fury was highly successful in the light-attack role, there were not many of them in the Navy's inventory. Further, they were being overtaken by a significant development in weapons delivery by the Navy attack community.

The Grumman A-6 Intruder

Ideally, the development of a requirement for a multimillion-dollar airplane should follow a logical, orderly, systematic process, driven by the detection and evaluation of some potential threat. If there were nothing in the inventory that could counter the threat, a new requirement would be generated, followed by approval, funding, and production. As

The Grumman A-6 Intruder. NASM collection.

a rule in the acquisition of weapons, a shoddy product results from a shoddy requirement. The Grumman A-6 Intruder was certainly the exception to the rule. There was nothing orderly about the development of its requirement, and the initial requirement was shoddy.

The requirement for the A-6 (initially designated A2F-1) was generated by the Marine Corps. The Marines wanted an aircraft that could take off in about five hundred feet of runway and carry two 500-pound bombs a relatively short distance. To meet this requirement, industry designers came up with a large wing and two powerful engines. They even rotated the tailpipes of the jet engines downward to help meet the short-field-takeoff part of the requirement. There seemed to be no real obstacle to producing the plane, but the Congress would not approve funding unless the Navy participated in the buy. The Navy bit the bullet and responded with a requirement for a long-range-strike capability that would include delivery of nuclear weapons, a considerable expansion of the original Marine Corps requirement. Most significant in the Navy requirement was the need to "kill on the first pass." That meant a weapons system superior to anything then flying in carrier aircraft. It was a requirement adhering to the principles of Admiral Sims, namely that the shots that hit are the ones that count.[13]

At that time in history, the late 1950s and early 1960s, two very significant and pertinent technological developments were taking place. First, radar was improving to the point where the image returned from a target could be studied in depth, and the characteristics of the target could be determined in some detail. Picking up a bridge over a river, for example, was easy. An operator could even identify various aspects of the bridge. Similar abilities were materializing that would permit the pinpointing of specific targets in a maze of radar returns. The radar operator could now not only detect a target, he could also determine many of the target's characteristics.

The second major technological development was the digital computer, which was fast replacing the inflexible analog computers in weapons technology. The speed with which such computers could absorb information, process it, and come up with the solution to a complicated mathematical problem was very evident and encouraging to those involved with the design of improved weapons systems.

The basic mathematics problem faced by weaponeers since history began is called the "fire-control problem." The variables are considerable: the location of the target, its distance from the attacking weapon, and the ballistics of the weapon to be used, be it a rock, a rocket, or a bomb. At what point should the weapon be released in order to get a "hit on the first pass?" If the launch platform for the weapon is an airplane moving at high speed toward the target, the updated range information has to be entered and rapidly processed in order to provide a correct solution for the release point of the weapon. That also means introducing the altitude of the airplane above the target and the force and direction of the wind. All of these variables were available and could be introduced automatically into a digital computer. Then a continuously updated solution to the rapidly changing fire-control problem was presented to the pilot or bombardier wanting to release the weapon.

Naval aviation had a requirement for an extremely accurate weapons delivery system, and industry was coming up with a technology that would produce a satisfactory result. The capability could also be exercised at night or in all-weather conditions. The radar and computer made environmental conditions in the target area relatively unimportant. But it was obvious that a pilot alone could not perform the task. The A-6 would be a two-place aircraft, with the pilot and bombardier sitting side by side in the cockpit.

With a good sensor system (radar) that could keep up with the rapid changes in ranges during a bombing run, the bombardier in the aircraft could concentrate on his target, using radar selection if needed. Because the on-board computer was constantly solving the fire-control problem, it was possible to put the release of the intended weapon on automatic, with a good probability of getting a hit on the target. As far as carrier aviation was concerned, it was a major step forward in the ability to hit a target under almost any conditions. Now, the pilot could generate a hit without visual reference to the target. Night and all-weather became the preferred delivery mode, because it provided a higher survivability factor for the aircraft and crew. The visions of mass formations of attacking aircraft were beginning to fade from the memories of the tacticians of carrier aviation.

The original wing design to meet the Marine short field requirement served the Navy's requirement of a long-range strike with a big payload very well (see table 2 for specifications). The introduction of the A-6 was delayed by the necessity to refine the technology necessary to produce what had been demonstrated in the laboratory. The Navy waited a long time for the weapon system, while other aspects of the airplane were fully developed. The first A-6s were only shells: airframe, power plant, appropriate cockpit and control systems, but no weapons system.

The first overseas deployment of the A-6 was to Vietnam in 1965 in Attack Squadron 75 (VA-75) under the command of Comdr. (then) Leonard "Swoose" Snead. VA-75 faced many problems, particularly with the weapons system. Each weapons system in the twelve-plane squadron had a different configuration. Navy maintenance men worked with contractor representatives to fix each airplane, establish configuration control, and realize the capability that was in the airplane. Some criticized the early deployment, feeling that the plane was not ready for combat duty, much less an early deployment. However, the information that came back from the combat theater provided the procurement people in Washington with the ammunition they needed to procure funds and develop solutions to the problems that arose. For example, low-light television and infrared sensors were integrated later into the fire-control sensor system, thereby helping to produce a better aim point for the pilot/bombardier and greater accuracy with the weapon being released.[14]

Stories of flights over Hanoi and other targets in North Vietnam are the stuff of legends and testify to the wisdom of the original concept. Although the missions performed by VA-75 flight crews during their Vietnam deployment involved the delivery of conventional weapons under night and all-weather conditions, there is a direct correlation between those tactics and those involved in the delivery of nuclear weapons. An overview of some typical missions during the Vietnam conflict provide an insight into the unique capabilities afforded by the A-6 Intruder.

VA-75, known as the Sunday Punchers, was formed with fifteen pilots, most of whom came from the A-4 Skyhawk program. There were five junior officers, all junior-grade lieutenants, and all graduates of the U.S. Naval Academy, class of 1960. In addition to the pilots, each of fifteen bombardier/navigators was assigned to fly with a specific pilot for all but exceptional missions.

Ground training began in September 1963, when the aircrews began studying the various systems in the airplane. The A-6 replacement squadron, designated VA-42, provided the training for both ground school and flight school for about ten weeks, after which time VA-75 completed its indoctrination in the aircraft and trained with their own complement of twelve aircraft. Accompanying these new aircraft were a significant group of technical representatives from Grumman and its subcontractors.

Initially the squadron was going to deploy to the Mediterranean Sea in the spring of 1965 as a member of Air Group 7, embarked in the USS *Independence*. After the conflict in Vietnam began to heat up, considerable interest was generated in the Navy in the capability of the sophisticated A-6 system in a combat role. Accordingly, the *Independence* was routed around South Africa, through the Indian Ocean, and subsequently to the South China Sea.

For the most part, tactical training for the A-6 was performed in preparation for warfare using conventional weapons. Periodically there were scheduled flights for nuclear weapons delivery training, but it was evident that conventional warfare was the mission of the moment. A typical mission would be planned to take three to four hours, commencing with takeoff from a departure point at sea, followed by a diverse route over land, passing eight to ten navigational points along the route as checkpoints (e.g., a bridge over a river, a small town, a highway intersection), and delivering the practice bomb to the target that had been designated.

There were two basic methods for delivery of the weapons. When utilizing the full weapons system as designed, the flight crew would first select the type of ordnance being carried on each of the five weapons stations: two on each wing and one on the fuselage centerline. For nuclear weapons targeting, the plan usually called for the A-6 to carry the weapon on the centerline station. This would allow the addition of four 2,000-pound fuel tanks on the wing stations, an additional 8,000 pounds of fuel. This additional fuel, added to the 16,000 pounds carried internally, served to increase the range of the aircraft by as much as one-third. The aircraft could then remain airborne for over five hours if most of the flight were conducted at high altitude, providing a realistic total range of 2,500 miles. Round-trip range was between 1,200 and 1,300 nautical miles.

Since so much of the typical flight was performed at low altitude, the range would be lessened proportionally. To compensate, VA-75 had the additional capability of refueling in flight from other A-6 aircraft configured as "buddy" airborne tankers. Practice included non-stop cross-country flights from the Naval Air Station in Oceana, Virginia, to the Naval Air Station in Alameda, California. These flights approached six hours in length.

The *Independence* was the first carrier equipped with an inertial navigation system (INS), which could be electronically plugged directly into the A-6 while the airplane was on the flight deck of the carrier. It would align the aircraft INS and automatically update the navigation information in the airplane. This meant that when the pilot was launched from the ship, the plane's navigation system contained the most up-to-date location of the ship. The navigational coordinates of the en route navigational checkpoints were then entered as well. This had a great impact on the ability to get to a specific target, providing the location of the target was known.

The weapon to be used, nuclear or otherwise, was selected on the armament panel in the cockpit. That selection automatically accounted for the ballistics of the specific weapon that was to be dropped. While the plane was in flight toward the target, the on-board computer would sample the winds aloft to make adjustments for what offset, if any, was needed to adjust the aim or release point for the launching or firing of the weapon. The pilot would arm the weapon and press the release switch, as opposed to a conventional trigger, or "pickle" switch. The weapon would release automatically when the system solved the targeting problem and the aircraft reached the release point.

In Vietnam, during the 1965 deployment, the automatic-release feature was seldom employed since rules of engagement usually required that targets be visually identified before weapon release. This often required flying over the target, particularly at night and during inclement weather conditions, in order to visually identify the target before weapon release. Then came a second pass over the target in order to deliver the weapon. This often placed the A-6 crew in harm's way. Targets where only one pass was performed, such as the infamous Than Hoa Bridge, were notable exceptions.

Outstanding successes marked the overall performance of the A-6 and the capability of the side-by-side aircrew configuration. That configuration gave the pilot and bombardier/navigator a much closer sense of teamwork in performing their mission. The aircrews were very loyal to each other and felt a close bond, both spiritually and physically.

The fact that the A-6 was an operational fleet aircraft from the fall of 1963 until the spring of 1997 is testimony to its ability to perform its mission successfully. It could deliver more ordnance at a greater distance to multiple targets, if required, with greater accuracy than any other jet attack aircraft in the fleet at that time. It was also a relatively safe aircraft, since landing speeds were under 120 knots. With typical 25 to 30 knots of wind over the flight deck during landing, the relative landing speed was less than 100 knots. There was never a carrier landing accident aboard the *Independence* during the maiden voyage of the A-6 to the western Pacific in 1965.[15]

Because of its size and long-range capability, the A-6 mission was often referred to as "medium attack." Whatever the label, it was an outstanding success. Subsequent deployments to Vietnam were increasingly successful, setting the stage for future improvements that capitalized on modern technology as it continued to evolve. Electronic warfare versions, the EA-6A and the EA-6B, were introduced into Vietnam in the late 1960s. Updated versions were part of the inventory in the late 1990s, when the Navy, Marine Corps, and Air Force were still using them, and they are forecast to be part of the arsenal well into the twenty-first century.

The Chance Vought A-7 Corsair II

Derived to some degree from the Ling Temco Vought (LTV) F-8 Crusader supersonic fighter, the Vought A-7A Corsair was designed as a replacement for the A-4. It brought some new features, including a fan-jet engine, which gave greater fuel efficiency, particularly at low altitude; a new computerized weapons system, which provided better accuracy than that of the A-4; and an Air Force Gatling gun, which was a major improvement in Navy gunnery capabilities. The Air Force mounted a major campaign for the introduction of their own version, the A-7D, which was a great improvement. The Navy enthusiastically supported the Air Force version, one of the few instances of a joint procurement program.

The ultimate Navy version of the A-7 was the A-7E, by all accounts an "honest" airplane and an easy transition from the more docile aircraft flown by student aviators in the Training Command. The airplane was certified to deliver several weapons in the nuclear arsenal, including the B-57, about 500 pounds, with a small yield; the B-61, 700 pounds, with a yield of 100 to 500 kilotons; and the B-43, 2,000 pounds, with a yield in the one-to-two-megaton range. The A-7 could carry these weapons on two stations externally. A maximum notional load then might be two B-43s and two 300-gallon wing tanks, which would give an increased mission range. The realistic combat radius for the A-7, flying a significant portion of its route at low level, was seven hundred nautical miles with no fuel tanks, or upwards of one thousand miles if carrying the two external 300-gallon tanks (see table 2 for specifications).

The single-piloted aircraft had some new features to help it get to the target. It had the first true "heads-up-display" (HUD), which projected significant operational information on the windscreen of the cockpit. That feature enabled the pilot to keep his head up and eyes out of the cockpit and still be able to read the essential information needed for a safe and successful flight. The airplane had a projected map-display system, which furnished the pilot with a cockpit color display of the area over which he was to travel. Cassettes of maps were provided for various theaters in which squadrons might operate. In addition, the airplane had a fire-control computer coupled with an air-to-ground radar, which had mapping modes as well as terrain-

Two Chance Vought A-7E Corsairs escort their predecessor, the F8U Crusader. NASM collection.

following and terrain-avoidance features, thus providing some all-weather flight capability. These systems, combined with an inertial navigation system, provided an excellent navigation capability in clear weather. Pilots attempted to use the radar with the mapping modes and the terrain-following and terrain-avoidance features for all-weather operations, but with some difficulty.

Another feature in the aircraft relating directly to the nuclear weapon delivery mission was an automatically deployed thermoshield. It was housed behind the pilot's head and included a light sensor. If the sensor detected a blast or very bright flash, it would automatically deploy the clamshell thermoshield to protect the pilot's eyes from the effects of a nuclear blast. Pilots seldom, if ever, had a full-scale test of the shield, but they did have to train to cut it away in case it inadvertently deployed during normal flight.[16]

The McDonnell-Douglas F/A-18 Hornet. NASM collection.

The McDonnell-Douglas F/A-18 Hornet

The A-7E had been phased out of service by 1992. The McDonnell-Douglas F/A-18 Hornet began replacing the A-7 in 1987, after prolonged, divisive argument within the Navy hierarchy. The objective was to procure an aircraft that would be cheaper than the expensive but highly capable F-14 Tomcat fighter and the A-6 Intruder attack aircraft. Eventually the F/A-18 was selected, despite its relatively limited range and payload capability. It incorporated state-of-the-art technology in terms of weapons systems, versatility, and reliability. The initial versions, the F/A-18 A, B, C, and D, were to be replaced by a larger and more capable F/A-18 E and F, with full production scheduled for fiscal year 2002 (see table 2 for specifications).

It is intended that the improved Hornet will be the mainstay of the carrier offensive/defensive capability for years to come. Capable of operating both as a fighter and as an attack aircraft because of the advances in computer and sensor technologies, the Hornet can be converted from fighter to attack version in less than an hour.

Addendum

Not everyone shared the Navy's conviction that carrier-based nuclear weapons forces were essential elements of the nation's nuclear weapons arsenal. Many detractors at various levels of the military and civilian establishments, at home and abroad, remained unconvinced of the worth of the Navy's light-attack capabilities.

During 1970–71, an opportunity arose for the Navy to demonstrate to a senior NATO commander the capabilities of carrier forces to support land operations in central Europe.[17] The planning conference that preceded the exercise provided an insight into the intense rivalry between the Navy and the Air Force over each other's share of the nuclear pie. The conference was held at the NATO headquarters in Brunsuum in the Netherlands and was attended by military planners from all of the participating nations. The U.S. Air Force was present en masse and seemed to be much more aware of their nuclear potential than the U.S. Navy was of theirs—and jealous of it, too. The Navy was outweighed and outranked at every turn. "The Air Force described in grand terms their ability to handle either nuclear or conventional warfare, anything the Soviets might throw up, and saw no need for the complications of another force involved."[18] It was not hard to see that they wanted no "interference" in their area of responsibility.

Rear Adm. William Houser was in command of a carrier task force in the Mediterranean at the time. As he departed Gibraltar with his task force, returning to the United States, he made a detour to the Bay of Biscay and North Sea areas, conducting tactical air operations with the shore-based NATO units. It was an excellent exercise, demonstrating that naval forces could add to the arsenals of the European commanders and deliver nuclear weapons.

In 1971–73, I commanded the U.S. Sixth Fleet in the Mediterranean. During this tour, I attempted to demonstrate the capabilities of the carrier task forces to support activities in central Europe. I requested permission from my U.S. superior at the top of the command structure, a U.S. Air Force general, to launch four A-7 aircraft from the Aegean Sea in the Mediterranean and recover them aboard a carrier operating off Bodo, Norway, in the North Atlantic. At the same time, four A-7s from the carrier in the Norwegian Sea would launch for the carrier in the Mediterranean. The next day all eight aircraft would return to their respective home bases. It was a relatively simple exercise in that Europe is not that large, and the aircraft had plenty of range and payload capabilities for the mission. After some time, I was granted permission to conduct the exercise, but only under the condition that I not publicize the event. I did not question that restriction but merely ordered the exercise, which went off very smoothly. It showed once again that carriers could support combat operations in the European landmass and contribute to either the combined or joint operations being conducted. Subsequent events in the Balkans certainly proved that point.

6. Delivery Tactics

Getting a hit on a target has fascinated man since he started to throw rocks. Accuracy has always been the objective, whether in games, hunting, or war. The Navy has continually sought better ways of hitting the target without jeopardizing the crew or the attacking vehicle, be it ship, submarine, or airplane.

When pilots flew their Spads in World War I, throwing grenades from an open cockpit on the troops below, they were using an early version of delivery tactics. Between the two world wars, experimentation was extensive. Various ideas were promoted. Some pilots reportedly used a wad of gum on the windshield of the airplane for a bomb sight. Initially, horizontal bombing was the accepted tactic, flying straight toward the target and dropping at a "guesstimated" distance to allow for the trajectory of the particular weapon being delivered. That tactic was practiced by the Navy for many years, and efforts continued to develop some type of bombing system that would encompass all the many factors that could influence the ability to hit a target.

Dick Ashworth recalls the efforts to conduct horizontal bombing from Guadalcanal during the early days of World War II while flying the TBF torpedo bomber, built by Grumman. Because the TBF had an excellent autopilot, it lent itself to some stability in the horizontal-bombing run. He proposed the idea to his boss, but by that time the glide-bombing tactic was in use and producing fair results.[1]

Horizontal bombing became the trademark of the large bombers of World War II—the British Lancaster and the American B-17 and B-24, and eventually the B-29. After the war, the U.S. Air Force B-36 and the B-52 initially dropped all bombs from high altitudes using specially designed bombing aids such as the Norden bombsight, developed before and improved considerably during the World War II. Although a Navy development, it was not used much by the Navy itself. The main combat aircraft of naval aviation, certainly those operating from carriers, had no room for such systems. The Navy's large, land-based reconnaissance aircraft, such as the PB4Y-2 (Navy version of the B-24), made their attacks at low altitude during armed reconnaissance flights. Their mission was to search, locate, report, and then destroy if time permitted. High altitude was not in their bag of tricks.

However, the main reason that the Navy did not use horizontal bombing with sophisticated bombing systems is that other forms of delivering a weapon were found to be more accurate and carried less risk for the crew, if the tactics were executed properly. For example, glide bombing meant dive angles of about 45 degrees from the horizontal. That angle of attack was used frequently until pilots learned that the shallower the angle of dive, the less accurate the delivery, and the greater the risk to the crew. Eventually, the true dive-bomber was developed, which came in almost directly over the target at an altitude of 10,000 feet or more, rolled over into an almost vertical dive, and aimed for the target. To the pilot, the dive angle felt like it was 90 degrees— he was actually hanging against the shoulder straps and seat belt— but it was really about 70 degrees. If he exceeded the 70-degree angle, he was forced to rotate the plane in the dive to get back on the target.

Special flaps were placed on dive-bombers to keep the speed down during the dive-bombing run. The Douglas SBD, of Battle of Midway fame, and its successor, the Curtiss SB2C, were equipped with special split flaps. When activated, they extended both up and down on the trailing edge of the wing during the dive. The A-1 aircraft used in Korea and Vietnam had large dive brakes that extended from the side of the fuselage when activated. Dive brakes slowed the aircraft in the dive in order to achieve more stability and a lower release altitude. Release altitudes were about 2,800 feet above the target. The speed of the plane at that point was less than 200 knots. With practice at compensating for wind and target movement, one could achieve some decent results.

After release of the bomb and the closing of the dive flaps, the plane accelerated. Pullout was executed so that departure from the target was at a very low altitude and with as much speed as possible. When dive-bomber attacks were coordinated with torpedo-plane attacks, and fighter aircraft covered both, the coordinated assault tactic was devastating to a target ship. Further, it was most effective in ensuring a safe departure for the attacking force. Many planes, particularly torpedo planes, were lost with their pilots in the early days of World War II before the coordinated air group tactic was developed.

Carrier aviation did not embrace horizontal bombing as a tactic of choice, although much effort was expended on the development of instruments that would improve the accuracy of delivery. For example, millions of dollars were spent for the development of the Norden bombsight. Both the U.S. and British air forces were deeply involved in the horizontal tactic. Dive-bombing with a B-24, a B-17, or a B-29 aircraft was out of the question. Therefore, those air forces had a great need for more and better bombsights. The U.S. Army Air Forces were the prime customer for the Norden sight. It was one item of technology that the United States withheld from the British during the war.[2]

Consequently, when Deak Parsons and Dick Ashworth were serving as weaponeers during the raids on Hiroshima and Nagasaki in the summer of 1945, the bombardiers in the B-29 aircraft were using the Norden sight, which "was the only thing the Air Force had."[3] With the introduction of the atomic bomb, the strategic bombing arm of the Air Force still had to use the high-altitude horizontal tactic, which was

A Curtis SB2C Helldiver, with a unique display of the dive-bombing flaps. U.S. Navy photo.

dictated by the explosive yield of the weapons. High altitude, a stable platform, a good aim point, and a good bombardier on the bombsight could produce good results. If the plane made a relatively steep turn away from the target immediately after release, the bombing run could be safe for the crew—as long as the explosive yield of the weapon was about twenty kilotons. So the big strategic bombers used high-altitude, horizontal-delivery tactics.

The smaller or so-called tactical aircraft—Navy, Air Force, and Marines—used glide or dive bombing, depending on the nature of the airplane being flown and the targets under attack. As a general rule, however, the steeper the dive, the greater the accuracy. This was particularly significant to naval aircraft attacking moving ships. Sticking a 1,000-pound bomb down the stack of a warship moving at 30 knots was challenging. It certainly was the dream of many carrier aviators during the early years of World War II, when the Japanese outnumbered U.S. naval forces in the Pacific.

The atomic bomb forced the Navy to change its delivery tactics. While it was entirely possible to blow oneself out of the sky with a conventional weapon by going in too close to the target, the atomic bomb assured lethal destruction if the pilot were close to the target at low altitude when the bomb was released. The Navy needed a way to get the bomb on the target without losing the delivery aircraft and its crew. For Navy heavy attack, this meant high-altitude horizontal bombing with an improved bombing system. The ASB-1 system brought improvements and respectable accuracy, certainly sufficient for the task at hand, since the immense destructive yield of the bombs compensated for the lack of accuracy. The P2V-3C, the AJ, and its successor, the A-3, were essentially horizontal bombers. One of the most significant nuclear weapons tests conducted in the postwar years proved that a B-52 strategic bomber could safely deliver a bomb with an explosive yield of one megaton from high altitude.

Light-attack aircraft, however, did not use the horizontal technique except under special circumstances, when the weapon was dropped from altitude, using radar. Even glide or dive bombing with such aircraft was not very successful. The altitude of release had to be in the range of 20,000 feet to permit recovery that was sufficiently out of the lethal range of the ensuing explosion. That high altitude of release prohibited acceptable accuracies. A better way had to be found to do the job.

One of the smart operational moves made by naval aviation was the formation of a few experimental squadrons. They had specialized missions, all aimed at developing the best way to employ new weapons systems. Experimental Squadrons 3 (VX-3) and 5 (VX-5) were formed to concentrate on the nuclear weapon delivery tactic. VX-5 was to come up with the tactic for getting the bomb on the target without blowing up the delivery aircraft and the pilot. VX-3 was to develop a way to get to the target to use the tactic developed by VX-5.

Loft/Toss Bombing

Whether the "loft" or "toss" delivery tactic originated with the Air Force or the Navy is a matter of conjecture. One can find evidence pointing either way. Regardless, the idea was a good one.

The need for the development of such a tactic brought Comdr. (then) Tom Walker back into the nuclear weapons program. Walker was the first commanding officer of Air Development Squadron 5 (VX-5), stationed at Moffett Field and then at China Lake in southern California. He and his squadron were charged with coming up with a delivery tactic that would get the nuclear weapon on or close to the target while at the same time providing an escape envelope for the aircraft and pilot so they could avoid the destructive power of the weapon.

The people assigned to VX-5 were top caliber, numbering about fifteen experienced officers and one hundred enlisted men. The average flight time per pilot was over two thousand hours, which was high, even for a specialized squadron. Some light-attack aircraft were assigned, and much of the effort was devoted to delivery tactics for the propeller-driven A-1 Skyraider and the F2H Banshee jet.

The instrumented ranges at the Naval Ordnance Test Station (NOTS), in Inyokern, California, were ideal for the test work. They afforded the flexibility and ability to measure the variables involved. Of utmost importance was the extent of atmospheric overpressure and atomic radiation that would exist in the target area after detonation of specific types of bombs. Walker had personal knowledge of weapons effects from experience at Los Alamos and Sandia Base. However, the most valuable source of information came from the Douglas Aircraft Company, whose personnel, with proper security clearances, were authorized by Chief Engineer Ed Heinemann to work with VX-5. Naval authorities approved this collaboration between the Navy and industry. It represented the kind of industry/military/civilian scientist collaboration that Deak Parsons had envisioned many years before.

Tom Walker and two of his key pilots, Lt. Comdr. Robert Selmer and Maj. Michael Yunck, considered the options and decided to concentrate on the loft or toss bombing maneuver for delivery of the weapon. The tactic had been addressed in theory, but measurements were needed. The tactic required an identifiable initial point (IP). The run-in was conducted at minimum altitude and high speed over the IP on a heading toward the target. Either at the IP or a calculated distance beyond it, the pilot initiated a pull-up using a prescribed G acceleration force and speed, and bomb release occurred automatically at a calculated angle of climb, approximately 45 degrees for the bomb to be lofted the maximum distance. Maximum distance was needed to give the pilot time to escape the destructive elements of the bomb. With known ballistics factored in, the bomb would arrive over the target at a designated altitude and detonate at that point. After bomb release, the delivery aircraft would perform an aggressive escape maneuver to diminish the impact on the aircraft of over-pressure and radiation from the bomb explosion. The initial escape maneuver took the form of a half-Cuban eight, in which the aircraft made the first part of a loop, then rolled out, diving for minimum altitude and heading directly away from the target (fig. 1). An alternative escape maneuver was a hard wingover to the same retirement heading, but the favored maneuver was the half-Cuban eight.

To check the practicality of the loft maneuver and establish the optimum set of factors to be used—speed, G forces, altitude, and angle of release of the bomb—appropriate measuring equipment and procedures were set up on the Charlie Range at China Lake. An IP was located on the run-in line at a known distance from one of the range targets. Flight paths from the IP to the target, for both the A-1 and F2H aircraft, were established, including pull-up point and escape route. The bomb was released when the aircraft reached the prescribed angle of climb, as determined by an installed gyro horizon in the cockpit.

The flying for the tests was an extensive operation that required and received the utmost in cooperation and participation from the naval ordnance test station (NOTS). The instrumentation of the range enabled NOTS to plot aircraft position throughout the bombing run and after bomb release. They could also plot the trajectory of the

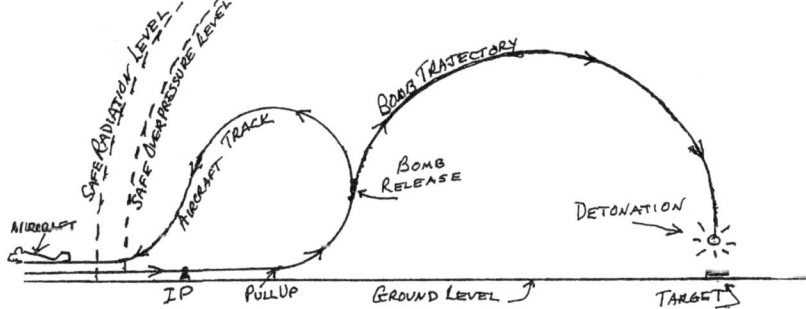

Figure 1. The loft/toss nuclear weapon delivery tactic as developed by Air Development Squadron Five (VX-5), 1951–53. IP = initial point. Sketch made in early 1997 by Vice Adm. Tom Walker, squadron commanding officer at the time of the development of the tactic.

bomb from release until it reached the target. Small Mark 76 practice bombs with smoke were used to mark the location of the bomb impact. Those locations were also plotted. Superimposed on the plot of the aircraft delivery, and to the same scale, were the overpressure and radiation of specific weapons plotted against time after detonation. By comparing the aircraft flight and weapons-effects plots, one could determine the distance required from the IP to target to provide safe escape for the aircraft and pilot.

Obviously, many variables were involved, and many aircraft flights were necessary to arrive at the optimum inbound flight path, pull-up acceleration, release angle, and escape-path maneuver. Measurements from these tests gave confidence that the loft or toss maneuver would enable the weapon to be delivered with an acceptable degree of accuracy while allowing the aircraft and pilot to retire safely.[4]

Over-the-Shoulder Bombing

VX-5 recognized that finding a satisfactory IP during the run-in to the target might not always be possible. The point might be missed during the run-in, so an extension of the loft/toss tactic was developed.

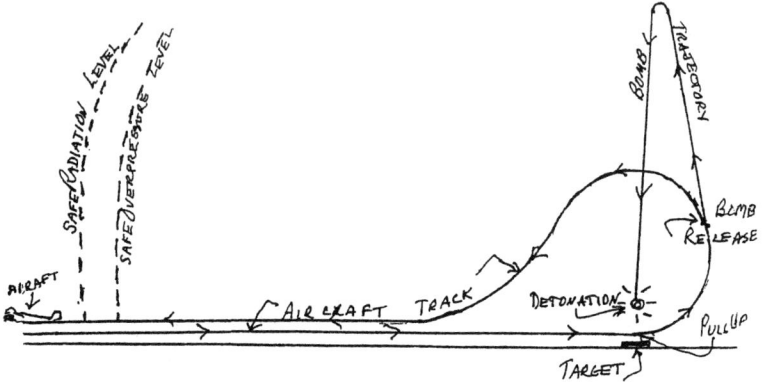

Figure 2. The over-the-shoulder (OTS) nuclear weapon delivery tactic as developed by Air Development Squadron Five (VX-5), 1951–53. Sketch made in early 1997 by Vice Adm. Tom Walker, squadron commanding officer at the time of the development of the tactic.

It was labeled the over-the-shoulder (OTS) tactic. It again called for a minimum-altitude, high-speed approach to the target, but with the pull-up starting directly over the target itself rather than at the IP. The same half–Cuban eight maneuver was used, except that the bomb release did not occur until the plane was past the vertical position in its climb. At a calculated point just beyond the vertical in the pull-up (about 110 degrees), the bomb would be automatically released. It would continue climbing after release to an altitude of about 10,000 feet for jet aircraft, reverse, and come back to the target. Following bomb release, the pilot rolled out and headed for the ground at high speed, executing the same escape maneuver as in the loft/toss tactic (fig. 2). The maneuver became known as the "idiot loop." Because Walker commanded the squadron that developed the tactic, he had some concern that eventually he might be known as the "idiot."

The squadron performed over ten thousand deliveries of Mark 76 practice bombs in developing the loft/toss and OTS techniques. This was possible in a reasonably short time because the range was adjacent to the air station runways, and the rearming of aircraft could be accomplished in minutes, without stopping aircraft engines between flights.[5]

VX-5 worked on other methods of delivering the nuclear weapon. For the A-1 propeller aircraft, dive-bombing was practiced, as in conventional bomb delivery, except that release altitude was much higher in order to provide safe escape distances. Still another tactic called for level flight toward the target by using the delivery aircraft radar, with release at sufficient altitude to provide safe escape distance. These flights were also performed at NOTS using the excellent facilities that had been set up for the loft/toss and OTS tactics.[6]

One problem facing the proponents of delivery of nuclear weapons from light aircraft was convincing authorities that it was effective. Demonstrations were conducted to display the delivery tactics. One such demonstration was conducted on the East Coast at Quantico, Virginia. A range was set up with an IP, a target, and a grandstand for observers from Washington military offices. About two hundred people attended.

The loft/toss and OTS maneuvers were demonstrated in impressive fashion using large shapes containing a conventional high-explosive charge, simulating the Mark VII nuclear weapon. Smoke trails from each bomb identified the trajectory and impact in close proximity to the target. All went well, although the dropping of a bomb using radar created some concern. That drop was scheduled as the last event of the demonstration and involved a horizontal altitude run-in to the target, with release by the pilot at an appropriate point. The target was augmented to enhance the reflections for radar detection.

The audience watched the radar-equipped aircraft approach in level flight at about 8,000 feet altitude. As the bright orange bomb left the aircraft, alarmingly, it seemed to be heading for the grandstand and not the target. It impacted about two hundred yards from the audience, scaring everybody. Since the target was about fifteen hundred yards from the grandstand, the drop had to be considered a "gross error." In the ensuing investigation, the pilot reported that everything had been fine in the cockpit, with an especially clear radar return from the target. Then it dawned that the bare metal roofs of the four buses that had delivered the Washington observers had provided the outstanding target radar return, which the pilot witnessed and used as his aim point! "The buses were parked about one hundred feet from bomb impact, which meant that it had been an excellent drop—but on the wrong target."[7]

The reaction of the pilot of the aircraft after his drop was related to a close friend in the squadron much later. "After releasing and rolling over to observe, he was horrified to see the device trajectory apparently heading squarely for the grandstand. He couldn't bear to look at impact and hightailed out of the area in complete despair with radio off to avoid hearing gruesome reports of the tragedy he was certain had occurred. Greatly depressed, he flew around until his fuel was almost exhausted. Then, fearing the worst, he landed. Learning that his drop had been a close call and not a tragedy, he pondered his good fortune and had the worst hangover of his life the next day."[8]

The Low-Altitude Bombing System

Although the loft/toss and OTS tactics developed by VX-5 were practical and successful, there was more work to be done. Data had been accumulated, and specific factors for the delivery had been developed: approach speed and altitude, G forces, bomb-release angle, and escape route. However, these factors were for specific aircraft carrying a specific weapon. They were "canned," applicable only to the A-1 and F2H aircraft. A bombing system was needed to accommodate the variables that would arise with other types of aircraft using the delivery tactics. In addition, the Navy needed a cockpit instrument that would enable the pilot to execute the maneuver precisely every time. After making many runs, squadron pilots could become quite consistent in their delivery, but errors could occur with new pilots, particularly when using other types of aircraft. Some instrumentation was required—a Low-Altitude Bombing System (LABS). That meant the introduction of some physics and mathematics to the mass of data that had been accumulated. It was not long in coming.

Lt. (then) Joseph Schwager was just finishing postgraduate training at MIT. A distinguished graduate of the Naval Academy with a special flair for mathematics, he was one of the first selectees as a bombardier/navigator for the heavy-attack program and was assigned to VC-5. After some frustration with the less than satisfactory bombing results being obtained with the P2V-3C, Schwager discovered that the pilot direction indicator (PDI) in the cockpit was wired incorrectly. Steering signals generated by the remotely located bombardier were transposed and prevented a correct bombing solution. His discovery was confirmed by Lt. (then) Robert Baldwin, who was a contemporary in the squadron. After a correction was made, bombing results improved, and Schwager became the bombardier for Capt. Chick Hayward, the commanding officer of VC-5. Later, he was assigned to VC-6, where Dick Ashworth was serving as the commanding officer. With support from both Hayward and Ashworth, Schwager attended postgraduate school, attaining a master's degree in physics from MIT. Seeking a challenge for the use of his talents and knowledge, he heard about the work that VX-5 had been doing on bomb-delivery tactics. He sought assignment to the squadron, which was approved. After reporting aboard, he took on the task of developing a low-altitude bombing system.

Schwager noted that the initial VX-5 loft activity had rightfully given highest priority to safe escape from nuclear weapon blast and radiation effects. That would logically be accomplished by maximizing aircraft separation from the weapon at detonation. For the loft/toss maneuver, that meant tossing the weapon from as far away as possible and then exiting the area. Realistically, however, an operational "maximum range" required a usable geographical reference, preferably *precisely* at the IP. That was almost impossible to obtain in all except a few circumstances. (With the modern-day global positioning system [GPS], that point could be easily established.) Some feasible geographic reference point, after the IP was reached, had to be established, whereupon a timed traverse was then used to arrive at the point for beginning the execution of the delivery maneuver. That predicament inspired the OTS solution, which used the target itself as the point for starting the maneuver. Maximum altitude attained by the aircraft during delivery became the means of attaining maximum range separation. Regrettably, however, OTS made the aircraft extremely vulnerable, since eligible nuclear targets were certain to contain intense close-in defenses.[9]

There were other residual problems. The Navy had to deal with a continuing extensive test program to qualify other current or future candidate aircraft for tactical nuclear weapons delivery. Those problems were a tormenting challenge for Schwager. He had observed and was particularly impressed with the degree of consistency pilots could achieve with consistent flight conditions and was motivated to consolidate and analyze the many aircraft and bomb plots that Tom Walker and his teammates had produced in their development of tactics. Whereas Walker and his crew had acquired some parameters for two specific models of aircraft through trial and error, Schwager wanted to set parameters for any loft delivery condition. That he did, providing solutions for most of the residual problems, including how to dramatically reduce, but not completely eliminate, the need for future flight tests.

Working on the OTS vulnerability problem, Schwager noted that in general, when the effects exposure from a specific weapon was acceptable at both the maximum range (MR) and OTS extremes, all other IPs, with variable release angles in between, were also acceptable. Hence, any suitable landmark within those bounds that avoided defense installations was an eligible precise IP for which the delivery formulation could provide a proper release solution and avoid the OTS vulnerability. Even so, Schwager noted that OTS could continue to be practical because "steeper is better" in evading defensive fire, and crisis situations could arise, requiring the use of the target itself as the IP.[10]

In short, formulae were developed for a low-altitude bombing system with a cockpit instrument for pilot guidance in the maneuver execution and automatic weapon release at the proper attitude regardless of the IP selected, aircraft used, or weapon delivered. These formulae were taken over by the Bureau of Aeronautics and the Bureau of Ordnance. A contract with industry was negotiated later, and eventually all carrier nuclear delivery aircraft were equipped with the LABS, including a very useful cockpit instrument.

Practicing the delivery tactic was fun with the LABS. A pilot approached the target at an altitude as low as he wanted, at a speed of 500 knots for jets. As he crossed over the IP or the target itself, depending on whether he was going to loft/toss or do the OTS delivery, he pushed a bomb-release pickle on the control stick and started a 4-G pull-up, now concentrating on the LABS instrument in the cockpit. The instrument gave an indication of wings level and vertical directional stability, plus the amount of deviation from the required 4-G force level. If the plane were steady in the pull-up, the crosshairs on the instrument remained in a perfect horizontal/vertical presentation. But with any variation in the flight regime, the reference marks moved from the desired presentation. When the bomb-release pickle was pressed, a whistling tone was broadcast in the pilot's earphones and remained on until the bomb released, at approximately 45 degrees for the loft/toss maneuver and 110 degrees for OTS. The tone stopped when the bomb had been released. At that point, the pilot could start his escape maneuver, rolling out or performing whatever routine he elected for escape. It was fun making low-level, high-speed runs on the target, finishing with a partial loop and high-speed getaway, only to rejoin the pattern of bombing aircraft and repeat the maneuver again. On an instrumented range, the range personnel would broadcast the significant aspects of the latest delivery, including the miss distance from the target. Thus, the pilot always had current information while practicing, which provided instant and continual incentive for doing better. It was a form of legalized flat-hatting, something that most pilots enjoy but rarely have an opportunity to practice.

Most impressive, particularly with the OTS maneuver, was the accuracy that could be obtained. To have a weapon delivered in that manner, rise to 10,000 feet, reverse course, and impact on or near the target was remarkable. A bull's-eye was not uncommon. The development of the maneuvers and the associated bombing system, coupled with the results attained by the pilots through training, were hallmarks of true professionals.

With the leadership of Tom Walker and the ingenuity of the many excellent people assigned to the squadron, including Joe Schwager, the loft/toss and OTS maneuvers became the Navy way. There was never any question that if a pilot were in a carrier aircraft carrying a 2,000-pound load under the belly, and the weapon had an equivalent explosive yield of one megaton, either the loft or OTS maneuver was the preferred method of delivery. The maneuvers aided in the identification of the target, were reasonably safe during the approach because of low altitude and high speed, produced excellent accuracy, and provided a safe escape. They were major developments in bombing tactics.

These tactics placed high wing loadings on the aircraft, which meant that the large A-3 aircraft, with its restrictions on G forces on the wing, might not be safe for anything but the high-level, horizontal-bombing technique. However, some of the leaders in the heavy-attack program, particularly Jig Ramage, felt that the time had passed for high-altitude bombardment. Some kind of low-altitude penetration and delivery was needed. Tests were conducted with the A-3, again at NOTS in southern California. A simple maneuver was developed. After a low-level run-in, pull-up, and bomb release, the aircraft did not complete the half–Cuban eight maneuver, as did the smaller planes. Rather, after weapon release at about 50 degrees pitch angle, the plane did a high-angle bank to reverse course and escape the blast. Ed Heinemann, the Douglas Aircraft designer, directed a test of the wing to see if it would take the stress. The wing was rated for 2.5 Gs, but tests showed that it could take at least three times that stress. The A-3 was still in business with a new delivery technique.[11]

Other tactics were developed. "Lay-down," that is, parachute-retarded weapon delivery, provided a means of flying directly over the target and releasing the weapon. As the weapon slowly descended on the target, the aircraft and pilot escaped at high speed. The tactics for obtaining hits on the target and at the same time providing a safe escape for the pilot and aircraft were major contributions to the carrier nuclear delivery capability. Air Development Squadron 5 served the Navy well.

Getting to the Target

Regardless of how clever and effective the tactics were for delivering the weapon, it was still necessary to get to the target to execute the tactic. This part of the problem was tackled by Air Development Squadron 3 (VX-3). In the early 1950s, Comdr. (then) Noel Gayler was the commanding officer. A bright, innovative officer with an impressive combat record in World War II, he was the man to take on many of the tactics problems facing fleet aviation squadrons. Under him was a group of outstanding pilots, some of whom were test pilot school graduates with a great deal of experience in that aspect of flying. Though promotion to flag rank may not necessarily be a valid indicator of competency, nevertheless an unusual number of officers in that squadron went on to positions of considerable responsibility. Gayler himself became the head of all armed forces in the Pacific Command.

Since flying at low altitude was the best way of avoiding detection by radar, it became obvious that low-level flight would be necessary as the delivery aircraft began to penetrate enemy defenses. This would match the delivery tactic as well, which was to be executed from a high-speed, low-altitude run-in. A tremendous amount of effort was devoted to learning how to fly long distances at low altitude, with the terrain flying by at a rapid pace.

Whitey Feightner was a key member in VX-3 at the time. He became deeply involved in developing the ability to fly a bomb-delivery aircraft safely to a target at low level for very long distances. Improved antiair defenses made this the only reliable tactic for penetration of enemy territory. Feightner says that the objective was to fly long distances "with no radio, at one hundred feet and below."[12]

One of Feightner's first questions had to do with the ability of a pilot in a jet to navigate at low level for a long distance without much low-level navigation training. The late Donald D. Engen, one of the most competent of all naval aviators, volunteered for the project. His mission was to fly at an altitude of 50 feet from Atlantic City, New Jersey, to a dam in central Ohio at a speed of about 300 knots. It started well, but as time wore on, the difficulty of the mission became obvious. He reported that extensive low-level navigation route training was a "must"; that naval aviation should plan to have routes and syllabi that would enable pilots to train adequately; that such flying could not be a one-shot affair. He had great respect for those thousands of Navy, Army, and Air Force pilots who subsequently trained in low-level navigation.[13] Based on Engen's report, Feightner knew that he had his work cut out for him. Low-level flights, particularly in jets, would require intensive training.

Developing tactics and getting fleet personnel trained to use them is one problem. Persuading people that the capability is necessary, particularly the politicians and bureaucrats in Washington, another. One of the more impressive demonstrations conducted by VX-3 during this period involved three F2H aircraft taking off from the USS *Midway* east of Cuba. The pilots—Michael Ames, Whitey Feightner, and Noel Gayler—were to fly to a target in Lake Erie and then return to the carrier. To add some realism to the demonstration, the entire North American Defense Command (NORAD) was alerted that an attempt would be made to penetrate the air defense zone and stage a mock nuclear weapon delivery on the target. These penetrating aircraft were to be detected and intercepted if possible. It was a good exercise for all concerned, with potential for providing some useful answers to many questions, not the least of which was whether low-level tactics were effective.

All that the NORAD system knew was that the flight would attempt to penetrate the area sometime during the day. The flight launched from the carrier at 9:30 A.M. local time and refueled from one of the ship's AJ tanker aircraft over water at an altitude of about 20,000 feet. They were about 150 miles from the East Coast at that time. After refueling and reaching a point about 75 to 100 miles from the coastline, they descended to very low altitude over the water, crossing the coast at a point just north of Savannah, Georgia, and remained very low all the way to Lake Erie. The pilots had planned the navigation route very carefully, an absolute must in long low-level flights. In this instance, the target was in a large lake, which would have been hard to miss. They chose en route landmarks such as bodies of water that could not change regardless of weather conditions. The flight was not intercepted during the approach to the coast or during the entire flight to the target. They were carrying the Mark VII shapes, which simulated the type of nuclear bomb the aircraft would carry in an actual attack. The shapes contained conventional high explosives but no nuclear cores.

The pilots used the OTS maneuver for the delivery of the shapes, which exploded as planned. At the postflight debriefing, they were informed that they had not been detected until they had dropped their explosive shapes on the target. The Air Defense Command then became aware of the flight. It was a beautiful day, and the F2H pilots could see the U.S. Air Force F-86 and F-84 fighter aircraft circling above the target at about 20,000 feet. Immediately after the shapes exploded, the Air Force intercept aircraft started down after the F2H flight. The flight remained at low level, as close to the ground as possible, maintaining maximum speed. When the interceptors got down to the low altitude of the penetrators, the latter started a high-speed climb, topping out at over 50,000 feet. That altitude was too much for the pursuers. The flight went into a cruise mode and watched as the pursuers attempted to get to their altitude, unable to complete an intercept.

The flight proceeded out to sea, rendezvoused with another AJ tanker, refueled, and returned to the ship. They had been in the air a total of 8.3 hours and covered a distance of over 2,800 nautical miles, which was a record for the time. "The F2H Banshee was a great airplane. You could pull the wings off if you were too aggressive, but it could perform. It certainly did on that day."[14] The success of the mission was mainly attributable to the hours and hours of practice that the squadron had devoted to low-level flying for long distances. The flight answered many questions and gave the Navy considerable confidence in its ability to perform the nuclear missions.

Training for high-speed, low-level navigation took some ingenuity. One problem was pilot recognition of checkpoints at low level. VX-3 modified the nose on one of their F2Hs and mounted a forward-looking camera, which could produce some very effective 8-by-10-inch negatives. They flew that airplane over designated training routes, taking pictures of the entry to the various navigation checkpoints along the way. By studying the pictures, the pilots became aware of the different perspective presented by low-level flying. It helped a great deal, and the accuracy of the navigation improved dramatically. The pictures gave the pilot a chance to get a preview of what he was looking for before actually conducting the flight. After working with the problem for sometime, Feightner came to some firm conclusions.

Low-level flying is a mind-set operation. You have to get people used to a different perspective, which means a lot of low-level flying. After several flights, the light suddenly dawns. From then on, it is relatively easy, but you have to have the right mind set to start with. That was a major problem. It was similar to getting used to the idea of long flights in single-engine aircraft. You had to be in the right frame of mind. Nobody thought we were going to be able to fly for twelve or more hours in the A-1 prop aircraft. But, after developing the technique and practicing a lot, everyone accepted the concept.[15]

The A-1 prop aircraft figured very heavily in the nuclear delivery picture all through the 1950s and early 1960s. Low-level flights in the A-1 were easier in some ways than in the F2H jet. For one thing, the ground went by at only three miles a minute, rather than six or seven in the jet. However, the flights were longer because the aircraft had great endurance. VX-3 worked on the low-level tactic for the A-1. Feightner recalls that the squadron made one flight in a stripped-down aircraft that lasted eighteen hours to prove to the fleet pilots that the aircraft and pilot were capable of that type of endurance. All delivery pilots were guaranteed that they could make at least "twelve- or fourteen-hour flights" in the A-1. Staying awake and alert on such flights was a problem.

> We had all sorts of gadgets. We had vibrating back pads for one thing. Frank Austin was our flight surgeon. He tried all kinds of things to keep people awake. We finally decided that we were better off not eating during the long flights; that water alone was enough. On those flights, some pilots did not eat a thing and were still quite alert when they returned to land aboard ship. Pilots were busy on those flights. Flying at low altitude has one advantage at least. It does not get boring. When we first started the long-range low-level flights, many pilots thought they were terrible. However, as they gained confidence, the flights became routine. People just went ahead and flew them.[16]

Another problem created by these low-level flights was the disruption of normal civilian life. Mules pulling a wagon would rear up in excitement as the planes flew overhead, close to the ground. After carefully planning a flight and getting it cleared from proper authority, the flight might fly over a turkey farm, causing the turkeys to pile up in a corner and smother each other. The squadron received many damage bills, particularly in New Jersey.[17]

Some of the best sea stories about naval aviation are stories of low-level "butt busters" or "sand blowers," as these flights were called often. One published story prompted a series of letters by many pilots who had experienced similar situations.[18]

In late 1953, a pilot flying an A-1 from a carrier in the Mediterranean launched and flew at low level to the east. The flight was supposed to terminate with a climb in altitude just before reaching the target, followed by a simulated high-altitude attack on the airfield at Afyonkarahisar in central Turkey. All went well during the flight until the pull-up to launch the weapon, when the engine had a serious malfunction and quit. The pilot was forced to make a wheels-up landing in a desolate part of that vast country. As soon as he exited the airplane, he spotted a camel caravan approaching. In subsequent events, he learned something about the Turks, their hospitality, and their willingness to help. Although the time in the air had been only a few hours, the rest of the flight required about a month to complete. Movement of the plane to a suitable airfield about sixty miles away took some time. Just getting a new engine to the area from the parent carrier was no small feat. The support from the Turks was superb. Finally, after completing basic repairs and performing some rudimentary navigation through Greece and Italy, the pilot was able to make it back home to the carrier. It had been an interesting butt buster in many ways.[19]

The A-4 was the light-attack workhorse for the nuclear weapons mission during the 1960s, augmented for a while with a small number of FJ-4B squadrons. Squadrons flying those aircraft conducted literally thousands of practice runs. Approaches to the target followed the patterns developed by VX-3. Delivery was by either the loft/toss or OTS tactic, depending on the target location and identifiable reference points. For those air wings that had both the A-3 and the A-4 on board, "buddy bombing" was employed. The A-3, having a better navigational capability, would lead the A-4 to the vicinity of its target before peeling off to proceed to its own target. Navigating to the target was always a major point of concern.

The arrival of the A-6 in the arsenal in the mid-1960s added more sophistication to the all-weather and night capability, but flight tactics for nuclear targets were essentially the same as for the A-4 Skyhawk. After launch from the carrier, the A-6 would fly at high altitude until it reached about 150 miles from landfall. Then the pilot would descend to 100 feet or less above the water to escape detection by enemy radar. The pilot would remain at that altitude, utilizing the radar altimeter to maintain the proper altitude and employing the vertical display indicator as the primary instrument for pilot terrain clearance information on a real-time basis.

As the aircraft passed each checkpoint along the route, the bombardier/navigator updated the computer with more precise positioning data to continually increase the probability of a direct target hit. In addition, en route to the target, the electronic counter measures (ECM) package was armed in the event of an enemy ground or air attack. Radar jamming and chaff packets were effective devices to divert radar lock-on by unfriendly guns or missiles.

When the aircraft approached the weapon-release point, the crew positioned the blast shield or curtain in the cockpit. The bombardier/navigator then armed the centerline weapon station and indicated to the pilot that the weapons system was "go." The pilot depressed the "commit" switch or trigger and commenced the delivery maneuver. Typically, the special-weapons delivery started at low level, five to ten miles before the target. With the OTS maneuver, the weapon would automatically release from the aircraft when the system had completed its solution.

If the system were inoperable, the crew would override the computer, and the delivery would be completed by manually performing all of the necessary in-flight functions before weapon release. The pilot would depress the bomb-release button, or pickle, on top of the control stick, instead of the trigger, or commit switch, located on the front of the stick, which was used during the preferred systems delivery.[20]

While VX-3 and its pilots mastered the low-level flight regime, it was not easy for the average fleet squadron. For example, a realistic mission for the A-7, flying a significant portion of the route at low level with no fuel tanks, would be about seven hundred nautical miles in radius. With the tanks, the radius would be extended to about a thousand miles — no short flight. When a pilot reported to a fleet replacement squadron in the early 1970s, his initial nuclear weapons training involved learning how to fly an accurate flight at 200 to 500 feet at 360 knots. New pilots learned to navigate by dead reckoning and the use of the airplane's inertial navigation system to determine a precise location while still flying at very low altitude. The visual, fair-weather, low-level flights became quite feasible. However, the all-weather flights were difficult, and much training time went into the use of the A-7's excellent air-to-ground radar. Radar training was in the rear of a T-39 jet training aircraft equipped with the A-7 radar system. Students sat behind radarscopes in the rear of the plane with an A-6 bombardier/navigator instructor who was assigned full time to the A-7 squadron. He taught radar operation and scope interpretation of radar images so the pilots could become proficient in radar navigation. Periodically, an attempt was made to perform the all-weather mission at low level. The trainee flew the route under the thermal shield in the airplane cockpit, which prohibited visual reference of any kind outside the airplane. For safety purposes, an instructor pilot in a second aircraft chased the trainee. Unfortunately, on occasion, there would be a communications foul-up or some other problem that made the situation hazardous. Flying the A-7 at high speed and low level, relying on radar navigation, was not easy, even with all the navigation aids that were in the cockpit. There were occasional accidents, after which the squadrons would cease the low-level all-weather training. Later, they would try again, but it was a spotty capability. Consequently, it was difficult to assume that anybody would be adequately trained for all-weather low-level navigation in the A-7. In visual weather conditions, fine, but in all-weather conditions, it was "iffy."[21]

Low-level navigation training was a critical aspect of preparing for the nuclear mission. That training was followed with practice for the delivery tactics that were to be employed, the loft/toss and lay-down maneuvers. Although the OTS maneuver was popular at one time, by the 1970s some squadrons opted for the loft/toss tactic to get more separation from the nuclear explosion. Some A-7 squadrons were tossing the weapon on the run-in, when about fifteen thousand feet from the target.

The lay-down maneuver was a delivery tactic for the big, heavy-attack A-3 but was also used for light-attack aircraft in case of systems failures or bad weather with low ceilings over the target area. A delayed fuse on the weapon was mandatory. In the A-7, pilots would fly directly over the target, manually releasing the bomb when the computer or manual sight gave an indication on the heads-up display that it was time to drop. This delivery tactic prohibited the use of an airburst of the weapon, but it was fine for a ground burst. The favorite tactic, however, was still the loft/toss maneuver.[22]

Accuracy of delivery was a factor that received considerable attention. In the A-7 program, to qualify for a mission, the pilot had to have a circle error of probability (CEP) of less than 400 feet. A CEP inside of 225 feet won the pilot an E for efficiency. Many pilots became quite proficient in the delivery tactic, attaining CEPs of 100 feet or less using the medium-angle loft maneuver. Given the distance that they were throwing the bomb, the results were remarkable.

Accuracy in navigation was as much a part of the competitive process as accuracy in delivery. Tests for accuracy in navigation were conducted in simulators, where an entire low-level route could be programmed. A chase pilot would measure timing variances from each of the programmed checkpoints and time on target.

It was obvious to the pilots that a high-priority mission for all Navy attack squadrons during the 1970s was the nuclear weapons delivery mission. It was clearly a mission that the pilots knew they had to execute correctly. The level of emphasis and attention to detail were most impressive, considering that the probabilities of the actual delivery of any nuclear device by any means seemed more remote each day. The nuclear mission provided a very competitive atmosphere, not only between individual pilots in the squadrons, but also between squadrons. In most units, qualification exercises were conducted as part of the operational readiness exercises, which took place before each deployment to the forward area.[23]

When studying the overall nuclear delivery plans, some pilots developed strong doubts as to whether or not they could return safely from the mission, especially because so many nuclear weapons were targeted in the operational area. The stockpile was immense in the 1970s, and more than one weapon was often programmed for the same aim point—designated ground zero. Even so, most pilots believed that they were well prepared and would perform successfully if called upon to deliver.[24]

7. Ships

The airplane, the thermonuclear weapon, the ballistic missile, and the nuclear-powered submarine all ranked among the technological wonders of the twentieth century. Each in its own way represents an unprecedented and unmatched capability in military arsenals. Notwithstanding these amazing accomplishments, the modern-day attack aircraft carrier represents, for many, one of the military marvels of the age. Other nations, such as Great Britain, Argentina, Italy, France, Spain, and Russia, have developed a limited aircraft carrier capability, but the United States remains dominant in that phase of modern warfare.

The modern aircraft carrier has evolved over more than eighty years. The United States can count in its weapons inventory an armada of mobile air bases, any one of which can travel over the oceans of the world at speeds of 30–40 mph. They can stay at sea for years, if necessary, by taking on needed supplies from modern, mobile, seagoing replenishment systems. Each carrier and embarked air wing is manned with a complement of five to six thousand men and women. On board is a mix of aircraft and weapons, the capabilities of each depending on the mission at hand. Each carrier is capable of carrying a large inventory of nuclear weapons, and this load of weapons can be

The USS *Essex* (CV-9), 27,000 tons, before conversion, which was completed in 1942. Naval Historical Foundation.

replenished at sea if required. Not constrained by international boundaries or other politically imposed restrictions, the carrier enjoys the freedom of the seas and can carry its might to a troubled area, providing a presence of U.S. force and will.

Starting with some daring experiments in the early 1920s, the U.S. Navy gradually developed the carrier and its associated aircraft and weapons systems into a potent force. The first carrier was the USS *Langley* (CV-1), a 1920–21 conversion of a collier, which displaced 11,000 tons and had 542 feet of flight deck. The *Langley* was followed in 1927 by the *Lexington* (CV-2) and *Saratoga* (CV-3), built on battle-cruiser hulls and displacing 33,000 tons, with almost 900 feet of flight deck. The USS *Ranger* (CV-4) followed in 1934, the first built from the keel up as a carrier, displacing 14,000 tons, with a flight deck of over 700 feet. The *Ranger* was followed by three of the *Yorktown* class (CV-5), displacing 20,000 tons, with flight decks over 700 feet

An early jet, the North American FJ-1, engaging the emergency barrier after failing to catch an arresting wire, 12 October 1948. U.S. Navy Photo.

long; and the USS *Hornet* (CV-8), displacing 20,000 tons and 800 feet long. The so-called big decks of World War II, the *Essex* class (CV-9), of which twenty-four were eventually built, displaced 27,000 tons initially and had flight decks almost 900 feet long. During conversions, which will be described later, these increased in displacement to 45,000 tons to accommodate nuclear weapons and improvements in embarked aircraft. The "small decks" of World War II were escort and light carriers with displacements ranging from 8,000 to 11,000 tons and flight decks in the 500–600 foot range.

Three *Midway*-class ships were commissioned immediately after the War with initial displacements of 45,000 tons, later increased to 50,000 tons as they were modified to incorporate nuclear weapons, the angled flight deck, steam catapults, and accompanying improvements. Flight decks were over 900 feet long. In 1955, a major im-

The USS *Midway* (CV-41), 45,000 tons, with straight or "axial" deck, completed in 1945. Naval Historical Foundation.

provement came with the *Forrestal* and *Kitty Hawk* classes, at almost 60,000 tons, with flight decks longer than 1,000 feet.

As U.S. naval aviation continued to evolve during the early years of the jet age, carriers became bigger and heavier. Beginning with the USS *Enterprise* (CVAN-65) in 1961, nuclear power began to replace fossil fuel as the means of propulsion. The size of the *Enterprise*—85,600 tons, with a flight deck of 1,100 feet—came close to meeting the mobile air base requirements of existing and future aircraft. Later carriers of the *Nimitz* class all came in at about 90,000 tons and 1,000-plus feet of flight deck, which provided the stability required for flight operations in any kind of sea or weather, day or night.[1]

There have been proponents of smaller, cheaper carriers. As long as aircraft continue to require great energy for takeoff and the absorption of great energy during landing, there will be a need for a stable flight deck—a runway that is not pitching and rolling with the heavy seas. Eighty years of experience have proven that the 90,000-ton carrier is the ideal all-weather mobile air base.

The evolutionary development of the carrier was costly in terms of dollars and people. In the 1950s, the British contributed some very essential concepts, which were incorporated by the U.S. Navy with enthusiasm and great success. Angled flight decks, steam catapults, and mirror landing systems were vital additions to a growing capability. There were many technical as well as political challenges along the way, which continue to arise as the nature of future weapons systems is debated.

As ship architects began to design and produce large commercial tankers displacing over 200,000 tons, some naval strategists gave serious consideration in the late 1960s to building a carrier of that size, with two runways and double the complement of aircraft. There seemed to be no problem in building a ship of that size, which would double the capacity and theoretically be more cost-effective. However, the size of the mobile air base was not the constraining feature. It was the air space surrounding the carrier. Having 200 airplanes on board would mean as many as 100–120 airplanes in the air at the same time during routine launch and landing operations, all flying in the same airspace—an untenable situation. So, the Navy wisely settled on the 90,000-ton size. It chose to build two 90,000-ton air bases and keep them dispersed in order to capitalize on all the air space that is available at sea, rather than concentrate on one 200,000-ton ship.

The USS *United States*

The attainment of a nuclear weapons delivery capability was perhaps the greatest challenge faced by the carrier aviation community in the jet age. One of the earliest perceived setbacks to that goal was the cancellation of the construction of the USS *United States*, in April 1949, within a few days after the keel was laid. This unexpected event created considerable consternation in Navy circles, since the ship had been a key factor in the plan to attain a realistic nuclear weapons delivery capability. Having to operate the AJ aircraft from the smaller decks of the *Essex*-class carriers presented many problems, some of which would seriously degrade the Navy's claim to a realistic capability to deliver nuclear weapons from aircraft carriers. A much more capable carrier had to be built, or the future of carrier aviation was in jeopardy. The bomb was creating pressure on the ship designers and architects to come up with something better.

Secretary of Defense Louis Johnson canceled the *United States* for several reasons, mostly political. Though not specifically germane to the cancellation of the ship, the events leading up to the selection of Johnson and his subsequent actions with regard to the military establishment provide an excellent insight into the reasons for the cancellation and Johnson's later removal in September 1950.[2] Had he not been removed from his post, the Navy's goals would have been more difficult, if not impossible, to attain.

The election of 1948 was a close contest, and before Truman was reelected, there were dark days for the Democrats. The Democratic Party was in financial trouble. Louis Johnson, who had been very influential with the American Legion, told President Truman that he would raise the money to finance a last-minute whistle-stop train tour around the country as part of the election campaign. Johnson stipulated that in return, should Truman win, he was to be given any job he wanted in the new administration. Truman agreed and was reelected. It has been contended that he gave credit to that whistle-stop tour as the key event in the close victory. As for Johnson, he wanted to be secretary of defense—immediately. That was the only job he wanted. So Truman sent for Forrestal, gave him his notice on 23 April 1949, and Louis Johnson became the nation's second secretary of defense.

Within a matter of a couple of days, Johnson moved in some of his American Legion cronies. It was the old political patronage game, and it marked the beginning of the massive buildup of the Office of the Secretary of Defense, which started under Johnson and expanded during the lengthy reign of Secretary of Defense Robert McNamara.

After Johnson canceled the construction of the *United States,* he rode roughshod over the Navy, the Marines, whom he hated more, and naval aviation, which he hated the most. He was not a man with whom one could argue or make a logical presentation. When the Korean War broke out, the extent of Johnson's attacks on the military establishment was exposed. His contention that he was cutting the fat but not touching the bone was revealed as untrue. "He had smashed the bone to splinters. Little was left but shards."[3] The military had virtually no strength when Korea erupted. Due to Johnson and his demolition of the military establishment, the country was not ready for war. But that lack of preparedness gave Truman an ideal opportunity to fire him, which he did. It took some time and much emergency action for the military to recover.

The crash program to achieve a nuclear delivery capability involved ships as well as aircraft and their crews. In fact, in many ways the ship was the major hurdle. There simply was no body of technical experience in shipboard operations of 70,000-pound aircraft. Simultaneous operations of jet- and piston-engine aircraft on an aircraft carrier presented a different set of problems. Further, no one had any experience in the storing of nuclear weapons. Getting them into carriers and keeping them safe as they were assembled, handled, and stored on board posed unprecedented problems.

The Navy was pushing hard for a new carrier. The cancellation of the *United States* was viewed as a major setback to some, for it was a key factor in the plan for delivering nuclear weapons. However, its cancellation was viewed as a godsend by those more knowledgeable about designing carriers. A simple follow-up to the *Midway* class was not the answer by any means. For example, the existing hydraulic catapults were at the end of their performance envelope. Something new and dramatic was needed. In addition, the size of the aircraft needed to carry a 10,000-pound payload would make operations on board extremely difficult, as experience with the AJ aircraft proved conclusively. There had to be a major redirection of aircraft carrier characteristics.

Capts. Deke Ela and James D. Small spent most of their active duty naval careers designing, modifying, building, and repairing aircraft carriers.[4] They did not share the view that cancellation of the *United States* was a disaster. In Small's opinion, the *design* of the ship was the disaster. That design called for an axial flush deck, with an island on an elevating platform. It had an electronics suite at each corner of the fight deck on an elevator of sorts. No decision had been made about the catapult to be used. There was much talk about how to design a slotted-tube catapult. The existing catapult of the time was the H-8, the most powerful hydraulic catapult ever built. It was an accident waiting to happen, and it did happen—twice—once in the USS *Leyte* (CV-32), and once in the USS *Bennington* (CV-20), a disaster in which 127 people were killed in 1954.[5]

Planners also talked about introducing a powder catapult, but there was not enough space in the ship to hold all the powder charges that would be required for the catapult and at the same time store bombs and ammunition for the embarked aircraft. The design provided for four catapults arranged at an angle to the centerline of the flight deck. There were two starboard catapults, one forward, and one aft, both angled to starboard. There were two port catapults, arranged similarly to port. In retrospect, the angled deck was there all the time—but no one recognized it. "It is too bad that our naval architects, naval aviators, or bystanders didn't see it—but they didn't."[6]

In Small's opinion, Secretary Johnson should go down in history as a great friend of the Navy. Had the *United States* been built, it would have been a classic example of what not to do. Newport News Shipbuilding and Dry Dock Company was building the ship and tried to avoid the cancellation by rigging a structure in the dry dock where the ship would be built in an effort to indicate that the construction had proceeded too far for cancellation. "Fortunately, the ploy failed."[7]

In retrospect, it is easy to see why Deke Ela and Jim Small were thankful that Louis Johnson had canceled the *United States*. Had it been built, it would have fallen flat on its keel and could have meant the end of carrier aviation.

The *Essex*-Class Projects 27A and 27C

Despite the success of U.S. naval ships during World War II, that war highlighted the need for a new aircraft carrier that could operate in the atomic world, and the necessity to modify existing carriers and other warships as well. For example, the first conversions of surface ships to handle guided missiles posed some fascinating problems for the ship architect. Submarines were undergoing tremendous changes with the introduction of air-breathing cruise missiles, nuclear power, and eventually ballistic missiles.[8]

For the carriers, the first task was the conversion of the World War II *Essex*-class carriers to accommodate nuclear weapons, a project called 27A. The project had to be a "conversion." It could not be called "modernization" because that term implied new construction work, and no new construction money was available when the project was planned in the late 1940s. However, there was money for converting existing ships for some new mission. This evasive tactic worked. The cost of the project was about 55 million dollars.[9]

The project consisted primarily of providing nuclear weapons handling and storage capability. Essentially, the same assembly process that existed at the nuclear laboratory in Sandia had to be duplicated in the ship. The weapons were not stockpiled in a magazine like conventional ordnance. The various components had to be placed in separate shops from which they moved to an assembly shop, where they were put together as a weapon before being stored. The whole assembly area was termed SASS (Special Aircraft Service Stores). All of this work had to be done under tight security measures.

The USS *Oriskany* was the lead conversion. It was literally drowning in manpower in the New York Naval Shipyard in the effort to complete the ship by mid-October 1950. All hands understood the importance of that upgrade. The SASS detail design and installation went well because it had been the subject of detailed engineering in the Bureau of Ships. There had been intensive liaison with the nuclear laboratory at Sandia. Supervisors were also able to minimize the number of engineers requiring high-level security "Q" clearance. Reducing security restrictions, many of which were almost ludicrous, can do a lot to generate progress.[10]

The ship designers were faced with some completely new design problems in handling this new form of weaponry. Comdr. John "Red" McQuilken had started the SASS design for the Project 27A conversions. The project required close liaison with the Armed Forces Special Weapons Project in Sandia and Los Alamos because the lead time from design to ship trials meant dealing with nuclear weapon geometries still on the drawing boards. McQuilken and his predecessor, Dick Mandelkorn, had to be forceful in getting the scientists at Los Alamos and Sandia to deal with shipboard realities. As part of their duties, they took the weapon-assembly training at Sandia, which helped them bring theoretical concepts into the real world of shipboard handling and storage.[11]

The nuclear weapons required an array of specialty shops that had to be arranged in a logical assembly-line process, all the while meeting existing safety standards. For accessibility, as many component shops as possible were located on the same level as the main assembly shop. The magazine for storing bomb shapes with their conventional high explosives was in the lowest level of all the SASS spaces, because it was the safest. Smaller stowage spaces on different levels had dumbwaiter access to the assembly shop. The whole operation, including the Special Weapons Unit (SWU) office, had to be grouped under a single guarded entrance for security. This array of dispersed components—assembly, checking, testing, and associated instrumentation—was not a model of efficiency. It was, however, a notable improvement over in-flight procedures with which Deak Parsons and Fred Ashworth had had to cope when assembling and arming the weapons for the drops on Japan and the tests at Bikini.

In the beginning, the SASS aspect imposed laboratory procedures on a traditional military operation. In a few years, these constraints were drastically modified because of new developments in tactical weapons (low-drag bomb shapes) and missile warheads. As operational readiness became the governing criteria in weapons-development activities, assembly operations became simpler and safer. But such was not the case in the initial SASS installations in the 27A conversions. For example, there was a requirement that, at all times from receipt on board to secure attachment to the aircraft, the store, or weapon, would have zero degrees of freedom of motion. This necessitated sway bracing while lifting the weapon, plus a range of stowage fittings to clamp and restrain each store. Restraint was designed to cope with excessive ship motion and a level of shock loading. Later modifications included the development of a universal cradle frame for all store types. The store remained attached to the frame until loaded aboard an aircraft. Thus, the handling system saw only one interface, the cradle frame. The system adjusted to cope with the rapidly developing modifications to nuclear weapons.

A bomb elevator in a watertight trunk (shaft) from the storage space to hangar level was fully automatic and self-leveling. From the hangar, a similar upper-stage elevator connected to the flight deck. In later installations, the upper stage was eliminated, because loading on the hangar deck was preferable from the standpoint of security, weather, and easier traffic, after a new deck-edge elevator replaced one on the centerline of the ship. The elevator platform contained an auxiliary elevator to lift the store. A positioner on the auxiliary provided the small adjustments for the critical attachment to the aircraft. Motions built into the auxiliary elevator later eliminated the positioner. The elevator hatches were hydraulic and interlocked so that the hangar and the armor box around magazine areas could not be opened simultaneously, nor could the elevator hit a closed hatch.

The SASS system was not without penalties to the ship's other characteristics. There was a reduction in the number of conventional weapons that could be stored. When the special stores were not on board, their spaces were not suitable for conventional weapons. However, the SASS magazines could be adapted to take a partial load of the new, conventional, high-explosive, low-drag ordnance that became prevalent during the Vietnam War. The SASS handling system required increased deck heights, a structural problem that meant further encroachment on limited space. Also, the special-weapons team Q clearances, security system guards, and special personnel administration reduced the crew available for other functions.[12]

Much of the assembly and storage aspects of nuclear weapons came under the Civil Engineer Corps of the Army after World War II. Thus, when the Navy wanted to modify the *Midway*-class carrier to include the nuclear weapons assembly function, it called upon the Sandia Corporation to determine the specifications for such modifications. The first liaison officer from Sandia was Capt. (then) Ken Cooper, U.S. Army, Civil Engineer Corps. Later, during the Sandstone series of weapons tests, the Navy called upon the Army civil engineers to test and validate the nuclear weapons handling capabilities aboard the *Midway* class. This test was conducted over a period of five days aboard a carrier at the Norfolk Naval Base. The tests were conducted in conjunction with personnel from the Atomic Energy Commission and resulted in some additional modifications to the shipboard installations in order to meet the AEC criteria for operations.[13]

One special aspect of early shipboard stowage had to do with nuclear cores—the highly sensitive material that made the bomb so effective when matched with its other components. Those cores had a life all their own. In the early days, their stowage was quite imaginative. A steel, box-shaped compartment about fifteen feet by fifteen feet was suspended under the flight deck overhang near the bow of the ship so that in case of emergency, it could be released and dropped into the water by pulling on a large lever. Access to this space was limited to only a few persons. The door was carefully guarded, and a secure lock was attached to the lever. Comdr. (then) Robert McNitt, the gunnery officer on board the *Midway,* recalls checking out this imaginative stowage facility, but he was not cleared for access to the cores. He had no responsibility for them and does not recall ever seeing one.[14]

During the conversion of the ships, ripping out existing structure in the original hull configuration was not particularly difficult and did not require any particular attention as far as security. However, before the conversion had progressed very far, the terminology "special weapons" came into use. Although never explicitly stated, there was no doubt that nuclear weapons were involved. Anyone requiring access into the magazine area known as the Special Weapons Spaces had to have an Atomic Energy Commission Q clearance. This applied to the mechanics fabricating storage fittings in the shops, those making the installations, and, of course, supervisory personnel, military and civilian. Access to these spaces was carefully and closely controlled. A Marine guard, or at least an armed guard with the required AEC Q clearance, had to clear everyone who entered the space against a list.

Similar security restrictions applied to testing the elevator for moving a 16,000-pound bomb. There was no doubt that this elevator was installed to handle nuclear weapons, since it had access to the special-weapons magazines and opened onto the hangar deck as well as having a large hatch in the flight deck. Tests of the storage and the elevator were made with bomb shapes. Everything was done behind closed hatches and temporary screens rigged on the hangar and flight decks. No general observers were allowed to watch the test procedures.[15] Security restrictions caused many of the difficulties in attaining a realistic delivery capability.

The 27A conversion also required strengthening the flight deck; providing new, more powerful catapults; a new aviation fuel system; and a system for handling 16,000-pound bombs, including a new, very large bomb elevator. "Big" was the active word for nuclear weapons, and the Navy had to build accommodations for something bigger than the Fat Man bomb. These modifications resulted in a significant increase in design displacement of the ship. This in turn resulted in the addition of a blister on the hull—a new shell about four feet outside the original hull—to accommodate the increased weight.[16] The original displacement of 36,000 tons had now increased to 45,000 tons.

While the 27A conversions were being implemented, radical improvements developed in carrier operations. Most significant was the adoption of the angled deck for launching and landing operations, coupled with the steam catapult. These improvements were of such significance that they had to be incorporated in all carriers involved in the attack mission. That meant a new conversion project for the *Essex*-class, called 27C, which incorporated all of the nuclear weapons features of the 27A conversions, plus the new improvements for the operation of aircraft. The *Midway* class had to be modified as well, incorporating all the aspects of 27A and 27C.

The design work on Project 27C conversions formally started in February 1952. Beyond the angled deck and steam catapults, the major characteristic changes were elimination of the centerline elevator, incorporation of a starboard deck-edge unit, and increase in flight-deck strength to suit. All applicable features of the Project 27A conversions were to be included as well. The first angled decks and steam catapults entered the fleet in February, September, and November 1955. The 27C conversions required additional blisters on the hull of the ship to compensate for the additional operational features.

Project 110 extended the SASS, angled-deck, elevator, and catapult changes to the three ships of the *Midway* class along with most of the other changes mentioned above. Modifications made to accommodate new generations of aircraft emphasize that there was a larger story than the nuclear weapon mission to be told, having to do with concurrent advances in weapons, delivery systems, and the carriers. None of these, *by themselves,* made the Navy's mission goals achievable, but all were essential to the Navy's ability to accomplish its many missions during the Cold War period, not to mention the many brushfires to which the Navy and Marine Corps were ordered to respond.[17]

The USS *Forrestal* (CVA-59)

The ashes of the USS *United States* were in the desk drawer, which brought relief to many of the ship architects but only increased the pressure from the leaders of naval aviation to come up with something

The USS *Forrestal* (CV-59), 60,000 tons, with the angled deck and the steam catapult, completed in 1955. Naval Historical Foundation.

better. Combat strike and support operations in the Korean War demonstrated unambiguously the Navy's role and mission capabilities vis-à-vis the Air Force. A new carrier gestation was inevitable. By the end of July 1951, the preliminary design and ship characteristics of Shipbuilding Project 80, the USS *Forrestal* (CV-59), were finalized.[18]

One of the most significant changes and dramatic improvements in naval aviation came in the design of the *Forrestal*. It was not placed in commission until 1955, almost ten years after the commissioning of the three members of the *Midway* class. When it arrived, it solved many problems and set the stage for the excellent carriers that followed—the nuclear-powered USS *Enterprise* and those of the *Nimitz* class. The *Forrestal* was fossil fueled and capable of operating the most sophisticated aircraft in the history of carrier aviation at the time, both safely and efficiently.

The USS *Nimitz* (CVN-68), 90,000 tons, with 4½ acres of flight deck and nuclear power for propulsion. Naval Historical Foundation.

The *Forrestal* incorporated three critical installations that many think saved the carrier and made delivery of nuclear weapons from carriers quite possible: the angled deck, the steam catapult, and the mirror landing system. If the *Forrestal* had not been successful, it is quite possible that the Navy would not have built another carrier. As it came about, the Navy had the capability to launch, land, house, and service the projected 70,000-pound airplane.[19]

As the Navy moved into the contract design phase for the *Forrestal,* the evolutionary aspects of the SASS shops were included. In fact, the *Forrestal* design included two sets of SASS spaces, one fore and one aft, which served as damage-control and redundancy factors. About half of each magazine—the M shop—could be used for conventional low-drag stores, but it was obvious that nuclear weapons were to be a principal armament in this new class of carrier.

The flush-deck concept of the canceled USS *United States* was still in force when Navy engineers signed off on the initial *Forrestal* drawings. However, as a hedge, an alternate arrangement had been completed, reverting to the old island structure, which included boiler uptakes, a bridge, and radar functions. Studies had shown clearly that the trade-offs were favorable. The costs in boiler uptake space, weight, powerful stack machinery, vulnerability, and questionable gas plumes offset the gains in the flush-deck landing facility.

By this time the Navy was eyeing the British angled deck. U.S. Navy barrier designs for a failed landing for the higher-performance and heavier planes were doubtful at best. However, the angled-deck concept could not be adopted without organizing a test program, which could not be executed within the deadline for releasing *Forrestal* plans.

A hastily prepared design was prepared for an angled deck with the details for the construction and installation on the USS *Antietam* (CVA-36), which was in the New York Navy Yard. The yard completed the job in mid-December 1952, only three months from go-ahead. The Bureau of Aeronautics had a dozen planes and test pilots from the Patuxent River Test Center on board, and they ran two days of landings at sea off Norfolk. It was a winner, and the idea was sold. It immediately became an element of the Project 27C conversion program and change orders to the design of the *Forrestal*. She would have an angled deck.

The lack of time for making a decision on the *Forrestal* catapults did not permit a U.S. trial installation, but the Navy was able to arrange for a British Royal Navy ship with a steam catapult installation to visit the United States for a demonstration. U.S. Navy pilots conducted enough launchings from the ship while it was tied to the pier at Philadelphia Naval Shipyard to enable the Navy to make the decision to buy the steam catapult. These catapults were designated C-11 and were specified for the *Essex*-class Project 27C conversions in March 1952.[20] Most importantly, they became a key factor in the design of the *Forrestal*.

As discussed earlier, the *Forrestal* was a critical factor in enabling naval aviation to mount a realistic nuclear weapons delivery capability. However, as history has shown, that was only a transitory period in naval operations. That ship, and its successors, went on to more significant roles relevant to emerging worldwide developments.

Nuclear Weapons aboard Ships

Initially, the SASS personnel—members of the ship's company—conducted all handling of nuclear weapons aboard carriers. Eventually personnel from the individual nuclear delivery squadrons were brought into the loading operation—the actual hanging of the weapons on the delivery aircraft. This meant additional responsibilities for the aircraft delivery squadrons. In a typical A-7 Corsair II squadron in the early 1970s, for example, there was always a great deal of emphasis on nuclear weapons safety and on adhering to all security regulations that had been issued for the handling of the weapons. There was probably nothing that drew more attention than the safety aspect of the program. Each operating squadron was ordered to have a personnel reliability program (PRP), a formal program to ensure that the people close to and handling the weapons were all the best available. There were about sixty such personnel identified in each squadron, all enlisted. Their personnel records were screened to make sure that they had final security clearances. Performance appraisals were checked, and violations of the Uniform Code of Military Justice, specifically drug or alcohol abuse, were also checked. Usually a record of drug abuse was sufficient to eliminate the individual from further consideration as a member of the nuclear team.

Qualified candidates were interviewed and volunteers solicited. Some candidates objected to being included on moral or religious grounds. Others did not want to be part of the program because they knew it meant extra work. Some were intimidated by nuclear weapons and just did not want to be around them. However, squadrons were always able to get a pool of thirty-five or forty to fill the positions needed for four loading crews, plus a yeoman in the administrative area to keep track of the records of the people involved. Once people were brought into the program, their performance had to be monitored. Any situation involving an infraction of rules, such as drug abuse, meant instant dismissal from the PRP. It was a dynamic program, designed to maintain a reliable cadre of people to load special weapons on the aircraft.

A squadron weapons training officer and nuclear safety officer had to attend one week of school in San Diego, learning more about the technical aspects and hazards of nuclear weapons as well as rules covering their handling. The nuclear safety officer had to make sure that the PRP program was in good shape and that recurrent training in the loading of the weapons was conducted. Periodic safety meetings with quizzes were held to make sure everybody knew their roles and weapons safety rules. The final responsibility was to make sure that the squadron could pass the nuclear technical proficiency inspection (NTPI), a major event in the command's schedule before it deployed to the forward area. These inspections covered every detail of the loading process and were practiced a great deal to eliminate any deficiencies. The drills continued throughout the deployment to maintain a high state of readiness, but the big inspection came just before deployment.

The loading exercises were referred to as proficiency loads, or "pro-loads." Loading teams consisted of six men, each team with a petty officer in charge as the crew chief. A loading truck with a man on each side contained the weapon. With each team was a loading officer, usually a junior officer who would also be the safety officer for that team. The teams would conduct drills about twice a month. Each team loaded the weapons onto the aircraft, ensuring that they met the established time limits and were safe in their operations. It was paramount that the teams not do anything that would jeopardize the safety of the ship or compromise the integrity of the weapon. Therefore, a lot of time was spent making sure everybody understood all of the procedures and that they were observed in detail.

The "two-man rule" was universal throughout the nuclear weapons community of all the armed services. With each weapon, there had to be at least two people present, each in good view of the other and aware of what the other was doing. The rule was strictly enforced to ensure that a situation did not occur in which there was only one person standing near a weapon.

During the actual loading, the team took the weapon from the SASS area on the loading truck, inspected the weapon to make sure that it was safe for operation, and then wheeled it out to the aircraft. They performed an electric circuit check on the aircraft wiring to make sure that it was satisfactory before they started the load. Next, the weapon was loaded on the aircraft, and another circuit check was performed to make sure that the weapon had not inadvertently armed itself while it was being loaded. Such drills might take about ten minutes to complete. Sometimes the actual weapons that were in the ship for delivery to targets were used for drills. During shore-based drills, only shapes (dummy weapons) were used.

The nuclear safety program, including the PRP and the nuclear loading drills, would culminate with an inspection—the NTPI—before every deployment. A team of outside professionals would come aboard and conduct the inspection, which consisted of a vigorous review of personnel records to make sure that the squadron had qualified people in the PRP. Training records were checked to make sure that each individual in the program had been attending the appropriate safety meetings and quizzes. They would also observe each of the loading crews during loads, looking for discrepancies. Squadrons strived not only to pass but to "ace" the inspection, with no discrepancies at all. The commanding officer of a unit failing such an inspection could lose his command—such was the serious emphasis placed on the safety aspects of the nuclear mission.[21]

The Future

Although the nuclear mission has never been executed, for some time it was accorded the highest priority in carrier warfare planning. The combination of aircraft, ships, and people produced a significant capability. That combination literally saved the carrier and naval aviation. What is the future of this mission in the new carriers coming into the arsenal?

There seems to be no question that there is a firm commitment by the Navy and the Congress to continue with carriers in the inventory. In the year 2000, new ships for the future were receiving attention and funding. CVN-77 was labeled a "transition ship," the intent being for it to take the carrier Navy from the current *Nimitz* class to the more exotic model, the CVNX. It is slated to replace the USS *Kitty Hawk* in the year 2008, which will be the forty-seventh year of service for the *Kitty Hawk*. Fifty years is emerging as the average life of aircraft carriers.

Plans for CVN-77 include propulsion plant improvements, with emphasis on the capacity of the electric plant and control systems. The combat systems, including radars, will involve the newest in information technology. There will be a major redesign of the island structure. Reducing the costs of construction and operations is being emphasized, with significant reductions in the size of the crew needed to man the ship.

Present planning calls for the CVNX series to consist of two ships. The first, CVNX-1, will incorporate major steps forward in technology. A most significant improvement will be the changeover to an electric propulsion plant. Nuclear power will provide the energy, but propulsion will change from steam to electricity. The increased emphasis on electricity will also permit introduction of an electromagnetic aircraft launch system, a new form of catapult. Electricity will be replacing steam as the capacity of the electrical system is greatly enhanced. As in CVN-77, there will be more emphasis on reducing the total cost of operations, including a reduction in crew size. The second in the series, CVNX-2, will incorporate new developments in technology, including an electromagnetic aircraft recovery system. There will be improvements in the hull for increased survivability, as well as the incorporation of advances in technology that will permit reduction in crew size and the total operating cost of the ship.[22] In summary, the Navy has an aggressive approach to the future of the carrier, continuing the emphasis on its role in our national security posture and its applicability to the likely combat scenarios of the future.

8. Testing the Capability

During the development of the atomic bomb, some people, both ordinary and extraordinary, realized that carrier aviation could have a role in nuclear warfare and took extraordinary measures to convert that idea into a reality. It wasn't easy. Lives were lost, careers were ended, and considerable effort and dollars were expended. However, there was no question that carrier aviation had become a factor to be considered in any nuclear warfare scenario. But did a truly reliable capability exist?

One of the facets of the military profession that is born from combat experience is the constant testing of individuals and equipment to ensure that a realistic combat capability exists, that individuals and units are not about to be sent into combat without being ready for the serious business at hand. Readiness must be demonstrated. Hence, there are constant inspections, ranging from minor checks on the proper wearing of the uniform to major tests of weapons systems as they are to be employed in the implementation of national policy, strategies, and tactics. Operational readiness inspections of individuals and units are routine and highly significant. They can make or break a unit commander, for he must prepare his unit for combat as well as lead it in combat itself.

In modern military history, the Strategic Air Command (SAC) was probably the combat organization that made the most out of readiness inspections. In *Revolt of the Admirals,* Jeffrey Barlow recounts the difficulties Gen. Curtis LeMay faced as he took over a command with a questionable capability of hitting the target.[1] LeMay's forceful leadership included a great many surprise readiness inspections of all units. SAC became famous for its alert drills, and the tradition was passed down the line to LeMay's successors, such as Gen. Thomas Power. The need for those inspections was learned by LeMay and Power during their extensive experience in World War II, in which the Air Forces created great destruction but also lost many fine young men in their combat crews. SAC always played for keeps. Warfare, particularly that involving nuclear weapons, was a serious business, and the leaders used inspections to test the readiness of the force.

Naval aviation also emphasized readiness inspections in preparation for combat. For example, it was common practice in the Pacific for all carriers and embarked air groups to spend a few days in Hawaii en route to the Korean or Vietnam Wars to test the combat readiness of units. Personnel and facilities to conduct the tests were made available. These high-priority exercises were omitted only in extreme circumstances, such as the crash deployments to Korea in the first days of that war. When a unit left Hawaii and headed westward, it felt confident that it was ready for the task at hand.

As the carrier Navy developed the nuclear weapons delivery capability, operational readiness inspections continued to be conducted, with much emphasis on that capability. During 1958–59, three such inspections, conducted in the Jacksonville, Florida, area, are illustrative of those routinely experienced by deploying air groups. These inspections were conducted by the staff of Commander Fleet Air, Jacksonville, Florida, and utilized the many training and test facilities under the control of that command.[2] They were not only very worthwhile, they were fun to plan and conduct. More importantly, they provided answers to questions such as, "Are we ready to perform the task assigned?" and "Who is best prepared?"

One inspection in 1959 was quite significant because of the senior personnel that were involved. The carrier was the USS *Saratoga* (CVA-60), a *Forrestal*-class carrier. The embarked air group included squadrons of A-1 (AD), A-3 (A3D), and A-4 (A4D) aircraft, all charged with the task of carrying out the high-priority nuclear weapons delivery mission. The commanding officer of the *Saratoga* was Capt. (then) John J. Hyland, a front-runner who later rose to four-star rank and commanded the U.S. Pacific Fleet. Rear Adm. George Anderson was the embarked flag officer, about to put on his third star and head for the Mediterranean to command the U.S. Sixth Fleet. Subsequent to that assignment, he became the chief of naval operations. In addition, on board the *Saratoga,* preparing to relieve Admiral Anderson, was Rear Adm. Thomas H. Moorer, who later moved on to become the chief of naval operations and then the chairman of the Joint Chiefs of Staff. It was not a bad audience for a test and demonstration of a group's ability to perform the nuclear mission. The results could have considerable impact on the thinking of these gentlemen as they moved upward to be key decision makers in naval affairs.

The inspection was designed for two days of operations. It required the active participation of the crew of the ship and the manning of many of the target facilities in the Jacksonville area. For the attack aircraft, the air plan was oriented strictly toward putting weapons on the target. There were tests for delivering conventional bombs, rockets, and strafing, but at this stage in the history of naval aviation, the issue of prime interest was the ability to perform the nuclear weapons delivery mission.

For that purpose, the armed services were provided with nuclear weapons training and testing devices called shapes, dummy nuclear weapons that included all features of such weapons other than the actual explosive components. They resembled the real thing. Certain missions in the operational air plans required the ship and squadron personnel to bring these shapes from the storage magazines, mount them on the assigned aircraft, and check out the wiring to ensure proper release when the pilot reached the target and executed his delivery tactic. These shapes did include a small explosive charge, which was used to mark the location of the hit relative to the center of the target. The routes to the target varied but were of considerable distance, requiring accurate navigation, location of the target, delivery of the weapon, and high-speed departure.

The score for measuring the readiness of individual units had nothing to do with morale, the physical appearance of the crews and aircraft, rates of launching or landing aboard the carrier, or smartness of operations. It concentrated strictly on Admiral Sims's old adage.

In the inspection, each squadron was tasked to fly a large percentage of its assigned aircraft, requiring attacks of a specified target a number of times. If availability of aircraft for a mission was low and the squadron could not mount the programmed launch, the score for that event was a "maximum" or "gross" error. In short, if you got hits on the target, you would pass the readiness inspection. Nothing else mattered.

The inspection measured the readiness of the overall group, but it also pitted the three models of aircraft against each other. While all scores in all the three inspections were quite good, the A-3, with its horizontal-delivery tactic, edged out the others by a small margin. It would be wrong to conclude that the A-3 and its system were better than the A-1 and the A-4. It was impressive, however, that the A-3 and the heavy-attack community earned some respect from these inspections. This was at a time when Jig Ramage had taken over the heavy-attack wing at Sanford and was instilling some carrier professionalism in the units.

At the completion of operations and the tabulation of scores, the results were presented to the flag officers, air group, and ship personnel. These exercises were about as realistic as one could get in measuring the capabilities of an air group to perform its combat mission. The performance in the nuclear warfare mission was particularly rewarding. There was no question from the results of these inspections that carrier aviation had arrived in the nuclear business. It was a viable nuclear weapons force with which not only the Soviets, but

The USS *Franklin D. Roosevelt* (CVA-42) and the USS *Wrangell* (AE-12) in the Mediterranean, 1963. Two hundred nuclear weapons and 36 delivery aircraft. U.S. Navy photo.

also the U.S. Air Force would have to contend. Admirals Moorer and Anderson and Captain Hyland agreed that the capability had been attained. It was a force that was ready for combat.[3]

The priority placed on the nuclear weapons delivery mission was impressive. Even in the middle of the Vietnam War, the nuclear role was never far from the thoughts of the leaders and their troops. Vice Adm. Dennis McGinn was a young pilot flying the A-7E:

During my days as a junior officer in a squadron deployed to Vietnam, I vividly recall participating in conventional air strikes against the enemy. In the middle of a combat period on the line at Yankee Station in the Tonkin Gulf, an occasional reveille would be held at 0400 in the morning. We would be required to go through a nuclear weapons loading proficiency drill—a pro-load. Getting the weapons up on deck from the secure magazines, matching them with the proper aircraft, conducting electric circuit checks, maintaining absolutely by-the-book security—we covered the full spectrum of prelaunch activities for the delivery of nuclear weapons. As a commanding officer, you could lose pilots over the beach, have a grounding of the ship, do about anything—and your career might still survive. But bust a nuke weapons inspection and your career was finished. Such was the professional intensity with which we pursued the nuclear mission. The SIOP [nuclear warfare plan] and its targets were paramount in the scheme of carrier aviation priorities. Even the intensity of the Vietnam air war could not gain a higher priority than the sobering constant vigilance of the Cold War.

Our attempts to be as realistic in training as possible were impressive. I recall a radar bombing training mission at Fallon, Nevada, when an A-7 pilot was flying on instruments under the canopy anti-glare shield. Communications with the safety chase pilot were lost. The terrain was mountainous, so standard operating procedure called for coming out from under the shield and returning to a visual flight profile when communications were lost. In this case, as the pilot was quickly pushing back and lifting the shield, it became entangled somehow with the ejection seat system, which inadvertently ejected the pilot safely from the aircraft. Since the aircraft was on autopilot, it flew on for hundreds of miles by itself, finally crashing into the mountains. It was carrying small inert practice bombs.

Later in my career, while serving as the executive officer of the USS *Coral Sea,* I recall being at Pier 11 at the Naval Operating Base in Norfolk, Virginia, late one evening as we prepared for a deployment to the Mediterranean. A critical part of the preparation was the loading of nuclear weapons in our special weapons magazines. Down the road, coming towards the pier about sunset, was a convoy of trucks with nearly one hundred nuclear weapons. They had been assigned to our ship for use against potential targets if a nuclear attack were ordered. That sight of all those special weapons in convoy was still a chilling reminder of the Cold War. It was tangible proof to me that we were serious about containment and deterrence.[4]

Rear Adm. John Beling recalls his experience while serving as commanding officer of the USS *Forrestal,* preparing the ship for a deployment to Vietnam for combat duty with conventional weapons. Beling had considerable experience with nuclear weapons, but he was headed for participation in a conventional war. Much to his surprise, in taking command of the ship he found that the ammunition magazines had been configured largely for nuclear weapons. He had plenty of storage space for them but was short on what he needed for the combat he was about to face. Some fast corrective action was taken to modify the spaces and better prepare the ship for the duty at hand.[5]

Vice Adm. Don Engen was commanding officer of the USS *America,* deployed to the Mediterranean in 1967. He was in the middle of a major nuclear weapons inspection, with nuclear weapons all over the flight and hangar decks. Suddenly came an emergency call for help from the USS *Liberty,* an intelligence and communication ship, which was being taken under attack by the Israeli armed forces. As Engen told the story, he could have delivered a nuclear weapon quite easily. Instead, he had the task of converting from a nuclear weapons exercise to the real world, in which a U.S. Navy ship was being taken under attack. A supporting strike was readied and launched, but shortly after takeoff, it was recalled by higher authority. One of the great mysteries in U.S. Navy history is why the supporting strike was recalled—a question that will probably never see a public response.[6]

The emphasis on the nuclear mission was serious. The capability was significant, and the people involved played the game for real, even though there was increasing doubt that the capability would ever be used. With all this capability of carriers to destroy the world, what targets would be selected for destruction? With what weapons? And what degree of success could be expected?

9. Targeting

The story of the targeting of nuclear weapons has not been told very often, at least by those who have actually been involved in the process. Students of nuclear affairs have produced several works on the subject, but those who have actually been involved in the process have stayed clear of writing or speaking about it. There are several reasons for that reticence.

First is the security aspect. The targeting of nuclear weapons was placed in a highly classified category from the onset. This classification became even more pronounced in 1960 with the establishment of the Joint Strategic Target Planning Staff (JSTPS). Its purpose was to produce two documents, a national strategic target list (NSTL) and a single integrated operational plan (SIOP). Even the acronyms NSTL and SIOP were classified "Top Secret." Almost forty years later, some who held the necessary security clearances are still not sure they can mention those terms in an unclassified context. This tight security discouraged many from addressing the subject, which was unfortunate because the targeting process provides answers to many questions. How much is enough? What works? What does not work? Are there conflicts in time of arrival on the same or adjacent targets? By keeping the subject so highly classified, very few people in the higher echelons, who needed to know what was going on, were able to discern the details. Even President Eisenhower, who showed much interest in the size of the stockpile and the nature of the war plans, failed to get into the intricacies of the targeting business. It would have provided him some exposure to a fascinating planning process. It might also have provided him with better questions to ask as he became concerned over the ever-increasing size of the weapons stockpile.

During my second tour of duty with the JSTPS at SAC headquarters in 1973–74, I had several conversations about security with the late Gen. John Meyer, USAF, who was the director of the JSTPS as well as the head of SAC at the time.[1] Meyer and I agreed that the secrecy surrounding the nuclear war plans often prevented us from giving senior people, in particular, the kind of information they needed to know. We reasoned that we could divulge some of the major points of the SIOP without jeopardizing the security of the details. Our principle was to let common sense prevail. We decided that instead of presenting the audience with formal scripted briefings on the subject, I would give an unclassified briefing of the SIOP, stressing the basic principles of the plan and the broad consequences of execution without going into the specific targets, tactics, timing of attacks, and systems being used.

The new approach worked well as we briefed executives in the Department of Defense, the Congress, and the academic world. The late Don Cotter, special assistant to the secretary of defense for nuclear matters, was particularly supportive. We were onto something of value—education as opposed to pure information. Two of our best listeners were Vice President Gerald Ford and the director of the Central Intelligence Agency, the late William Colby. The discussion with them went on for about three hours, with just the two of them, General Meyer, and me in the room with some instructional aids. It was an educational give and take, covering the many questions that occurred to them—things they felt they needed to know. President Ford asked the best questions of any individual I ever faced during my several years of talking about the SIOP. He was interested and rightly so.

When he succeeded Richard Nixon as president, he was the only man with the authority to execute the SIOP.[2]

Educating people about the SIOP was an interesting experience. We took the program to the academic world, starting first with the university system in the state of Florida. We invited some of their academic leaders to JSTPS headquarters in Omaha and explained what we had in mind. We reasoned that it was difficult for future leaders to understand about defense policy and arms control if they did not know much about arms, particularly nuclear arms. The college level appeared to be a good starting point in the process, and the objective was to give faculty and students correct information. Florida was very interested in at least making a trial run at one of their campuses. Of course, they needed funds to get started.

Shortly after General Meyer and I retired from active duty and not long after our educational efforts at the JSTPS, I met with Gen. George Brown, USAF, who was serving as the chairman of the Joints Chiefs of Staff. He was supportive of the idea, saying it would be an extremely valuable contribution. I sought funds from the Ford Foundation, whose leader, the late McGeorge Bundy, showed considerable interest. After his final analysis, however, he offered, instead, to provide two professors from the "elite" academic community to hold a couple of seminars for Florida educators on the subject. "Elite" was his word, not mine, and I did not let him forget it in subsequent discussions on the dangers of nuclear warfare. Our program to educate died, and I regret my lack of success.

For the academic world to be uninformed about nuclear targeting was understandable. It would be hard to become knowledgeable about nuclear weapons targeting when the Department of Defense classified the subject so strictly. What bothered me most, however, was the degree of misinformation that existed. Some of the knowledge in the academic community was just plain incorrect.

Immediately following retirement, because I dared to intimate publicly that we might have more weapons in the stockpile than we needed, I was invited to several universities to participate in or lead discussions of the nuclear issue and to give lectures on the subject. Education was the objective. I did not ask for a fee, and none was offered, which gives an indication of the value the academic world placed on my revelations about their misinformation. I was on the dais at Harvard, Cornell, and Stanford, among other less "elite" institutions.

The session at Stanford was particularly revealing. My talk on nuclear weapons was delivered at a faculty bag lunch session in an auditorium where one hundred or so attendees ate while I talked. Their questions revealed a tremendous misunderstanding of the impact of nuclear weapons and their destructive capability. For example, the bulk of the audience believed that the majority of the U.S. strategic arsenal was programmed against the Soviet urban/industrial base, that the leadership of the U.S. was immoral in its targeting, and that all the United States intended to do was kill people. They were wrong on that issue. While our guidance told us to destroy the urban/industrial base, we could do that with relatively few weapons. It was the counterforce strategy—the destruction of the enemy's ability to destroy the United States—that required so many weapons, and did a very poor job of it to boot. Such a misunderstanding highlighted the need for the program General Meyer and I had envisioned. I suspect that many academics still do not understand that a counterforce capability is impossible to obtain—by either side.

A second reason for the reluctance to discuss the SIOP and reveal the answers the targeting process provided was that the closely held information added to the parochial advantage of certain elements of our society. The individual armed services could benefit. If the civil authority and senior leaders in the military were not aware of the process of targeting and the answers that process could provide, they could be convinced that expansion of our arsenal was essential. Build the threat, highlight our own weaknesses, and the stage was set for obtaining more funds from the Congress. If the Navy said that we needed forty-five Polaris submarines and there was no way to check the reasoning because of security restrictions, the Navy benefited. The original number of Polaris submarines sought by the Navy was forty-five. The number settled for and produced was forty-one. Some good studies and experience with the program through targeting established that far fewer were needed.

The defense industry also benefited a great deal from the security restrictions. If Congress and the general public were convinced that ICBM sites were vulnerable, then industry would gain from developing hardware and systems that would negate that vulnerability. If greater accuracy of delivery was perceived as the only solution to hard-target destructive capability, then several companies in the defense industry were going to be handed some lucrative contracts. Security of information about the targeting process concealed answers about what was needed and what could be spared.

If no one knew the details of the nuclear targeting plan, extreme positions could be taken—and they were. The interservice rivalry and politics that were played with the nuclear issue were fierce, particularly in the early days of the SIOP, when Gen. Thomas Power headed the Strategic Air Command. He did not like naval systems unless he could control them. Targeting their weapons was not enough, and he kept pressure on to denigrate the accepted capability of naval systems or gain operational control of their use.

Another reason for the lack of public exposure of the subject by the personnel involved is that nuclear weapons targeting is not a very sexy subject. You have to really be interested in the details of the nuclear business to get involved in the finer points of the targeting process. Many, including people in high places, simply were not interested, particularly as time went on and the subject became old hat. Also, there was steadily increasing doubt that nuclear weapons would ever be used, under any conceivable scenario.

I recall leading a briefing team from JSTPS headquarters to the Pentagon in 1973–74. We were to brief the Joint Chiefs of Staff on the details of the latest SIOP to obtain their approval for its implementation. As a preliminary, we conducted a briefing for at least one hundred military and civilian authorities who held the proper clearances and were responsible to some degree for the preparation of the guidance for the plan and its eventual approval. The briefing, conducted as scheduled, lasted about forty-five minutes. It was carefully scripted, and every sentence contained some significant aspect of the war plan.

At the conclusion of the briefing, I stood and asked the audience if there were any questions. There was dead silence. We had just presented the high points of a targeting plan that would unload about eight thousand nuclear weapons on various targets in the world and kill millions of people. There was not a single question from this supposedly responsible group. Therefore, I said, "All right, I have some questions for you." I then conducted an oral quiz, asking some basic questions about the contents of the briefing. How much of the stockpile was devoted to countering the enemy's capability to destroy us? How much was devoted to targets in the urban/industrial base? What level of damage could we expect to achieve against hard targets such as ICBM sites? All of the answers had been laid out in the briefing, but the level of interest in the subject was obviously low. The prevailing attitude seemed to be, "Nuclear weapons are dumb, and they are boring."

Initial Targeting

The selection of the targets to be attacked with nuclear weapons in Japan during World War II was done by a high-level group, and the secretary of war himself got deeply involved. Even President Truman made at least one decision when he supported Secretary Stimson in negating Kyoto as the prime target, the first choice of General Groves and his supporting scientists. They wanted a pristine target on flat terrain where they could measure accurately the effects of their work. Stimson said no: Kyoto was the cultural center of Japan, and destroying it would alienate the Japanese forever.[3] So targets more military in nature were selected. The list was not long.

The new threat emerged with the signing of the surrender document with Japan. Almost immediately, in September 1945, the Joint

Chiefs of Staff came up with a list of ten targets in the Soviet Union that, if destroyed, would be enough to defeat the Soviets. In the fall of 1945, a Joint Chiefs of Staff study concluded, "Twenty Soviet urban areas contained a commanding proportion of the Soviet war-supporting industry, e.g., aircraft and munitions production plants, and steel and ball bearing production centers. These were the target areas initially selected for further study."[4] The problem? The production of weapons took so much effort and time that there would have been none in stock if the decision had been made to attack the targets. It took a long time to get weapons in sufficient quantity to make the targeting process big business, particularly for aircraft carriers.

During the 1950s, each individual command authorized to use nuclear weapons did its own targeting. As the number of weapons multiplied, the need to coordinate the plans of the individual commanders became evident. Duplication and conflict of timing of attacks on targets became a problem. Coordination conferences were held to resolve the conflicts, but they were not very successful. As a result, many weapons were programmed against many targets, without much liaison between the units carrying the nuclear loads. Things got out of hand as the size of the stockpile increased. The solution advocated by the Air Force and championed by SAC was the creation of a strategic command (StratCom), an organization that would have responsibility for target planning and *operational* control of all strategic nuclear forces. That included aircraft carriers, but more significantly, it would also involve the Navy's new submarine-launched ballistic missile (SLBM) system, the Polaris.

Adm. Arleigh Burke, the chief of naval operations at the time, was in many ways the most significant individual in the creation of the SLBM system. The idea of having the Navy's most promising new weapon under the control of the commander of SAC made him furious. A fierce fighter, he resisted the move and enlisted all the support he could.

Gen. Thomas Power, the commander of SAC at the time, was most articulate and rather coy in his arguments. He would point out the advantages of such a command and then suggest that it was perfectly all right with him if an admiral commanded the new StratCom. However, since the Air Force, specifically SAC, was slated to deliver a vast majority of the nuclear megatonnage, he thought it only logical that an Air Force officer be the leader.

Beside himself, Burke went to President Eisenhower to make a desperate appeal. The concept of a single strategic command was of very serious concern to the Navy. It would have required the aircraft carriers, when in their strategic nuclear weapons role, to take their orders from the new commander, a strategic bomber leader. However, the Polaris SLBM system was the hinge pin. Everyone knew it was going to be a great addition to the arsenal—a genuine threat to the Soviets, but also a real threat to the Strategic Air Command.

The issue was resolved after some bitter controversy in the summer of 1960. At that time, President Eisenhower authorized the establishment of the Joint Strategic Targeting Planning Staff, to be located in the headquarters of the Strategic Air Command in Omaha, Nebraska. The director of the staff would be the commander of the Strategic Air Command, wearing a second hat of authority. To give a "joint" symbol to the organization, a billet was established for a deputy director to be a Navy vice admiral experienced with nuclear weapons. That first deputy was Vice Adm. E. N. "Butch" Parker, a nonaviator with an enviable record, who had headed the Department of Defense nuclear agency.

In short, before the creation of the JSTPS and the development of the NSTL and the SIOP, the individual commands did their own planning and targeting for the use of the weapons assigned to them. Planning for the use of the carriers was in the hands of the field commanders. After 1960, the plan was integrated. Pilots received their target assignment, weapon assignment, route of transit, and time of delivery from the SIOP, produced in Omaha.[5] The decision to create the JSTPS made sense and was long overdue. Officers with appropriate backgrounds from all the armed services were ordered to Omaha, and the individual unified commanders—the major claimants of nuclear weapons—had senior representatives in the staff headquarters to look out for the targeting interests of their commands. It was a fascinating period in the nuclear weapons business.

The First SIOP

The first SIOP was completed by inauguration day in 1961. President Eisenhower approved the plan and passed it on to President Kennedy for use if needed. The plan went into effect in the spring of 1961. There is little doubt that it was an updated version of the strategic bombing strategies used by General LeMay in World War II, but instead of the iron bombs and incendiaries from B-29 aircraft, the new plan employed jet aircraft and cruise and ballistic missiles with nuclear weapons. The first SIOP was really an extension of the basic SAC emergency war plan. It integrated the weapons from other commands, thereby creating a system for catastrophic destruction with maximum efficiency. As the magnitude of the plan became more apparent, it had the effect of deterring the United States as well as the Soviet Union, because their mutual destruction was assured.

The aircraft carriers were in that first SIOP, along with a few Regulus cruise missiles to be launched from submarines. It included the first submarine-launched ballistic missiles, deployed on station in the USS *George Washington*. Embarked in the carriers and included in the plan were A-1 propeller aircraft, as well as A-4 and FJ-4B light-attack and A-3 heavy-attack jet aircraft.

The aircraft to be launched from the carriers enjoyed a high level of damage expectancy in the planning process. They represented a formidable force, particularly to the Soviets, who were always worried about "those carriers."[6] Surprisingly, in the first SIOP, the propeller-driven A-1 had a high probability of achieving the desired results—better than most. It was a reliable airplane, and it traveled at low level to the target, giving it a high penetration reliability. In addition, the targets to which it was assigned were generally elements of early warning air defense systems such as radars, which were on the periphery of the vast target area. The A-1 did not last long in SIOP plans, however, for it was needed in Vietnam for conventional warfare purposes, first by the U.S. Air Force and then the South Vietnamese. The Navy A-1, owned and operated by other than Navy pilots, saw its last days in Vietnam.

Perhaps the most significant aspect of the first SIOP was that it presented in one plan a clear picture of the carnage that would be visited on the world if even one option in the plan were executed. It brought together the efficient destructive capability of 3,500 weapons, the majority of all the U.S. strategic nuclear forces, and highlighted, as had not been done before, the total impact of an efficient approach to blowing up the world. Unfortunately, because of security restrictions, a relatively few people were aware of the details and the magnitude of the consequences of execution.

Intelligence

The key to good targeting is good intelligence. Determining how to get to the target also requires good intelligence. Never were these factors more significant than in building the nation's nuclear war plans.

The leader in supplying intelligence for the nuclear weapons targeting was SAC, the command that initially would carry the bulk of the attack. Even though there were still many problems within the force, such as a lack of weapons and the limited range of the bombers in getting to the targets, the emphasis was rightly on SAC. That emphasis was recognized in the allocation of assets for processing the raw intelligence material.

At the end of World War II, when the Joint Chiefs of Staff came up with their ten targets in the Soviet Union, SAC or any force would have had a difficult time carrying out an attack. One restriction was the lack of intelligence. That intelligence got no better for several years. Many who were assigned targets in the mid-1950s were presented with little in the way of information on the location and nature of the target to be attacked. Artists' sketches of enemy airfields were common. No photographs were available, just sketches or blueprint drawings. The location of the target was defined merely by latitude and longitude. The situation was reminiscent of the experience related by General Groves, who used a *National Geographic* map of Japan to brief Secretary Stimson and others on the target selection for the 1945 attacks on Hiroshima and Nagasaki.[7] It was stretching the point to call it intelligence.

Some authorized and unauthorized overflights of potential target areas added a bit to our knowledge, but not much. The famed U-2 spy aircraft produced some useful data, but there were few flights in its short career over the Soviet Union, and the take of material from those flights covered only a small part of the Soviet territory. Many U-2 flights were aimed at locating the sites where the Soviets produced nuclear weapons material.[8] Satellite recognizance had some possibilities, but in the late 1950s, it was just coming into the fold, and the quality was very poor, at least compared to the take from the U-2 aircraft. However, it was to be the prime source for future targeting, and emphasis was placed on that form of intelligence collection. Money and people were assigned in large volumes. Initial priorities for the new satellite reconnaissance capability were Soviet ICBM sites.[9]

In order to work with satellite intelligence, one had to have the necessary security clearance for a program called Talent-Keyhole. Personnel billets to receive these clearances had to be approved by the White House. The number of billets cleared for such work reflected where the emphasis on satellite reconnaissance would be placed. On 18 August 1960, the planned allocation of billets was listed as follows: CIA, 286; U.S. Army, 289; U.S. Navy, 100; and U.S. Air Force, 479. In addition to those for the USAF, two hundred more were allocated for SAC alone. Just two months later, in October 1960, as an indicator of the increasing significance of satellite intelligence, additional billets were requested. When the totals were added, the Air Force, including SAC, had 1,569 billets; Navy, 221; Army, 531; and CIA, 418. An additional 93 billets were added for JSTPS, which would put more billets in SAC headquarters.[10] It was obvious that the Air Force would dominate satellite intelligence, which was becoming the main source of intelligence for targeting nuclear weapons. The unified commanders who had carriers in their forces—Atlantic, Pacific, and Europe—were not on the Talent-Keyhole billet clearance list. They would get their satellite intelligence for nuclear targeting through JSTPS in Omaha. That arrangement made sense. Although there was some bickering in the higher echelons, things worked well at the working level as the troops diligently became involved in the actual targeting process.

SAC dominated the satellite-intelligence business and created a highly competent and significant capability. Regrettably, there was some misuse of their dominant authority, which resulted in the creation of the alleged "bomber and missile gaps." Interpreting some fuzzy satellite picture as a missile site when it could just as easily have been a new housing project did not enhance SAC's reputation for complete trust and confidence in the product. However, the intelligence organization put together by SAC was impressive. With the establishment of the JSTPS, all commands benefited a great deal from the SAC creation.

Despite the apparent abuses of the capabilities, one can have nothing but the highest regard for what SAC and the Air Force, in cooperation with the CIA, produced in the way of a national intelligence organization. Their detection of the first Soviet nuclear weapon explosion, their introduction of specially configured reconnaissance aircraft for electronic warfare, their highly successful operation of the high-altitude, high-speed SR-71 aircraft, their concentration on the improvement of satellite capabilities—all have been great contributions to the security of the United States and the world. No one can take away the pride they must feel and justly deserve for developing that intelligence-gathering capability.

The Targeting Process

As JSTPS was established, it adopted the SAC targeting process, a professional approach to the business of warfare. One of the most professional aspects of the process was the computation of the probability of achieving a prescribed level of damage. The term for the objective was "damage expectancy." It was, in essence, a mathematical determination of the kill probability (Pk) of the mission. A computation was run on every sortie in the SIOP to determine its probability of arriving at the target and achieving the damage desired. If the probability of success were low, the mission was planned again with a different route or the assignment of a different target. Sometimes missions were added and targeted against the threatening defenses in order to increase the probability of success. From such probability computations, the number of weapons needed to achieve the prescribed level of damage could be determined—a measure of "how much is enough." The damage expectancy was a product of the probability of the weapon arriving at the target compounded by the probability of it exploding and creating the damage attributed to its designation.

A key factor in determining the probability of arrival at the target was the survivability of the platform being used for launch of the nuclear weapon. Land-based systems, particularly bombers, did not score high on the survivability factor. Hence, the development of base-dispersal plans and airborne alerts—measures to enhance the survivability of the nuclear weapons delivery systems. The aircraft carrier, being mobile, enjoyed a higher probability of survival than fixed land bases. The ultimate in survivability, of course, was (and still is) the submarine-launched ballistic missile, for the anti–submarine warfare problem has yet to be solved to a degree necessary to jeopardize the survivability of on-board SLBMs before they are launched. The survivability factor, degraded by launch reliability, in-flight reliability, and penetration ability, all combined to produce the probability of arrival.

The probability of the weapon exploding as designed was high, based on the many tests of weapons that had been conducted. That explosion probability has been a much-debated issue as the United States enters the twenty-first century. The congressional hearings on the Comprehensive Test Ban Treaty (CTBT) have highlighted the need for reliability—knowing the probability of a weapon performing as designed.

The reliability of nuclear weapons can diminish in storage, hence the need to test the weapons occasionally. The proponents of reliability exert pressure for such tests. Adversaries, stressing arms-control agreements, argue that other means can be used to determine reliability, that we do not need weapons testing. They contend that computers can provide the necessary answers, but few specifics on the nature of such tests have been published. Consequently, there is considerable doubt about the verity of that contention. Besides, they say, actual explosive testing is politically "destabilizing." The debate goes on.

The targeteer in Omaha needs that weapon reliability factor to complete his probability computations and to provide a measure of the ability of the SIOP to produce the results dictated by the civil authority. If weapons tests show that 5 percent of the time a weapon will not detonate as designed, that factor is entered into the damage expectancy computations. However, if the factor is uncertain and guesstimates must be used, the tendency is to call for more weapons to ensure the desired result. Therefore, failure to test can work in reverse for the proponent of reductions in the stockpile. More uncertainty means more weapons as a hedge.

For a pilot to go through extensive training, fight through to the target, complete the delivery, and then have the weapon fail to explode is not very efficient—and also very demoralizing. While survivability of the launch platform is significant, the reliability of the weapon is paramount. Failure of the weapon is reminiscent of the Navy torpedoes in the early submarine patrols of World War II. After struggling to get into a position to fire and taking the risk of being destroyed, the submarine commander finally launched his weapons and then eagerly awaited the explosion. When the weapon malfunctioned, for whatever reason, morale took a nosedive. Frustration was rampant in the early days of World War II U.S. Navy submarine warfare.

In the early 1960s, one of the positive factors introduced by Secretary of Defense Robert McNamara and his "whiz kids" as they became infatuated with nuclear weapons strategy and tactics was their insistence on good reliability factors. They stressed operational readiness tests to determine factors that could be used reliably in mathematical determinations of mission success. If a Polaris submarine was expected to fire sixteen missiles in rapid succession—"ripple fire"—a test needed to be conducted firing sixteen missiles to verify the launch reliability of each missile.

The United States has never fired an intercontinental ballistic missile from an operational missile silo. Most such firings have been conducted at Vandenberg Air Force Base in southern California from test and development silos. There has been some question that the missiles launched from an operational silo in Wyoming or North Dakota will perform as expected. Several attempts have been made over the years to conduct such tests from at least one operational silo, using inert weapons, of course, but the opposition has been effective in preventing such endeavors. The people of Oregon do not like the idea of a huge missile flying overhead in peacetime. Therefore, the reliability factor of the ICBM has always been a little suspect.

One impact that unreliable operational factors have on the weapons stockpile is the call for more weapons. If there is some question about whether a weapon will explode upon arrival at the target, more weapons are targeted. The CTBT may be a great arms control device, but unless it surely provides for an alternative means of determining weapon reliability, it sets up a call for more weapons, not less—in opposition to the objectives of arms control measures.

In spite of all the rhetoric about testing, the fact is that with the large number of weapons programmed in the SIOP, many could fail to arrive or explode upon arrival, and the result would still be about the same: massive destruction with millions dead. Add to that the impact of the Russian plan, and the world is in trouble, with or without a CTBT.

The targets assigned to the carriers in the SIOP were a point of contention for a while. The Navy argued that they were not getting high-value targets. But what was a high-value target for a nuclear weapon?

The authorities dictating the guidance and damage criteria for nuclear attacks in the early days of nuclear weapons concentrated on the urban/industrial base. They were termed "soft" targets, for they could be destroyed easily. The rationale was, destroy the industrial capability, and you can bring them to their knees. That was the logical choice for a "system" of targets, because the delivery vehicles, particularly the missiles, were not accurate enough to take on more precise aim points. Guidance ordering the destruction of 70 percent of the industrial floor space left a lot of room for error in planning an attack, but it still would create a lot of collateral damage, which meant killing people. If the directing authority prescribed in addition that a certain *high-confidence* level be attained in the destruction of that floor space, the stage was set for an increase in the number of weapons required, which in turn meant more collateral damage and more people killed.

In contrast, take on the task of destroying an ICBM in its hardened silo—a "hard" target. The computed damage expectancy for a single mission turns out to be very low. Therefore, more weapons are applied to the target in an attempt to obtain the damage prescribed, thereby setting the stage for a further increase in the size of the stockpile. With the massive numbers of weapons planned for targets, pilots had good reason to question their own survivability or the probability of completing a return to the parent carrier.

As delivery systems became more accurate, calls emanated from the controlling authority for a more moral strategy. The desire emerged to attack the enemy's ability to attack the United States—a "counterforce" or "damage-limiting" strategy, which meant going after the hard targets. The problem with that strategy was that the nuclear-threat targets such as ICBMs were difficult to destroy, even if U.S. missiles arrived before the enemy missile had been launched. The decisive factors, however, were all those weapons based in submarines, Soviet as well as U.S. If that capability cannot be destroyed, there is no chance of attaining a high probability of counterforce success. Former Secretary of Defense James Schlesinger, one of the more informed students of nuclear warfare, often made that point in public statements as early as 1974. He contended that attaining a counterforce capability was impossible for either side. If the antisubmarine problem is not solved, and more than half of programmed weapons are based in submarines, Schlesinger's point was well made. The eighteen Trident SLBM systems in the U.S. arsenal in the year 2000 represent a highly reliable containment/deterrent force, largely because they enjoy a survivability factor of 100 percent. The laws of physics associated with the detection of quiet submerged objects such as submarines seem to predict that the high survivability factor attributed to the submarine will continue for a long time.

The SIOP and the Carriers

The creation of the SIOP had a major impact on operations of aircraft carriers. It was just as important for the various services to be in the SIOP as the new plan was put together as it had been to have a nuclear weapons mission at the end of World War II. If one of the armed forces was not integrated in that plan, it had no real justification for funding, since nuclear weapons were the cornerstone of U.S. strategy for implementing the containment/deterrence policy. Therefore, each command having carriers in their arsenal committed those carriers and associated weapons to the new SIOP. Those commands were CinCPac for the Pacific carriers, CinCLant for those operating in the Atlantic, and CinCEur for those in the Mediterranean, including those weapons that were earmarked for NATO. Although the ships were not under the operational command of CinCSAC, they were going to take their orders from him in the targeting of their nuclear weapons as he put on his hat as the director of the JSTPS. The plan began to have a major impact on the movement of carriers.

If the plan were to be truly integrated, weapons had to arrive on their assigned targets at a precise time. That meant that aircraft had to launch from predetermined geographic locations to ensure that the carrier aircraft arrived on target at the time specified by the integrated plan. The more tense an international situation, the closer to those launch points the carriers had to be. The Navy had been extolling the flexibility of the carrier, its ability to be anywhere on the oceans of the world at any time. Ironically, with the SIOP, those ships were tied to an operational war plan that required them to be within range of a fixed launching point. Those ties were often quite frustrating to some carrier commanding officers.[11] Freedom of the seas was now restricted by the necessity to be a contributor in the overall scheme of nuclear warfare.

The sanctity of these launch points was extraordinary, and throughout the Vietnam War, the carriers had to consider their location in respect to them. There was concern at high levels that failure of the carriers to reach the launch points would bring charges of inability to compete. Authority to vary or "stand down" from those restrictions was granted occasionally, with appropriate accommodations made in the SIOP to compensate for the possibility that the carrier might not be on station. However, in times of tension, when nuclear weapons might be needed, the carriers had to head for their prescribed launch points to be in position to launch on schedule. It was an onerous restriction, but necessary, if one really believed in the idea of an integrated attack using thousands of nuclear weapons, each one theoretically playing a role in attainment of the prescribed objective.

Many improvements in nuclear weapons targeting were made with the first SIOP. For example, many carrier aircraft missions increased their probability of success as new targets and better intelligence were fed into the planning. These missions in turn improved the penetration ability of other systems, such as SAC bombers. Some missions, like those of the Air Force B-66 medium-range aircraft operating out of England, were greatly improved. As those missions were subjected to the SIOP planning process, it was determined that their original probabilities of success were very low, and their chances of returning safely were almost nil. Changes in those missions were made for the benefit of all concerned.

Other changes took place. For example, the Air Force Snark cruise missile, planned for launch from Presque Isle in Maine, was supposed to travel several thousand miles to a target in the Soviet sphere. The probability of its arriving was very low. Therefore, it was unilaterally removed from the arsenal after the first SIOP was published. This was when Secretary of Defense Robert McNamara and his systems analysts began involving themselves, not only in the policy and strategy for nuclear warfare, but also in the details of the targeting process. Other systems were eliminated as well, showing that unilateral arms control could be accomplished quite easily, not only reducing the size of the nuclear arsenal but improving the operational plan as well. Complicated diplomatic negotiations with the Soviets were not necessary to make those reductions.

Target assignments and routes for penetration improved with the implementation of the SIOP. Since there were top-caliber carrier aviators in Omaha planning the strikes, missions were designed to meet the capabilities of the carriers and their embarked air wings. Training was oriented to prescribed launch points and specific routes to assigned targets. Some exercises were timed endurance tests, with accuracy checks for the entire ship's system, running through the launch plan for a specific SIOP option. Drills included the planning of missions, adjusting to changing assignments, handling the unique communications traffic, preparing weapons for loading, and launching to fly the prescribed SIOP schedule. Like any competitive exercise that requires adherence to specific standards, they were worthwhile, although sometimes irksome to the crews.

About three or four weeks before a major deployment, delivery crews spent a couple of hours each day planning the mission in detail. Squadron air intelligence officers briefed the details of the mission and the target. There were numerous surface-to-air-missile sites and antiaircraft gun emplacements en route to the targets that had to be considered. Because a number of nuclear explosions from other delivery vehicles could occur along the route, they were key factors to be considered in the planning process. After completion of the planning sessions, the maps and supplies were returned to the air intelligence officers for storage in the appropriate secure vaults.

Periodically during deployment, the aircrews would return to the air intelligence offices to review the maps and flight data to become more thoroughly prepared for the mission. After all the planning was completed, the crews felt that they could fly the missions in their sleep, without the maps and supporting documentation.[12]

It is interesting that despite all the planning and the improvements in targeting that came with the SIOP, few pilots had much faith that, "if the balloon went up," the actual operation would happen as planned and practiced. One major unknown factor was the impact of targeting so many nuclear weapons against a high density of targets, to be delivered by various delivery systems. The magnitude of the attack caused some doubt about the ability to successfully deliver and return home safely. However, the SIOP drills were conducted with great seriousness. They were usually the finals of the three-day exercises that were common at the time.[13]

The A-6 Intruder aircraft added a tremendous capability to the carrier nuclear weapon delivery mission and was a favorite with SIOP planners. With its added range and penetration capability, Moscow showed up on the carrier target list, whether launching from the Pacific or the Mediterranean. During the deployment of the first A-6 squadron (VA-75) to the Pacific, many SIOP targets for the A-6 were in the Soviet Union. Some pilots felt that missions were planned so that, in all probability, there would not be enough fuel to return to the carrier. Consequently, a friendly airfield was considered as a landing site on return. In the event there were problems in flight or the aircraft were low on fuel, pilots were instructed to find a "safe haven" as a bailout point "somewhere in Russia."[14]

By the 1970s, target materials and training facilities were much improved. For example, in August 1973, Attack Squadron 147 (VA-147) was flying the A-7E, based on board the USS *Constellation* in the Pacific theater. The carriers were still committed to the SIOP, and the *Constellation* had an assigned role with a prescribed launch point in the western Pacific. Each pilot in the squadron had a designated target. Well before the deployment, intelligence folders were received, covering specific targets. As with the A-6 squadrons a few years before, pilots planned routes to the targets with timed checkpoints and radar predictions for each of the turn points and for the targets that they were assigned. They could select a couple of different initial points for weapons delivery.

New simulators aided preparation for flights in the 1970s. For the A-7E, the pilots could fly an entire mission in a weapons-system trainer at the Naval Air Station in Lemoore, California. They could load the appropriate intelligence information for the planned flight into the simulator, including the projected display map for the region and the radar perspective of the route and target area. Then they could fly the entire route in the simulator, gaining an indication of what they were supposed to see on radar during the actual flight.[15]

As part of the integrated plan, the squadron intelligence officers pointed out where other weapons were programmed along the planned routes. From the 3,500 weapons planned in the first SIOP, by the early 1970s the number had risen to over 8,000 and was still climbing. Appropriate indications of where and when another nuclear weapon might be detonated were made on strip charts. Pilots also reviewed procedures for returning to the force or proceeding to alternative landing sites. Again, even though intelligence procedures were much improved, few if any pilots believed that they would be able to return to the *Constellation* at the conclusion of their missions—not with all those nuclear weapons going off in the operational area.[16]

With the submarines and ICBMs taking over a major part of the nuclear weapons delivery load, the bombers and tactical aircraft could be eased out of the program. In 1974 a "reserve" force was established in U.S. nuclear warfare planning. The carriers were perfect for that role. They were not needed as full-time players on the team any longer, since there was enough destructive power in all the other systems in place. Accordingly, the carriers were withdrawn from the SIOP in 1976. Many emerging international scenarios required the carrier presence in more conventional roles. Freedom from the restrictive aspects of the SIOP was a welcome relief. A fascinating chapter in carrier nuclear weapons history was ending.

By 1978 the carriers, no longer in the SIOP, were free to operate without the launch-point restrictions. However, the pilots still had to train and prepare for the nuclear mission. Most significantly, the detailed nuclear weapons technical proficiency inspections were still conducted, with the same disastrous results for the commander of a squadron whose unit failed to pass. The major difference resulting from withdrawal from the SIOP was that delivery pilots deployed without an assigned target or nuclear weapons target folder. There were no preplanned missions. Instead, pilots had to learn contingency planning—to develop a delivery mission from scratch. They exercised by responding to a call for a contingency nuclear delivery mission. Upon receipt of such an assignment, they would also receive the necessary intelligence for the mission. A team would prepare a plan for delivering the weapon on the target or targets. After the planning was complete, pilots would brief the appropriate authorities on how they intended to execute the contingency requirement. Although no longer in the SIOP, they were certainly still in the nuclear delivery business. The proof was the requirement to continue to conduct those unpopular safety and loading drill exercises.[17]

10. The Past, the Present, and the Future

The A-6 and A-7 aircraft, combined with the modern carrier and readily available, highly efficient nuclear weapons, represented a very significant deterrent that concerned the Soviets considerably. Their replacement, the F/A-18, had the capability to deliver the latest weapons in the arsenal. Inherent in the F/A-18 were improved all-weather capability, reliability, and remarkable advances in the ability to deliver new, precision weapons. Notwithstanding the F/A-18's impressive capabilities, the fact of the matter is that *its nuclear weapons delivery capabilities no longer exist*. If the president of the United States wanted a nuclear weapon of any kind delivered on a target using an aircraft carrier and its embarked aircraft as the means of delivery, the Navy could not comply. How did the United States go from a posture of no capability in 1945, to an emergency capability in the early 1950s, to a very significant capability in the 1960s through the 1980s, to no capability in the late 1990s?

The answer lies in part with arms control actions. There has to be some question about the value of the arms control negotiating process: has it been a catalyst or detriment to the reduction of nuclear weapons? Some of the arms control treaties have brought agreements to reduce the number of weapons, but the negotiating process has also forced us to keep weapons in the stockpile that could have been eliminated much earlier. For example, without arms control the United States most certainly would have eliminated the Titan intercontinental ballistic missile much sooner than it did. The necessity of keeping weapons in the stockpile as bargaining chips for the arms controllers has sometimes added to the size of the stockpile, rather than decreasing it. It seems apparent to some that the arms control bargaining concept—that a nation never reduces without getting the opponent to give up something as well—has kept the stockpile at a level that is questionable.

While "unilateral" is a bad word in the arms control process, the size and quality of the U.S. stockpile and associated delivery systems made unilateral reduction actions quite feasible—for both the United States and the Soviets. For example, when President Nixon was preparing to make his visit to Moscow in the early 1970s, some of those involved in the targeting of weapons considered the issue of arms reductions. They postulated that a sound political tactic would be for Nixon to announce to the world that he was going to Moscow to discuss nuclear arms reductions; that he would offer to reduce U.S. strategic stockpile by one thousand weapons—and he would let the Soviets pick the weapons the United States was to destroy. Such an announcement would gain world attention, give Nixon an upper hand in any dealings with the Soviets, and not effect the impact of the SIOP one iota. The overall effectiveness of the U.S. war plan would have been the same, that is, massive destruction with a high probability of success. When damage expectancy curves have reached the asymptotic stage, much can be given up with only a minimal impact on the result.

President Gerald Ford's action in a meeting in Vladivostok with the Soviets in 1974 offered some possibilities of reducing numbers of weapons. "Had the parties involved signed a simple agreement at the time, formalizing the numbers agreed upon, a cap might have been put on the nuclear buildup. The United States would have had to add weapons to the arsenal to reach the Vladivostok figures, but at least an upper limit would have been established. It would have been a start toward weapons reduction, a distinct advantage for the United States at that time because of the better technology in U.S. systems. But that is not the way of arms control negotiations. There can be no simple formula or agreement. The 'process' must prevail, including much debate about where and when to hold talks."[1] Although the action by Ford and his negotiators was somewhat encouraging, the professional arms control community and the defense hawks of the nation criticized it adversely. Therefore, nothing really came of that effort, but some U.S. nuclear weapon targeteers were impressed. They could see that the proposed reductions would have little or no effect on the results achieved by the overall nuclear warfare plan, a fact that few in the public realized because of the restrictive security measures on the targeting function.

Next came a bold gesture by Secretary of State Cyrus Vance during his trip to Moscow in 1977. He proposed radical reductions in the numbers of weapons—reductions that would not have adversely affected the damage expectancy of the U.S. plan enough to mention. "The Soviets rebuffed Vance, which should have been a good indicator of the Soviet view of arms control negotiations."[2]

Then came some dramatic action by Presidents Reagan and Gorbachev in Iceland in October of 1986. They kept the professional arms negotiators out of the room. Reagan held a firm position, particularly on the Strategic Defense Initiative.[3] Although no specific treaty or agreement came from the meeting, the stage was set for some significant progress toward actually reducing the number of weapons in the arsenals of both sides. Some of the eventual agreements called for unilateral action, others bilateral. But "reductions" rather than "control" was the ultimate achievement.

The arms control process as practiced before (and since) Iceland had not been very effective in the actual reduction of the stockpile. Something better could be done, and Reagan led the way. Again, the critics were aghast. At the time, Strobe Talbot, later under secretary of state, was writing for *Time* magazine. In his comments about the nature of the agreements between the two principals, Talbot labeled Reagan the "amiable dunce." Although the press and the professional arms control community were upset over the Reagan/Gorbachev actions, once again some of the U.S. targeteers were impressed. At last, someone in authority in both the United States and the Soviet Union was beginning to pay attention to the ridiculous size of the nuclear weapons arsenal.

The Reagan/Gorbachev actions set the stage for reductions in nuclear arms. George Bush became the president of the United States in 1989. Following up on the Reagan initiative, he and President Gorbachev reached an agreement. "When the Soviet Union was falling apart, both Bush and Soviet President Mikhail Gorbachev took unilateral actions to pull back tactical nuclear weapons. Bush announced on 27 September 1991 that the United States would eliminate its entire worldwide inventory of ground-launched tactical nuclear weapons and would remove all nuclear weapons from surface ships and attack submarines. Gorbachev followed on 5 October with a similar pronouncement."[4] The unilateral initiatives were never codified. There was no treaty over which to haggle or to be tabled in the halls of legislative bodies. Instead, it was an agreement between two leaders to do something concrete.

The unilateral reductions ordered by President Bush included the weapons in aircraft carriers. His actions essentially meant removing our forward based systems (FBS), which included the Air Force tactical aircraft on nuclear weapons alert in Europe. Some in the targeting business considered the FBS to be the best of the nuclear weapons arsenal, if the United States actually became involved in a nuclear weapons exchange. Many of those weapons systems were mobile, therefore highly survivable. They were accurate, and they were relatively close to the significant targets. They would be the first to arrive in any nuclear weapons exchange between the super powers. The new Pershing II, in the hands of the U.S. Army, was particularly impressive as an intermediate-range ballistic missile. Most importantly, those forward based systems were most probably the first that would be used, by both sides, in any nuclear weapons exchange. Eliminating them from the plans was an appropriate step if you were looking for stabilization of the nuclear weapons environment.

As for the aircraft carriers, they had already assumed a backup role in a nuclear "reserve" force. Although delivery crews were trained, and weapons-handling crews still maintained a high degree of nuclear weapons readiness, the significance of the role had been greatly reduced as other uses for the carriers became a priority and many new systems were in place for maintaining a nuclear-ready force.

With the Bush initiative, not only were nuclear weapons removed from the carriers, but other significant actions were taken as well. Training of delivery crews was terminated. There would be no more loft/toss and "idiot loop" maneuvers. The storage magazines and handling equipment were still available, but the bomb assembly and handling personnel were no longer on board. By the late 1990s, both the A-6 and A-7 aircraft had been retired to aircraft storage sites, replaced by the new F/A-18 aircraft, which became the mainstay of both the offensive and defensive elements in the carrier air wing inventory.[5]

As for restoring the capability in the carriers, which some might consider in an emergency, that would take some time. Although the nuclear weapons storage and handling spaces are still available in the carriers, they are really intended for the new precision weapons, not the nuclear weapons. Those spaces could still be used for nuclear weapon assembly and storage if the need arose, especially since the present-day weapons are relatively simple to assemble and store, at least compared to the weapons of the past. Although the Marine security detachments on the carriers have been reduced in size, in an emergency, they could assume the security role.

The F/A-18 C and D aircraft models still have the wiring and bomb racks for nuclear weapons delivery. They are physically capable of the delivery mission, although they could not cover long ranges without support from refueling tankers. There is no special software program for the on-board weapons computer that replaced the old Low-Altitude Bombing System. A specially trained team would have to modify the computer software in the aircraft to provide a delivery-release capability. Professional estimates indicate that it would take about one year to restore the capability, whether the F/A-18 became the delivery vehicle or the old A-6 was taken out of mothballs.

Should the nuclear weapons delivery capabilities ever be restored to carrier aircraft, there would be considerable improvements in the overall capability to put a bomb on the target. For example, the ability to get to the target is now vastly superior to that in the past. The low-level navigation requirement that demanded so much training of pilots is no longer a problem. The Global Positioning System (GPS), utilizing a network of orbiting navigational satellites, enables the pilot to navigate to a position for the loft/toss or OTS delivery maneuver with extreme accuracy. The intelligence information on target systems is much better today. Targeting personnel can be far more selective in the choice of suitable targets and in the number that would need to be destroyed. The early SIOP requirements to attack large-target systems such as the urban industrial floor space or nuclear-threat targets no longer exist. Instead, targeteers can be more selective, using "nodal target analysis." Better intelligence means a higher probability of getting accurate hits on the targets. In the evolution of the target intelligence function, we have gone from the bombing encyclopedia to target systems to nodes of target systems. Incidentally, better intelligence should make a case for smaller nuclear weapons arsenals. With the precision delivery capabilities that now exist, the ability to take out the hard targets, such as ICBM sites, has improved. However, even though we continue to develop an impressive antisubmarine capability, there is no assured way to eliminate all the nuclear weapons that are loaded and ready in the ballistic missile submarines.

Vice Adm. Dennis McGinn, who had considerable responsibility for establishing the requirements for naval aviation in the late 1990s, expressed some thoughts about restoring the nuclear capability. "Most significant is the fact that presently, there is no training of pilots or enlisted personnel for the nuclear weapons delivery mission in the aircraft carriers. If we wanted to reinstate the capability, we would have to start that training over again. Such action is not advisable in my opinion. *We now have other, more appropriate weapons systems that can handle the nuclear job very well,* whether employed by the Navy or the other armed services. I would not like to see the nuclear delivery mission put back into our Navy's carrier roles and mission basket."[6] Once again, technology has had a major impact on the strategies and tactics needed for implementing policy.

What about the future? With new aircraft and new carriers in the plans, what role will the nuclear weapon play in their war-fighting capabilities? The short answer is none—if the military has a decisive voice on the issue.

Although the new carriers planned for the future, the CVN-77 and the CVX-1 and -2, will incorporate some major improvements in the overall capability to perform any mission assigned, there are no plans to incorporate the nuclear weapon delivery mission. The storage spaces on board will be perfectly adequate for the weapons, but there are no plans to fill them with those munitions. Even the new aircraft destined to operate from those carriers for many years are not being equipped with the nuclear weapons delivery capability. The F/A-18 E and F models will have significant increases in capabilities. However, while their predecessors, the F/A-18 C and D models, had the wiring and wing racks for nuclear weapons, the new aircraft will not be so equipped. The reason for this complete abandonment of the nuclear delivery mission is simple. *There are better ways to accomplish the objective of deterrence than using nuclear weapons.* Modern weapons systems with their standoff capabilities and proven accuracy can deter, without the devastation that is associated with nuclear weapons exchanges. Nuclear weapons are dumb and dangerous, for everyone. They create an environment that prevents any user from being a winner. They are weapons of the past, for aircraft carriers at least. They played a major role in keeping the aircraft carrier alive, but their significance in national security affairs is diminishing, at least in the arsenals of major powers.

Dennis McGinn had more to say on the subject: "The carrier is far more suitable for the kind of warfare we have faced in the recent past, and it will be required for that type of operation in the future. That fact, coupled with the existence of better ways of doing the nuclear mission, obviates the need for nuclear weapons in the aircraft carriers. In a very real sense, we can achieve strategic deterrence much more effectively by using a variety of very precise and lethal conventional weapons."[7]

In reflecting on the history of nuclear weapons in carriers as he experienced it, first as a delivery pilot and then as a senior officer involved in planning for the future of naval aviation, Admiral McGinn commented: "Naval aviation played a tremendous role in winning the Cold War. Consider the effort and assets the Soviets had to devote to dealing with the U.S. Navy, especially the aircraft carriers. They could not concentrate simply on the central front in Europe. They had to worry about whether the carriers would attack from the Atlantic, the Pacific, the Mediterranean, or the Indian Ocean. Those carriers could surround the Soviet Union. And while creating that kind of threat, the carriers were also playing a major role in containing the spread of communism in South East Asia and Korea."[8]

11. Reflections

In reflecting on the fifty years in which nuclear weapons were associated with aircraft carriers, some significant aspects come to mind. As in any large undertaking, people emerge as the major factor in the equation. In the case of naval aviation and nuclear weapons, Deak Parsons dominates the landscape. His early accomplishments in the field of ordnance did much to aid the military's war-fighting capabilities. His vision and brilliance, coupled with his ability to educate, were paramount in the military exploitation of nuclear energy and the development of some exotic weapons systems. His premature death at age fifty-two deprived the nation of his talents. He was on the verge of making major contributions. Had he survived for ten or twenty years more, it is arguable that the world would have ever heard of Hyman G. Rickover. Further, nuclear energy might have been developed for peaceful purposes in a far more standardized, safer, and readily acceptable manner.

Many others fought for a proper role for naval aviation in nuclear affairs. Admirals Radford, Burke, and Griffen, supported by Denfeld, who sacrificed his career, are examples of leaders who placed principle well ahead of their own careers. Then came Spike Blandy, bringing the gun club traditions of the past into the new world of nuclear energy; Dick Ashworth, with his concern for the future of the Navy, not himself; Rivets Rivero and his unique abilities and innate intelligence, to take some of the load off Parsons; Dan Gallery and George Miller, with their thoughtful concepts on strategies for waging nuclear warfare; Chick Hayward, with his flamboyance, drive, political savvy, and leadership; Jig Ramage, with his early belief in the need, who laid his career on the line to bring it to reality; Tom Walker, Noel Gayler, Bill Leonard, Don Engen, Whitey Feightner, Joe Schwager, and their many shipmates, devising ways of getting the weapon on the target; Deke Ela, Jim Small, Red McQuilken, Dick Mandelkorn, and the many ship architects who faced the pressures and produced carriers that would meet the challenge.

Then there was Ed Heinemann and his superlative aircraft designs; George Spangenberg and his role in the evaluation of aircraft, winners and losers; Tom Blackburn, Tom Connolly, Bob Townsend, Joe Jaap—the early heavy-attack wing and squadron commanders living with monumental operational problems; Dave Purdon, representative of those who gave their lives in developing the capability; Paul Stevens, Bill Spiegel, Dick Davidson, Doc Gullege, Dick Dunleavy— who spent so much time and effort in their careers honing the heavy-attack concept; Bob Hunt, Charlie MacDowell, and their contemporaries in the early days of light attack; Ace King and Bill Chapman, with their belief in the fading Fury, which was being overtaken by the "hit on the first pass" A-6 Intruder with Swoose Snead. There was Frank Ault, the perceptive instructor on the details of the weapon; and Frenchy LeBlanc and his contributions in the testing of nuclear weapons and their components. Following in the steps of the leaders were the hundreds of young men like Joel Febel and Doug Miller, who spent most of their active duty careers intimately involved with the nuclear weapon and its unique characteristics.

There were the many aircraft squadron commanders and commanding officers of carriers who operated the nuclear delivery forces, along with the logistic chain of ammunition ships that carried the "next load." They all played a role. Finally, there were those special troops, mostly in the enlisted ranks, who lived with the weapons, giving them tender care in the assembling, loading, testing, and storing. The number of people involved in the process was staggering and has to number in the thousands—all dedicated to the development and perfection of a capability that was never used.

A good case can be made that the development of the nuclear capability by these people probably saved carrier aviation and, in turn, naval aviation overall. If the carrier had not survived, the other roles employing naval aviation, namely antisubmarine warfare, reconnaissance, and logistic support, would have been taken over by the Air Force, for those missions were performed largely by shore-based naval aviation. Their transfer to the Air Force would have been a logical move. But with the carrier carrying the torch of naval air, its survival meant the survival of the whole naval aviation capability.

Many will contend that the Korean War saved the carrier; that the need to provide tactical air power in support of U.S. and Korean forces was a major factor dictating the reactivation of some of the World War II carriers, manned to a considerable degree in the early phases by a recall of the reserves. But Korea merely provided a respite—a breathing spell for naval aviation to evaluate the future and refine the plans for developing the nuclear weapons delivery capability. By the end of the Korean War, the carrier operations of World War II were outmoded. Something better had to be developed, and the pressure for that development came from the need for a capability to handle and deliver the nuclear bomb. As the aircraft designers produced an airplane that could carry the load, the ship architects came up with a carrier that could provide an efficient and safe air base for the aircraft. The end product was spectacular, resulting not only in a credible nuclear weapons delivery capability, but also, more importantly, an aircraft carrier that was suitable for the more significant missions that have occurred and may occur in the future. The prenuclear carriers had a questionable future. The postnuclear carriers appear to have no limits. It would seem that the bomb saved the carrier and hence all of naval aviation.

Sea Power

One clear lesson has evolved during the development of a nuclear weapons capability by the U.S. Navy. That has to do with the very nature of sea power itself. "Sea power" is an idea that embraces the economic welfare and health of our nation—its lifeblood. It is a culture, essential to a maritime nation. The United States was founded by maritime activity, settlers emigrating from Europe and elsewhere. It prospered eventually from the seafaring nature of its economy. It became a trading nation. Combatant naval forces were established with operating principles that guaranteed the viability of the maritime trading fleet, so essential to the economy.

The carrier nuclear weapons struggle was a phase in U.S. sea power history, using the oceans to project power in a highly effective manner. The eventual assumption of that role by the submarine force, freeing the carriers for other essential duties in the maritime environment, was most fortunate. It was another example of the value of sea power. The nuclear struggle reinforced the knowledge of the flexibility of sea power, the ability to be anywhere, anytime, with a wide variety of capabilities in the military/diplomatic arena of national and international affairs.

Personnel Policies

A second lesson from the carrier experience has to do with personnel policies. General Groves was fascinated with engineers from West Point and the Naval Academy. He wanted and got some of the most outstanding that were in the system. Hyman G. Rickover insisted on only having people from the top 10 percent of the graduates from the Naval Academy enroll in the Navy's nuclear power program. He got them, often over the objections of the Navy personnel planners and the individuals involved, several of whom had other ideas about how they wanted to spend time in their naval careers.

Vice Adm. William P. Lawrence was the superintendent of the

Naval Academy from 1978 to 1981 and an outstanding graduate—a leader, an academic, and a fine athlete. He was shot down during the Vietnam War and held as a prisoner of war for several years. Later, as the superintendent of the academy, he was faced with the onerous task of delivering to Rickover only the top 10 percenters from each graduating class. He stated that fulfilling that order was one of the most painful experiences of his life.[1] Some of the top 10 percenters had come into the Navy to fly airplanes or drive ships. Assignments to nuclear power were something they did not want, and forcing them into that environment against their wishes was questionable. The Navy undoubtedly lost some potentially great leaders in their early years by promising one career and then forcing them into another.

The decision to have only the best and the brightest in naval aviation's initial nuclear weapons delivery program seemed like a good idea at the time. Getting them into the program was fine, but not providing a clear career path for the future caused problems. Some solved these problems by leaving the service. Their careers were not oriented toward a full contribution. Their abilities to contribute were curtailed by the high priority placed on the nuclear mission and their lengthy retention in it, which prohibited them from broadening their career experience. Had the United States ever used nuclear weapons after the Japanese experience, it is quite possible that those assigned to the Navy nuclear weapons program at the start would have had a more pronounced impact on the future of the Navy. However, the nuclear mission was never employed, and some of the younger of the best and brightest may have suffered, which in turn deprived the Navy of the additional service and contributions that they might have provided. Similar comments may apply to those who were forced into nuclear power programs.

The experience gained from our carrier nuclear program seems to counsel that in similar situations in the future, the long-range effects on career patterns should be considered. High priorities can apply only for a short time before they start to have an adverse impact on the long-range abilities of individuals to contribute.

Psychology in the Cockpit

Another lesson related to personnel has to do with the psychological aspects of flying. Bringing experienced all-weather patrol plane personnel into the aircraft carrier environment was a debatable concept. Chick Hayward was undoubtedly right that carrier pilots were not as experienced in night and all-weather flying as members of the patrol plane community. However, the results obtained as the program progressed cast doubt on his decision to have a mix of carrier and patrol communities in the carrier nuclear business. Are pilots of such similar psychological makeup that they can be interchanged indiscriminately and merged into a single coherent unit without difficulty?

When VAH-1 was created with Paul Stevens as the commanding officer, the squadron was formed by simply taking a patrol plane squadron with multiengine pilots and commissioning it as a new squadron about to initiate one of the most challenging, radically different capabilities in naval aviation. The assumption seemed to be that if you could fly a patrol plane, you would perform well in this new venture with heavy jets. Fortunately, Paul Stevens invoked a different principle and carefully evaluated the *total* characteristics of his charges, not just their flying background. Dedication to the mission and a desire to excel were the paramount characteristics he was seeking, and from that principle, he fostered a winning team.

One must wonder whether lengthy service in one environment can develop habit patterns and psychological reactions that are difficult to modify as one shifts into another environment requiring different reactions. The experience in the heavy-attack program as it moved into the AJ and A-3 aircraft raises some question about the issue.

It is comforting to think that all aviators are alike, that the characteristics and abilities of each are equal, be it in the Army, Navy, or Air Force. But that is far from the truth. Although there may be some common denominator that lured them into the aviation profession, people are different in psychological makeup. Those differences have an influence on their abilities to perform in various situations.[2]

Habit patterns are formed in the early days of doing anything, and this is especially true of aviation. That may be a feature that Chick Hayward overlooked or did not appreciate when he was putting together the people who were going to fly the heavy-attack mission. He wanted experienced pilots, half of them with time in multiengine patrol plane duties, like himself. He brought in excellent people who had done well in other than carrier operations. They had developed habit patterns in the cockpit, some of which may not have been compatible with the emerging requirements for heavy jets on mobile air bases. Chick Hayward may have been wrong to bring experienced senior patrol plane pilots into the carrier community. There were plenty of exceptions, such as Paul Stevens, but as a general policy, the idea may have been wrong.

As Jig Ramage moved into the heavy-attack program and tried to get it oriented more to carrier duty, he established a policy of carrier-experienced pilots only as his senior leaders. He made exceptions, but his concept was to have the leadership imbued with carrier habit patterns. He was ready to take any young pilot with any background and teach him the rudiments of the A-3 aircraft and aircraft carriers, because psychological habits are much easier to mold or modify at an early age. But for leaders, he wanted those who had proven they could operate comfortably and sharply around the carrier, people who had developed a carrier jet aircraft psychological habit pattern.

There was a time before World War II when all naval aviators gained experience in all facets of flying, namely patrol, carrier, scout/reconnaissance from cruisers and battleships, instructor duty, and so on. But that went by the board with the war in the interest of graduating pilots faster and in greater volume for the individual flying communities. A return to that pre–World War II concept was precluded by the increasing complexity of the modern airplane, its cost, and the necessity to vastly improve the safety record. Hence, specialization became the norm. The need for greater attention to the psychological makeup of the individual in his or her assignment to specific types of aircraft had to be considered. The carrier nuclear experience provided evidence of the need. It is hoped that any similar program in the future will consider the psychological makeup of the individuals being assigned, as well as the specific aircraft qualifications they have acquired.

Testing

A good case can be made that the fifty years of the carrier struggle was one of the most intensive testing periods in military history. Included were tests of the individual components and capabilities of the nuclear weapons that were being developed; tests of delivery tactics and systems associated with getting the weapon on a target; tests of the major components going into the new and converted aircraft carriers, such as the angled deck and steam catapult; tests of individuals and units on their knowledge of how to handle such weapons safely; and tests of the many aircraft that were introduced from 1945 to 1990. Most significant among the latter were the tests of the AJ aircraft, in which political pressure caused established procedures to be bypassed, resulting in some serious problems and loss of life. Hopefully, leaders of the future will benefit from the AJ aircraft experience and adhere to established, proven procedures for the introduction of new weapons systems. Testing is such an essential part of military readiness that temptations to bypass the practice must be viewed with much concern.

Secrecy

The severe security classification policies imposed by General Groves as he set up the Manhattan Project have been followed continuously for all aspects of the nuclear weapons business. In 1999, there was official concern about technical information allegedly taken from our nuclear laboratories. However, one must wonder whether our stringent security policies have been essential since the first nuclear bombs were delivered on target. Those policies did not keep the Soviets, British, or Chinese from knowing what we were doing and developing their own nuclear weapons. Perhaps security restrictions did more harm than good.

Scientist Edward Teller, known as the father of the thermonuclear weapon, is reported to have said, "All classified information should be declassified within six months—the maximum time that any scientific or technical information can be kept secret."[3] If a technical idea is good, others are going to discover its intricacies in a short period. If it is not a good idea, who cares whether it is classified or not? Maybe declassification of a developing concept can lead the opposition to think it is not of much value. How does Teller's concept of the security of scientific information relate to the concern about allegations that the Chinese stole nuclear weapons secrets from the labs in New Mexico? Teller once served on the nine-member Pentagon Task Force on Secrecy, which concluded,

> With respect to technical information, it is understandable that our society would turn to secrecy in an attempt to optimize the advantage to national security that may be gained from new discoveries or innovations associated with science and engineering. However, it must be recognized first, that certain kinds of technical information are easily discovered independently, or regenerated, once a reasonably sophisticated group decides it is worthwhile to do so.
>
> In spite of elaborate and very costly measures taken independently by the U.S. and the USSR to preserve technical secrecy, neither the United Kingdom nor China was long delayed in developing hydrogen weapons. In addition, classification of technical information impedes its flow within our own system and may easily do far more harm than good by stifling critical discussion and review or by engendering frustration. There are many cases in which the declassification of technical information within our system probably had a beneficial effect and its classification has had a deleterious one.[4]

That may have been a Pentagon study, but anyone who has worked in that building in the past fifty years knows that it has not had much effect on the classification of materials in the Department of Defense.

The high-security classification placed on nuclear weapons as they entered the carrier aviation program caused a restriction in the flow of information—information that might have been useful as the Navy developed a plan for gaining a delivery capability. If the strategists had been aware from the start of the possibilities of smaller, lighter weapons with increased yields becoming available sooner rather than later, the Navy might not have moved so desperately and impatiently into the heavy-attack program with the P2V and the AJ aircraft, a program that called for stowage on the carriers of 10,000-pound bombs. Spawned by more knowledge of the nuclear weapon, we could have arrived at a better capability, and sooner, without all the rancor between the heavy- and light-attack delivery advocates.

How about all those restrictions on naval architects and their teams of yard workers who modified Navy carriers and other ships to house a nuclear stockpile? Was it really necessary to have been so secretive about what those men were building?

The restrictions imposed on the control and custody of the weapons was based on secrecy and lack of trust that the military could maintain proper control over the weapons. Keeping the weapons in the custody of the Atomic Energy Commission and then getting them into the hands of the military in the event they were to be used created an absurd Rube Goldberg process that was unnecessary, one that could have been eliminated with less concern about security and more about the ability to get the weapon on the target. The twenty-year struggle to transfer custody of nuclear weapons assigned to the military could have been avoided, just by removing some of the secrecy constraints and relying a bit more on trust.

Consider the case of Rear Adm. Robert B. McNitt, who early in his career was assigned responsibility for all aspects of the armament—conventional and nuclear—on board a major combatant. He was not allowed to have anything to do with the key element of the bomb, the nuclear core. Such was the degree of secrecy assigned to the program. Refusing to allow the gunnery officer of a carrier access to the nuclear core stowage spaces was an example of bureaucratic foolishness at its peak.

Undoubtedly, there are secrets that need to be kept in an imperfect world. Adm. Noel Gayler, former head of NSA and a well-informed officer on matters nuclear, as well, pointed out that some information has no business being revealed.[5] But scientists seem to push for a greater exchange of information. In the case of nuclear weapons, less secrecy after the Manhattan Project completed its work could have helped in many ways.

Senator Daniel Moynihan had considerable exposure to the subject of secrecy during his years in the Senate, when he concentrated on intelligence matters. Like others who have lived with the restrictions of security classification, he questioned the value, the almost paranoid tendency of our nation to keep things close to the chest. He concluded, "A case can be made . . . that secrecy is for losers. For people who do not know how important information really is. The Soviet Union realized this too late. Openness is now a singular and singularly American, advantage. We put it in peril by poking along in the mode of an age now past. It is time to dismantle government secrecy, this most pervasive of Cold War–era regulations. It is time to begin building the supports for the era of openness that is already upon us."[6] We fail to share for various reasons, the most insidious being the desire of bureaucracies to gain and keep power. We operate on the principle that the one who knows the most must be the most important and powerful—so do not tell anyone else what you know.

The bureaucratic secrecy associated with nuclear weapons certainly gave the Navy trouble as it struggled with its delivery program. Secrecy inhibits the flow of knowledge and is a policy that may be desirable in only exceptional cases. Perhaps the Navy carrier experience with nuclear weapons provides evidence that tendencies to classify should be reevaluated.

Civilian Authority and Control

At least twice during the fifty-year nuclear weapons history, the role of civilian authority—the well-established principle of civilian authority and control of U.S. military forces—came into play.

In the late 1940s, as the Navy and Air Force tangled over the mission of delivering nuclear weapons, civilian authority had to step in and referee. In this instance, both the executive and legislative branches of the U.S. government got involved. The B-36 aircraft versus the super carrier controversy resulted in the Congress authorizing the Navy to proceed with the nuclear mission. That authorization was essential before funds could be appropriated in the federal budget. The admirals had revolted, and the generals in both the Army and the Air Force, along with some civil authority in the executive branch, were engrossed in an argument that only the civil authority could resolve. Careers were destroyed, starting with the chief of naval operations himself. The price was paid by the military in other ways, but the only solution was for the civil authority to step in and make a decision, which opened the door for the Navy to become involved in the nuclear mission.

The second instance was in 1960, when the Air Force, led by the Strategic Air Command, waged a major campaign to create a "strategic command," a unified command that would embrace all so-called strategic forces capable of contributing to an overall strategic nuclear force. That command would have been comprised of at least four elements: the land-based bombers, based both in the United States and overseas; the intercontinental ballistic missile force; the aircraft carriers, if committed to the nuclear force; and the emerging Polaris submarine-launched ballistic missile systems. It was not beyond the realm of imagination that SAC would also have control over some NATO operational forces in Europe that would be involved in nuclear warfare. The objective was to gain operational control over all "strategic" nuclear weapons delivery forces, merging them into a single force, under command of one officer, probably a member of the U.S. Air Force.

Adm. Arleigh Burke's emotional response as chief of naval operations forced a compromise, authored by Secretary of Defense Thomas Gates and approved by President Eisenhower. That compromise was to deny operational control of the forces to one commander in exchange for the control of the targeting of those forces—the construction of a national strategic target list and the preparation of a single integrated operational plan. There is no way that the military forces could have resolved that issue by themselves. The civil authority at the highest level had to step in. Even after the compromise was implemented, some leaders in the Strategic Air Command continued to devote effort to the creation of such a command, feeling that the targeting function was a step in the direction they wanted to go and that the single command would follow. However, the rapid emergence of the highly successful submarine-launched ballistic missile systems (Polaris, Poseidon, and Trident) countered efforts to have the Air Force take over. Those delivery systems were highly effective at the beginning and continued to evolve, until now, more than half of the weapons in the U.S. strategic nuclear force are based in those submarines.

Ironically, a single strategic command (StratCom) was created much later, bringing together operational control over the SLBMs, the ICBMs, and the bomber force. The Strategic Air Command was eliminated. Command of this new force was assigned to the Navy and the Air Force on a rotational basis. Headquarters was located in the former SAC headquarters in Omaha, where the targeting function for the force continued to be performed. The incumbent sat at the desk where Gen. Curtis LeMay had held forth so effectively for so many years, a sure indication that StratCom was in existence.

Civil control of the military is essential, as these two instances demonstrate. Unfortunately, there have been abuses of this authority that have been disastrous in some ways. For example, when Louis Johnson took over from James Forrestal as secretary of defense, he used the office as a political patronage opportunity, staffing the very small organization with old political cronies. At the same time, Johnson emasculated U.S. military forces as he sacrificed national military assets in his move to become the president of the United States. The Korean War and U.S. lack of preparedness for doing battle brought Johnson down, but his abuse of the civil authority was shameful.[7]

The second major abuse occurred during the regime of President Lyndon Johnson, when he allowed Robert McNamara and his team of bright young whiz kids to inject civil authority into the minutest details of our defense establishment. Determining military requirements, selecting contractors to build weapons systems, developing tactics for nuclear and conventional warfare, and even selecting targets for the Vietnam War were in their repertoire. They were aided by the president himself at times. This major abuse of the civil authority principle cost the nation considerably more than the fifty thousand lives that were lost in the combat arena.

History has shown that there are lessons to be learned by military and civil authorities alike as they continue to maintain the principle of civilian authority and control. The lesson for the military is that they must be prepared to pay the price for such control. The lesson for the civil authority is to use caution and good judgment in exercising the authority that custom, tradition, and the law have established as essential to our national defense.

Arms Control

A major question that arises from the carrier nuclear experience and the overall nuclear weapons program has to do with arms control, specifically unilateral versus negotiated action. As the United States began more effective targeting of its strategic weapons and built the first SIOP in 1960, it was able to make several unilateral reductions in the delivery systems that were committed to the plan, without reference to other nations. Some cruise missiles and bombers that would have had difficulty reaching their targets, as well as marginally effective systems, were eliminated. In doing so, the United States not only brought some reductions in nuclear arms systems but improved its nuclear war plan as well.

Then the arms control mission erupted with well-intentioned negotiations to bring about some control over the continually expanding arsenals of the superpowers. Treaties were negotiated and considered by the executive and legislative authorities. These treaties have addressed not only the number and characteristics of weapons in respective stockpiles but also the development of new weapons, the proliferation of weapons, the testing of existing and new weapons, and the development of defensive systems for use against nuclear weapons attacks. With the negotiation process came a stalemate in reductions, because many weapons were kept in the arsenal as bargaining chips.

Malcolm Wallop, former U.S. senator from Wyoming, has written, "Arms control agreements are ever the substitute for *difficult political commitment*" (emphasis added).[8] It was not until Presidents Reagan and Gorbachev closed the doors to the professional arms control negotiators and made some "difficult political commitments" regarding nuclear weapons that some real progress in nuclear arms control began. Those commitments set the stage for President Bush to remove many nuclear weapons from the arsenals of the United States and NATO. His dramatic unilateral action, which took the tactical nuclear weapons from the carriers and other forward-based programs, represented real progress in harnessing the nuclear weapons race.

It is significant that Bush and Gorbachev chose to eliminate the weapons that were most likely to be used. Forward-based systems (FBS) always had a higher probability of being used than the big "boomers" of the sacred triad. Bush's action, fostered by Reagan and Gorbachev, was directed at the right systems in the arsenals if he really wanted to put a safety lock on the nuclear trigger. The Soviets, with Gorbachev leading, took similar unilateral actions. That bit of "political commitment" became known as the Bush/Gorbachev agreement.

Interestingly enough, the crisis in Yugoslavia over Kosovo had the Russians reportedly threatening to bring back tactical nuclear weapons.[9] There is no treaty to argue about, since the actions by Bush and Gorbachev were just part of an agreement, which is considerably different from a treaty. Should the civil authority of the United States consider countering the Russian threat with a resurrection of the forward-based force, I hope that they will consider the history of the nuclear weapon and realize that there are now better ways to do the job—that the weapon is a loser in real warfare.

There is good reason to believe that the present arms control process is a questionable venture. It keeps some intellectuals occupied, but the bottom-line results have not been impressive. Hasn't the use of nuclear weapons as bargaining chips in the negotiating process really prevented the reduction in the stockpile, reductions that made sense from a military point of view at least? Are unilateral reductions such a bad idea? The U.S. Missile Defense Act, passed by both the House and Senate of the U.S. Congress in early 1999, contains the following sentence: "It is the policy of the United States to seek *negotiated* reductions in Russian nuclear forces" (emphasis added). Why do we have to negotiate the reductions? If we have more weapons than we need, can't we just get rid of some of them without requiring the Russians to make similar reductions? What is so magical about the negotiation process?

As one studies the existing situation between Russia and the United States at the beginning of the twenty-first century, it seems apparent that the stage is set for some more difficult political commitments—more unilateral actions to bring down the size of the arsenal. However, the negotiators and many hawks find unilateral action unsatisfactory. So, the United States continues to keep a stockpile of such size that it has to be questioned. In 2000, there were eighteen Trident submarines with twenty-four missiles in each submarine and up to eight weapons on each missile—192 weapons in just one submarine—more than General Goodpaster thought the United States needed in the entire arsenal. The Congress has ordained that the number of Trident subs be reduced to fourteen, but even that seems excessive to some. If the United States has more than is needed, unilateral reductions seem advisable, which would probably be a relief to the Russians and would not hurt U.S. nuclear weapons deterrent/containment capability.

In addition to its awesome capability in the Trident subs, the United States has the other two legs of the sacred triad: the big bombers and the ICBMs. Couldn't the United States start a gradual unilateral reduction of those forces as well—weapons that serve as targets in the

United States for a potential enemy and jeopardize the safety of people living near them?

Reflecting on this issue, one has to question an existing U.S. arms control format that requires bilateral reductions and prohibits unilateral action. Closer attention of the negotiators to the targeting process and the answers it provides would help in any case. Further, attention to the damage criteria specified for the implementing plans, which generate much of the requirements for weapons, could aid a great deal.

The Usefulness of the Nuclear Weapon

The usefulness of the weapon itself will probably be debated forever. Within a few years after the two weapons ended the war with Japan, the United States had in its nuclear weapons arsenal thousands of weapons of varying capabilities. It now seems ludicrous that the United States would embrace the idea of launching a strategic attack with ten thousand nuclear weapons possessing an unbelievable destructive power—an attack that would result in the immediate deaths of over one hundred million people on either side. How did national leadership ever get to the point where they thought that kind of military response would solve any of the world's problems? But they did, with pressure from some to add even more weapons to the stockpile. Some contend that it was the massive stockpile that actually caused the Soviets to end the Cold War—and they may be right. But ten thousand so-called strategic nuclear weapons?

There can be no question that the nuclear weapon contributed to stability through its deterrence characteristic. Perhaps the large size of the stockpile was a key factor in that deterrence. The gross number of weapons in the stockpile was about all that could be considered, since security measures, coupled with disinterest in the qualitative aspects, kept the quality-measurement factor from being used. Qualitative measures could have meant considerable reduction in the size of the stockpile.

The pressure on the Soviets to keep up with the ever-increasing size of the U.S. stockpile had to have a major impact on their economic situation. Then came the pressure for the Strategic Defense Initiative, the final economic straw. Soon the Cold War was over. Perhaps the size of the stockpile may have played a useful political role, but for the military planner, a much smaller number of weapons would have been quite satisfactory.

There will probably always be a debate on the size of the stockpile. How much is enough? General Butler wants all eliminated. General Goodpaster would settle for one or two hundred. And some still want "lots of weapons." There is a certain level of comfort in knowing that the United States sits under the high-quality umbrella of the Trident missile system and its invulnerable submarines.

Short of a massive retaliation or preemptive tactic, use of the weapon was deemed feasible in other scenarios—cases where serious consideration was given to the idea. President Truman faced the possibility during the Berlin crisis in the late 1940s and actually moved bomber aircraft to England. The problem then was the lack of weapons to do anything. Even if the weapons had been available, there is doubt that any would have been used. There seemed to be better ways to solve the issue, such as the Berlin Airlift.

In the Korean War, President Truman faced MacArthur's idea of creating a nuclear radiation barrier along the Yalu River, the border between China and North Korea. Although he was the man who had approved the use of the weapons against Japan, he would not approve MacArthur's suggestion. President Eisenhower considered the use of the nuclear weapon against North Korea after he assumed office in January 1953. He was determined to finish that war, but he did not get enough support for using a nuclear weapon and would not approve the requests to do so. The United States tolerated the deaths of almost forty thousand service men but would not use the bomb. In 1954 Eisenhower withstood pressure from the Joint Chiefs of Staff, the National Security Council, and the State Department to use the nuclear weapon against China. He was adamant in denying approval.

During the Cuban missile crisis in 1962, General LeMay is reported to have recommended that we "nuke 'em." The capability to carry out his recommendation existed in the aircraft carriers and accompanying ammunition ships that were on station. But a better way was found to solve the crisis, specifically the naval blockade of Cuba. During the Vietnam War, Secretary of Defense McNamara and his staff studied the nuclear weapons capability with fascination, first determining that there had been no "missile gap," as contended by President Kennedy in the 1960 election campaign. Having worked over the basic strategy and the details of the implementing operational plans, they ordered enhanced confidence levels for destruction, operational tests for improving the validity of the reliability of weapons and their delivery systems, flexible response options, and various nuances in the national plans for use of the weapon. However, their interest was centered on the massive attacks—the big plan—not regional conflicts. Therefore, in the case of Vietnam, despite serious consideration by some military leaders for use of the bomb, no approval from the civil authority was forthcoming. Again, the United States chose the deaths of fifty thousand servicemen and political defeat in lieu of using the nuclear weapon. As one lived with these actions, it became apparent that although the nuclear weapon had tremendous destructive capabilities, it was fast becoming a purely political weapon, not one that military forces could use. Its destructive powers were so great that it actually deterred the power possessing the weapon. It has been said many times that any military commander who bases his combat strategy on the use of the nuclear weapon has taken his first step towards defeat.

What is the threshold level of loss at which a nation will respond with a nuclear weapon? Almost forty thousand deaths in Korea and another fifty thousand in Vietnam did not seem to be high enough. Suppose half of those deaths had been women, authorized to participate in combat. Would the United States have reached the threshold for the use of the nuclear weapon? Would those contending that women should be allowed to participate in combat have had second thoughts about their beliefs? Or would they have been leading demonstrations echoing General LeMay's cry of "nuke 'em"?

The weapons in the stockpile included those with destructive yields of fifteen megatons or more, weapons that were difficult to deliver reliably and were only suitable for blowing up whole cities at a time. Some, with a relatively small explosion, could be fired from artillery pieces on the battlefield. Others were designed specifically to counter submarines or attacking aircraft. Some were designed to clutter the atmosphere so that communications would be disrupted. Nuclear weapons that can penetrate the surface of a target before exploding are still in the U.S. arsenal.

Delivery capabilities and accuracy improved constantly, so that by the year 2000, nuclear weapons could take out some hardened command posts and ICBM silos—the so-called hard or counterforce targets. However, for all their improved accuracy and versatility, they have never been used. As President Eisenhower commented, public opinion has more power than the destructive capability of all the nuclear bombs.

As discussed in chapter 3, Generals Goodpaster and Butler and Admiral Gayler have seriously questioned the usefulness of the nuclear weapon—at least the need for the massive U.S. stockpile. Some very experienced and prestigious leaders throughout the world have supported them in their contentions. Is there still a role for a massive stockpile of weapons that have such questionable possibilities for use?

Senior leaders are not alone in their doubts. Those living and working closely with the weapons have also been skeptical. For example, Vice Adm. Robert F. Dunn had duties ranging from being a nuclear weapon delivery pilot to many senior positions of responsibility in which the nuclear mission was of some concern. He summarized the dilemma of the prospects of using the atomic bomb.

From my time as a midshipman until late in my career when the Cold War was winding down, we studied, trained, and planned for nuclear war, but the prospects were never high on our list of worries. The various special weapons schools, the loading, the planning, navigating, and practice delivery maneuvers and even the long hours spent on alert loaded with war reserve weapons were hardly ever more than drills or requirements to be met. Seldom did we think about the awesome power of the bomb or the responsibilities for death and destruction that might occur. Nor did we give much thought to the associated politics, whether international or interservice. Instead, our concerns were our people, our airplanes, and our personal and materiel readiness for conventional war.

By the time I was senior enough to be assigned positions of responsibility wherein I might have been more concerned with the pros, cons, and effects of nuclear war, there had been two major shifts in approach. First, all strategic nuclear war planning and capability had been assigned to the ballistic missile submarines, the Air Force long-range bombers (B-52), and the intercontinental ballistic missiles. Second, as we became more confident in our conventional capability and as the Soviet Union began to show signs of deterioration, the thought of using tactical nuclear weapons receded to deep background in our minds. In short, save for filling in the check marks in training and readiness requirements, we gave it pretty short shrift.[10]

In the U.S. Sixth Fleet in the Mediterranean in 1971–73, being prepared for nuclear warfare was not the number one priority. Antisubmarine warfare presented a great challenge at the time, and it drew on the energy and resources of the fleet. Locating a Soviet submarine in the Mediterranean was difficult, and it became the number one priority. A second priority was improving operational relationships with the NATO forces in the Mediterranean area. Serving as the NATO Support and Strike Forces, the Sixth Fleet concentrated on getting the British, Italians, Turks, and Greeks to work together in "combined" operations. In addition, bilateral exercises were conducted with the French and Spanish, forming relationships that would be most useful in time of conflict. However, as Dunn has pointed out, nuclear weapons were low on the priority list, although the fleet continued to keep a "ready nuke" posture. The SIOP was in effect, and the Sixth Fleet carriers were still in the plan.

Why and how the United States moved to a defense posture built around thousands of weapons that had such questionable military usefulness is an interesting story, particularly as one studies the groups of individuals who either deliberately or inadvertently contributed to the size of the stockpile. The massive destructive capabilities of those weapons deterred any superpower from using them, in either a preemptive or retaliatory mode. The mutual destructive capabilities led to a stalemate. Massive exchanges between the superpowers became highly improbable.

This leads to the question of whether there are scenarios for the future that might trigger the use of such weapons. One scenario has India and Pakistan starting a nuclear weapons exchange. If such an exchange actually occurred, would the United States or Russia respond with the use of a single nuclear weapon, or more than one? What would be the target? What would be the objective? Aren't there better ways of responding than with a nuclear weapon?

Another scenario involves the use of such a weapon by a terrorist organization. A worst-case situation could involve the detonation of a one-megaton bomb in the center of Manhattan. Would the United States respond with a nuclear weapon? Against whom? Against what target? For what objective? Is the bomb the proper response in such a situation? When the United States retaliates, particularly with a nuclear weapon, it had best be sure that the party it is attacking is guilty of the offense.

An emerging scenario that warrants attention is that dealing with relations between the United States and China. Any nation that has one billion people, mandated population-growth constraints, vast territory, and significant natural resources must be considered in any scenario addressing the future. How do nuclear weapons play in the Chinese scenario?

Some addressing the China problem give the impression that China is another "evil empire." Evidence cited includes China's interest in Taiwan, support of North Korea, and violation of human rights. Most recent are concerns that the Chinese have taken over control of access to the Panama Canal. Also cited are Chinese claims to the island chain near Japan, Taiwan, and the South China Sea.[11] Of considerable significance and growing alarm is the view that China is building intercontinental ballistic missiles capable of attacking the United States.

Consider the idea of China launching an ICBM attack against the United States. What would be their motive, their objective? How could such an attack possibly improve their economic situation, a critical issue, considering they have more than one billion people to support? They need the support of the United States for economic purposes. Why would they take actions with an ICBM attack that would not only sever economic ties but also alienate much of the rest of the world?

If such an attack did occur, how would the United States respond? With a retaliatory attack with nuclear weapons? Against one billion people? Wouldn't economic sanctions be more appropriate and more damaging to the Chinese than killing one hundred million or more of their populace? After all, Chairman Mao is quoted as saying that he was "willing to lose 300 million people if China had to fight a war."[12] Economics is their battlefield, not the nuclear fields of Armageddon. One utopian thought for the future has China and the United States becoming economic allies, building an economy that is so healthy that it can help solve many of the problems of developing nations. A healthy economy—money—is a prime requirement for world peace, not nuclear weapons.

If military action against the Chinese were required, would it not make more sense to use the conventional precision weapons that are in the arsenal of the Western powers—weapons that were demonstrated so well during the Desert Storm action against Iraq and perfected during the Kosovo campaign? Those weapons could be delivered against Chinese targets by aircraft carriers as well as other forces, without all of the horrendous consequences of the nuclear weapon.

The idea of a nuclear exchange between major powers is highly questionable, at least to many who have lived with the weapons. Knowledgeable, responsible officials have stated that *there are better ways to do the job*—to deter an adversary from taking action that is not desired for whatever reason, or to retaliate for actions taken that justify a military response.

In discussing better ways, emphasis is placed on the new precision weapons, which can be launched a good distance from a target and still achieve pinpoint accuracy. There seems to be no question that weapons can be placed in precise locations with high reliability. "Precise" is the operative word now, not "mass." The old "yield versus accuracy" philosophy is still in play, because the improved accuracy obviates massive yields. The United States has weapons that can be placed precisely where it wants them to explode. If the warhead on the delivery device is a nuclear weapon, there will be mass destruction—from heat, blast, and radiation. That destruction is often not desirable. It creates radiation problems if occupancy of the destroyed area is required, and it generates a need for major funding and other resources for restoration. Maybe there is something better for the future.

As the world entered the twenty-first century, some pundits and historians evaluated the past and dared to predict the future. Albert Einstein was selected as the man of the twentieth century by *Time* magazine. His theory of relativity and the formula that energy equals the product of mass times the square of the speed of light ($E=mc^2$) is the evidence that nuclear energy was a most significant discovery and development in the 1900s.[13]

Predictions for the twenty-first century venture that it will be the biochemical century; that great improvements will be made in medicine and food; that cures for many maladies will be discovered; that human longevity will increase dramatically; that fuel-celled cars will be operating; that hydrogen will be a key factor in energy programs.[14] Most sobering is the belief, voiced by President Bill Clinton, that the new biochemical century may also bring technological advances in the development of biological and chemical weapons, possibly more dreadful in their consequences than the nuclear weapons of the past.[15]

Other predictions contribute to the validity of the premise. For example, Gen. Colin Powell, while serving as the chairman of the Joint Chiefs of Staff, made the following comment in 1993: "The one thing that scares me to death, perhaps even more so than tactical nuclear weapons, and the one that we have the least capability against is biological weapons."[16]

Gen. Gordon Sullivan, president of the Association of the U.S. Army, also expressed his concern.

Despite the end of the Cold War, the threat posed to the United States by weapons of mass destruction has actually increased. Biological weapons are perhaps the most serious threat that will face our armed forces—and our nation—in the near future. These weapons are comparatively easy and cheap to make; anyone who can brew beer can create rudimentary biological weapons. They are also potentially quite lethal and could have effects far beyond those of nuclear weapons. The combination of ease, low cost and high payoff has made biological weapons increasingly attractive to rogue states and such transnational entities as terrorist organizations and other fringe groups. With the advances made in genetic engineering and biological sciences, more effective weapons can be made by industrial states that may wish to challenge us.[17]

For decades, we have referred to weapons of mass destruction (WMD) as nuclear, biological, and chemical. The nuclear aspect has been exploited in many ways and made quite public. On the other hand, the biological and chemicals aspects are still not well understood. As weapons, they have incurred widespread rejection. The idea of their use evokes gruesome images of suffering, because of the poisonous aspects of such weapons in the past.

Biological weapons spread disease and often require some time to take effect. They are difficult and dangerous to handle, particularly while being dispersed. Chemical weapons, on the other hand, have an almost immediate effect. They have some features that warrant attention. "Binary munitions are operationally safe, free of complex and costly production, handling, transportation, maintenance and disposal problems and potentially more politically acceptable for storage in areas now denied to current chemical munitions containing lethal agents."[18] The 155 mm artillery binary munition is impressive.[19] If that form of weapon were incorporated with the precise delivery systems now in existence, the potential for use has features that contest the nuclear weapon.

Possibly the scientific community, which did so much to exploit the atom, could develop and perfect a biochemical warhead that neutralizes rather than destroys—a weapon that would incapacitate the populace without killing or creating permanent health problems: a humane weapon, if there is such a thing. Such a weapon with a neutralizing agent delivered with great precision would be readily acceptable by those who have had experience on the battlefield in the past—the soldiers in the infantry.[20]

In short, the era of the nuclear weapon may be ending. It is so frightening that its use has never materialized since August 1945. Scenarios for the future do not give assurance that it will ever be used again, but if it is, there seem to be better ways to respond—political, economic, or military—than with another nuclear weapon. Adding to the questionable future of the nuclear weapon is the emerging threat of even more frightening weapons from the biochemical century. There is hope that the biochemists will make significant progress in the development of more humane weapons and of effective counters to any technological threats that develop.

It is comforting that the United States has a reliable nuclear weapons deterrent in the highly survivable nuclear powered submarines armed with the most capable Trident ballistic missile, backed by the land-based ICBMs and the long-range bombers. Under this Trident/triad umbrella, the nation should be able to find a better way to deter, persuade, or even retaliate than using nuclear weapons. The best use of the bomb may be the provision of this umbrella.

The Bottom Line

My last reflection on the carrier nuclear experience has to do with the capability of the carriers and the weapons. The fleet of aircraft carriers in the year 2000, centered on the USS *Nimitz* class, with plans and facilities to incorporate future technological improvements, is certainly a solid element in our defense establishment. There is finally in existence a capability that has been envisioned for years, a stable mobile aviation base that can stay at sea for years at a time if required, manned with competent people and an offensive/defensive capability that is not hampered by weather, night conditions, or international political constraints.

The marriage of the bomb and the carrier faced some rough waters in the beginning. There was not even a honeymoon. However, with hard work, good leadership, and many sacrifices, a healthy effective relationship developed—one that served the nation well. Eventually, for political reasons, the marriage was terminated by presidential mandate, thereby allowing the carrier to again enjoy the freedom and flexibility so inherent in its nature. The nuclear weapon has continued to mature, growing more sophisticated, but still serving a limited although important role in national defense. It has continued to provide a security umbrella under which much of civilized life can prosper as it struggles with the emerging problems of the twenty-first century. Following the mandated separation of the carrier and the nuclear weapon, the carrier appears to be more attractive than ever and highly relevant to national defense. The bomb, on the other hand, while still robust and highly efficient, may be losing much of its relevance.

Notes

Introduction
1. I was just completing my tour of duty as the commanding officer of the 50,000-ton aircraft carrier *Franklin D. Roosevelt*. We had concentrated on night and all-weather operations, and our ship seemed to be a good candidate for receiving the Flatley Award for operational competence, easily won if a carrier conducted frequent flight operations at night—safely.
2. We were fortunate, but it was undoubtedly the lowest moment in my professional career. After ascertaining that all was under control, I turned on the ship's intercommunications circuit, asked for quiet, and then apologized to the crew for the early and rather unique reveille. I hastened to point out that I was the cause of the collision; that the officer-of-the-deck, the helmsman, the bridge crew, the engineering watch—all had performed in a highly professional manner; that I alone was responsible, and I apologized for putting a stain on our reputation as a professional operating outfit.
3. As with any collision, an investigation was conducted. The investigating officer was a senior captain, the commander of a division of destroyers. He came aboard, and we met in my sea cabin. He asked a couple of questions, and I told him that everyone had performed perfectly, that I was the sole cause of the mishap. That concluded the investigation, and we spent the rest of the time talking about golf handicaps. However, I seriously considered ending my career. I was

forty-six years old; it was time to start thinking about another way of life.
4. Vice Adm. Herbert Riley, USN, "Oral History," U.S. Naval Institute, Annapolis.
5. Following the atomic bomb drops on Japan, Blandy was placed in charge of a newly created division on the Staff of the Chief of Naval Operations. It was named the Atomic Operations Division, initially designated with the code number OP-06. While in this position, Blandy was appointed by the Joint Chiefs of Staff to head up the initial atomic bomb tests held at the Bikini Atoll in the Pacific in the summer of 1946. Spike Blandy, a key member of the gun club, added much to our understanding of the capabilities and impact of atomic weapons.
6. This all came after Burke's outstanding performance as the leader of a destroyer division in combat in the Pacific and as the chief of staff to Vice Adm. Marc Mitscher in the employment of the fast carrier task forces during World War II. He also distinguished himself as a captain by being a major participant in the so-called revolt of the admirals in 1949, wherein the Navy, particularly naval aviation, battled for a role in strategic warfare.
7. Adm. Arleigh A. Burke, USN, "Winning Naval Battles," *Wings of Gold*, fall 1984, 20. Association of Naval Aviation, Alexandria, Va.
8. Horacio Rivero entered the Naval Academy with the class of 1931. He was from Puerto Rico and initially had some difficulty with the English language. However, he graduated with distinction and was nominated for a Rhodes scholarship at Oxford. In those days, if a graduate were accepted at Oxford, he had to resign his commission and leave the Navy. Rivero wanted to be a naval officer, so he rejected the nomination. During the early years of World War II, following graduate schooling at the Massachusetts Institute of Technology, Lieutenant (then) Rivero negotiated and let the contracts with industry for all of the fire-control radars procured by the Navy for use in its ships during the war.
9. Personal conversation between the author and Admiral Moorer, spring 1997. Moorer's World War II experiences were unique, to say the least. Shot down by the Japanese while flying a patrol plane in the western Pacific, Moorer and his crew were rescued by a Philippine freighter, only to have to abandon the freighter when it was taken under attack by more Japanese aircraft. The freighter sank, but Moorer and his crew survived by sailing a lifeboat to an island in the area, where they were later rescued by an Australian warship.

10. Much of the material about Rear Admiral Parsons is from personal conversations with people who knew and served with him, and a biography, *Target Hiroshima: Deak Parsons and the Creation of the Atomic Bomb,* by Al Christman (Annapolis: U.S. Naval Institute Press, 1998). Parsons entered the Naval Academy with the class of 1922. His prior schooling consisting mostly of what he had received from his well-educated mother. He had a bent for the academic world, particularly science and physics. Following graduation, his assignment as an ensign was in the battleship USS *Nevada,* later the prime target in the first Bikini atomic bomb test. He then received his postgraduate education, followed by three more years in an old battleship, the USS *Texas.* Throughout some early battleship tours, Parsons strove to improve the ordnance capabilities of the ships, particularly antiaircraft defense. His studies and experience eventually led to the development of the proximity fuse, a revolutionary achievement that contributed much to the improvement of antiaircraft defenses. Not only a brilliant physicist, Parsons was also personable, a true gentleman, highly respected by his civilian peers and revered by his military associates, both senior and junior.
11. Connolly was in the class of 1933 at the Naval Academy. He served in large patrol flying boats during World War II. Following the war, he commanded one of the early nuclear-capable carrier aircraft squadrons. Much later, he headed naval aviation and was the champion of the Navy's famed F-14 Tomcat interceptor aircraft.

Chapter 1. The Beginning
1. Most of the material concerning Vice Admiral Ashworth's role in the development of the atom bomb and its delivery on targets in Japan is taken from his excellent manuscript, "Oral History," on file at the U.S. Naval Institute, Annapolis. Coupled with that are numerous conversations and written correspondence between the author and Ashworth, covering several years.

    Vice Adm. Frederick Lincoln Ashworth is a naval officer from the old school, a true officer and gentleman, sometimes referred to as the most "humble" naval aviator in our nation's history. He was graduated from the U.S. Naval Academy in 1933, served a tour of duty in a battleship, and was designated a naval aviator in 1936, serving in carrier-based squadrons. Before World War II, he completed postgraduate training in aviation ordnance engineering, thus gaining entry into the

elite gun club of the Navy. World War II flying assignments included command of Torpedo Squadron 11, conducting combat operations out of Henderson Field in Guadalcanal. He then had duty as a staff officer with the Commander Amphibious Force, Pacific Fleet, participating in the invasions of Tarawa, Makin, the Gilbert Islands, Kwajalein, Roi Namur, and Eniwetok.
2. Lt. Gen. Leslie Groves, *Now It Can Be Told* (New York: Harper & Brothers, 1962).
3. Ashworth, "Oral History."
4. Ibid.
5. Paul Tibbets, "Enola Gay, and the Bomb," interview by George E. Hicks, *Aviation History,* September 1995; and C. V. Glines, "The Bomb that Ended World War II," *Aviation History,* September 1995.

Chapter 2. Policy and Strategy

1. Michael O. Wheeler, "The Evolution of Harry Truman's and Dwight D. Eisenhower's Views on Nuclear Weapons as an Instrument of National Security Policy, 1945–1955," paper presented at the Annual Meeting of the Society for Historians of American Foreign Relations, Georgetown University, June 1997, endnote 5.
2. Ibid., endnote 3.
3. Conversation with Gen. Andrew Goodpaster, USA (Ret.), 20 August 1998. General Goodpaster served as the executive secretary to President Eisenhower for almost the entire Eisenhower administration.
4. Demetrios Caraley, *The Politics of Military Unification* (New York: Columbia University Press, 1966), 100.
5. Ibid., 49.
6. Ibid., 151.
7. Information Planning Associates, *Cold War Navy* (Falls Church, Va., 1976), chapter 1. A report prepared for the chief of information, Department of the Navy.
8. Ibid., 4–8.
9. Ibid., 4–20.
10. Jeffrey G. Barlow, *The Revolt of the Admirals: The Fight for Naval Aviation, 1945–1950* (Washington, D.C.: Naval Historical Center, 1994). Barlow presents a complete account of the arguments about the atomic bomb delivery mission.
11. William S. Parsons, "Nuclear Energy for the Navy," memo to his immediate superior in the Navy Department, 28 March 1946. Author's files.

12. Jerauld Wright, "Authorization for Carrier Planes to Carry Atomic Bombs," memo addressed to the operations directorate, Navy Department, Office of the Chief of Naval Operations, 12 June 1946.
13. Personal official letter, Rear Adm. Jerauld Wright to Vice Adm. W. H. P. Blandy, 2 August 1946, Navy Department, Washington, D.C.
14. Telephone conversation between Vice Admiral Hayward and the author on 23 February 1999.
15. Ashworth, "Oral History."
16. Rear Adm. Daniel Gallery, "Oral History," U.S. Naval Institute, Annapolis, 212. Gallery attended the Naval Academy, graduating in 1921. He participated in the Olympics in 1920 as a wrestler, reaching the quarterfinals, the first loss of a match in his wrestling career. He spent about seven years in surface ships before joining naval aviation. Eventually, he attended postgraduate school, majoring in aviation ordnance, thereby qualifying as a member of the gun club. His interest was in bombsights and rockets.

    Rear Admiral Gallery's career as a naval officer was colorful. A prolific writer, he wrote sea stories, a biography, and serious articles on the future of warfare. He is famous for deliberately planning and executing the capture of a German submarine during World War II. The submarine is now on display at the Chicago Museum of Science and Industry.

    It is highly doubtful that Gallery could have survived the political climate of the 1990s, for his actions in support of the Navy were sometimes anything but politically correct. He was often in hot water with the civil authority in the Department of Defense because his concepts did not always fit with the party line. He certainly did not concur with the proposed strategy for nuclear warfare that was being adopted by the civil authority. He was very serious in his contention that the Navy, with carriers and submarines, was a more appropriate force for the delivery of atomic weapons than the Air Force, with its long-range bombers.
17. Barlow, *Revolt,* 326.
18. Gallery, "Oral History," 133–34.
19. Greg Herken, *The Winning Weapon: The Atomic Bomb in the Cold War, 1945–1950* (Princeton: Princeton University Press, 1981), 290.
20. Rear Adm. George Miller, "Oral History," U.S. Naval Institute, Annapolis, 40–100. A graduate of the Naval Academy with the class of 1933, Miller's wartime service included one spectacular event, saving the cruiser USS *Houston* following not one but two separate torpedo

attacks on successive days off the island of Okinawa. Many lives were lost, but many were saved as well. The story of George Miller and the saving of the *Houston* was a particularly inspiring lesson for personnel going through ship damage-control training. For his heroic acts, Miller was awarded the Navy Cross. He was a good man who devoted his career to concepts in which he believed very strongly. Further, he did it without rancor or bitterness toward the opposition, for whom he always had respect. He was truly thinking of the good of the country, not himself or the U.S. Navy.
21. This information is based on an airborne-alert flight by the author in 1959.
22. Personal conversations between the author and Admiral Moorer, 1998.
23. Ashworth, "Oral History."

Chapter 3. Weapons

1. Adm. Horacio Rivero, USN (Ret.), "Oral History," U.S. Naval Institute, Annapolis.
2. Ibid.
3. Vice Adm. Frederick Ashworth, USN (Ret.), letter to the author, 4 November 1996.
4. Ashworth, "Oral History."
5. Chairman's Office, *The Effects of Atomic Bombs on Hiroshima and Nagasaki: The United States Strategic Bombing Survey* (Washington, D.C.: U.S. Government Printing Office, 1946).
6. Adm. Thomas H. Moorer, USN (Ret.), conversations and correspondence with the author, November and December 1996.
7. Office of the Historian, Joint Task Force One, *Operations Crossroads: The Official Pictorial Record* (New York: Wm. H. Wise, 1946), 8.
8. Vice Adm. John T. Hayward, USN (Ret.), "The Atomic Bomb Goes to Sea," *The Hook*, summer 1981. Tail Hook Association, San Diego. Gen. Giulio Douhet of the Italian army was an early air power strategist.
9. *Operations Crossroads*, 8.
10. Ashworth, "Oral History."
11. *Operations Crossroads*, 9, 105, 106.
12. Ibid., 118.
13. Ibid., 8.
14. Ibid., 161.
15. Ibid., 6.

16. Ibid., 7.
17. Chuck Hansen, *U.S. Nuclear Weapons: The Secret History* (New York: Crown Publishers, 1988), 123.
18. Ibid., 52.
19. Dr. Henry Lowenhaupt, letter to the author, 20 July 1999. Late in World War II, Lowenhaupt, a young researcher with a doctorate in chemistry at Yale University, suddenly found himself drafted. He had been researching isotopes, and the Army, realizing it had a prize, placed him on General Groves's staff as a sergeant in civilian clothes at Oak Ridge, Tennessee. His first assignment was to develop intelligence on the German atomic effort and later to study the massive effort under Stalin in the Soviet Union. He became a key member of the technical intelligence community and has devoted much of his adult life to that vocation.
20. Doyle L. Northrup and Donald H. Rock, "The Detection of Joe 1," *CIA Historical Review Program* 10 (fall 1966). A declassified version was released on 18 September 1995.
21. Henry Lowenhaupt, oral and written communication with the author, 1998 and 1999. Following the war, Lowenhaupt was moved to the Central Intelligence Agency and became part of the organization that kept tabs on Soviet nuclear activity. At one time, this included targeting for the U-2 intelligence plane, which brought home some very useful data until one plane was shot down by a Soviet missile. That was the famous Gary Powers incident, which caused some embarrassment for President Eisenhower. As it became obvious that the Soviet Union would never accept any form of international control over the atomic issue and was bent on developing its own capability, more attention had to be paid to Soviet actions.
22. Hansen, *U.S. Nuclear Weapons*, 60.
23. Ibid., 68.
24. Ibid.
25. Ibid., 81.
26. Capt. Georges LeBlanc, USN (Ret.), audiotape to the author, fall 1997. Following his fascinating experiences with testing, LeBlanc was assigned to Air Development Squadron 5 (VX-5) at China Lake, California. He was involved mainly in the development of delivery techniques for conventional weapons, techniques that stood him in good stead later during combat service in the Vietnam campaign in 1967 and 1969.

27. Hansen, *U.S. Nuclear Weapons*, 105.
28. Greg Herken, *Cardinal Choices: Presidential Science Advising from the Atomic Bomb to SDI* (New York: Oxford University Press, 1992), 135.
29. Ashworth, "Oral History."
30. Robert Norris and Thomas Cochran, *US–USSR/Russian Strategic Offensive Nuclear Forces, 1945–1996* (Washington, D.C.: Natural Resources Defense Council, 1997), table 1.
31. "Nuclear Notebook," *Bulletin of Atomic Scientists,* July/August 1987, 64.
32. Alain C. Enthoven and K. Wayne Smith, *How Much Is Enough? Shaping the Defense Program, 1961–1969* (New York: Harper and Row, 1971), 207–10.
33. Hansen, *U.S. Nuclear Weapons*, 110.
34. Gen. Andrew Goodpaster, USA (Ret.), remarks dated 23 April 1998 and presented at a conference of the National War College Alumni Association at MacDill Air Force Base, Tampa, Florida, obtained from the Alumni Association, National War College, Fort McNair, Washington, D.C. General Goodpaster has to be classed as one of the great military officers of the twentieth century. A distinguished graduate of West Point in 1939, he rapidly established his abilities as a thinker, earning a doctorate from Princeton after World War II. He served in operational assignments involving combat, eventually rising to become the supreme commander of NATO and U.S. forces in Europe. In his many tours of service, he has been ever conscious of the nuclear weapon and its challenges, utilizing his authority to improve the readiness of our forces, including NATO, for the use of such weapons if they were ever needed. Quite possibly, Goodpaster's greatest contributions are a result of his service as executive secretary to President Eisenhower. He served the president for almost the entire eight years that Eisenhower was in office.
35. Adm. Noel Gayler, USN (Ret.), personal conversations with the author over a period of many years. Also, *Honolulu Advertiser,* January 1989.
36. Gen. George Lee Butler, USAF (Ret.), address to the National Press Club, Washington, D.C., 2 February 1998 (Washington, D.C.: Webber Professional Media Consulting, bwebber@erols.com); R. Jeffrey Smith, "The Dissenter," *Washington Post Magazine,* 7 December 1997.
37. Ashworth, "Oral History."
38. Correspondence ("Top Secret" declassified) of the Manhattan Engineer District, 1942–46, National Archives of the United States, 3.

39. Ibid.
40. Ashworth, "Oral History."
41. Correspondence ("Top Secret" declassified) of the Manhattan Engineer District, 1942–46, National Archives of the United States, 3.
42. Appendix D to a now unclassified official Navy document titled "The Custody Dispute," from the files of Vice Admiral Ashworth. It is an excellent eleven-page account of the custody dispute between the Atomic Energy Commission and the Department of Defense, which lasted for over twenty years.
43. Ibid., 9.
44. Ibid., 10.
45. Ibid.
46. Lt. Gen. Ernest Graves, USA (Ret.), *Engineer Memoirs* (Alexandria, Va.: U.S. Army, Office of History, U.S. Army Corps of Engineers, 1997), 35. Graves's career found him rotating between straight civil engineering and nuclear engineering tasks. A traditional army officer, his grandfather graduated from West Point with the class of 1872, standing number one; his father was in the class of 1905, standing number two; and Ernest graduated with the class of 1944, standing number two. His oldest son graduated with the class of 1974, standing number one. That is probably a record of many sorts. Following duty assembling nuclear weapons, Graves went on to receive a Ph.D. in physics from the Massachusetts Institute of Technology. Subsequently, he was assigned to a nuclear weapons research organization that built a nuclear reactor at Fort Belvoir in northern Virginia. In 1959 Graves became a research associate in the Plowshare Program at the Lawrence Radiation Laboratory in Livermore, California, where he learned about the peaceful uses of nuclear explosives, including a study of the feasibility of constructing a sea-level canal across the Isthmus of Panama. In 1973 he became the director of military applications in the Atomic Energy Commission and was responsible for all U.S. nuclear weapons development, testing, and production, and also cooperated with the British government's nuclear weapons program. His early days as an assembler of nuclear weapons set the path for his illustrious career.
47. Don Micco (historian of the Navy Nuclear Weapons Association, Geneva on the Lake, Ohio), letters and articles to the author, 1998.
48. James N. Gibson, *Nuclear Weapons of the United States: An Illustrated History* (Atglen, Pa.: Schiffer Publishing), 90. Also see Hansen, *U.S. Nuclear Weapons,* 137.

49. Hansen, *U.S. Nuclear Weapons,* 106, 107, 154.
50. Ibid., 110.
51. Capt. D. K. "Deke" Ela, USN (Ret.), letter to the author, 25 June 1997.
52. Conversation between Dr. George Kistiakowsky, President Eisenhower's science advisor, and the author at Harvard University in 1975, following discussions about the nation's national nuclear warfare plan.

Chapter 4. Heavy Attack

1. Al Christman, *Target Hiroshima: Deak Parsons and the Creation of the Atomic Bomb* (Annapolis: Naval Institute Press, 1998).
2. Official letter from Rear Admiral Parsons, then deputy commander of Joint Task Force 7, to the chairman of the General Board, Department of the Navy, Washington, D.C., 23 April 1948. Author's files.
3. Record of conversation between Commodore (then) Parsons and Admiral Purnell, 19 September 1945. Author's files.
4. Ashworth, "Oral History."
5. Vice Adm. John T. Hayward, "Oral History," U.S. Naval Institute, Annapolis.
6. "Flight Log," *Foundation,* fall 1996, 43. Naval Aviation Museum Foundation, Pensacola, Fla.
7. Ashworth, "Oral History."
8. Hayward, *"Atomic Bomb Goes to Sea,"* 22.
9. Rear Adm. E. L. Feightner, interview with author, 22 January 1997.
10. Feightner and Herzberger, conversations with author, 1998.
11. Feightner, interview with author, 22 January 1997.
12. Ashworth, "Oral History."
13. Herken, *Winning Weapon,* 334.
14. Ashworth, "Oral History."
15. Capt. Frank Ault, USN (Ret.), letter to the author, 24 March 1999. Captain Ault was one of the many outstanding officers brought into the heavy-attack program at an early stage. Standing high in math in his Naval Academy class of 1943 and a carrier aviator, he was a natural for selection to this new atomic bomb delivery program. He spent some time with Hyman Rickover during his career and considers that one of his own marks of distinction is to have been branded by Rickover as "the most irreverent officer" he had ever interviewed for entry into the Navy's nuclear propulsion-power program.
16. Ibid.

17. Ibid.
18. Ashworth, "Oral History."
19. Radford later became head of the Pacific Fleet and led the Navy team in the roles and missions controversy, which evolved into an argument over the B-36 strategic bomber versus the "super carrier," the USS *United States*. Eventually, President Eisenhower selected Radford as chairman of the Joint Chiefs of Staff.
20. Ashworth, "Oral History."
21. George Spangenberg to the author, 15 November 1996, 21 December 1996, and 9 July 1999. Spangenberg has a prominent place in naval aviation history. Starting as a newly graduated aeronautical engineer at the Naval Aircraft Factory in Pennsylvania in the mid-1930s, he soon found himself deeply involved in some fascinating aviation projects, in which he performed exceedingly well. World War II brought him to Washington, D.C., where for many years he was the "evaluator" of contractors' proposals to the Navy's Bureau of Aeronautics for the development of aircraft to satisfy the Navy's requirements. Naval aviators admired him and respected his forthright contributions. They designated him Honorary Naval Aviator number twelve at his retirement, the first civil servant employee to be so honored.
22. Capt. William Scarborough, USN (Ret), "The North American AJ Savage," *The Hook,* fall 1989, 28. Tailhook Association, San Diego.
23. Ashworth, "Oral History."
24. Scarborough, "North American AJ Savage," 34.
25. Ibid., 37.
26. Ashworth, "Oral History."
27. Capt. Kenneth "Doc" Gulledge, USN (Ret.), audiotape, 12 January 1997, and letter to the author, 4 February 1997. Gulledge is another example of the emphasis on quality in the selection of personnel for heavy-attack duties. A member of the Naval Academy class of 1942, he joined VC-7 in 1952. He logged almost six hundred hours in the AJ aircraft and liked its flying qualities. He thought that it was stable in the carrier landing, but on almost every flight, some difficulty occurred. He went on to command one of the A-3 squadrons stationed in the Pacific and thought it was one of the best carrier airplanes ever designed for the Navy.
28. Ibid.
29. Ashworth, "Oral History."
30. Edward H. Heinemann and Rosario Rausa, *Ed Heinemann, Combat*

Aircraft Designer (Annapolis, Md.: Naval Institute Press, 1980), 201, 206, 207.
31. Paul F. Stevens, *Low Level Liberators* (Nashville: Paul Stevens, 1997). Paul Stevens is unique, even for a naval aviator. Commissioned in 1941, he was flying a patrol plane out of Midway Island during the Japanese attack on Pearl Harbor. Later combat took place in the New Guinea–Bismarck Sea area as he was flying in the famous Black Cats program—patrol aircraft that specialized in night operations. His second combat tour was as executive officer of a land-based patrol squadron flying the PB4Y-1 Liberator, a four-engine armed reconnaissance aircraft. He and his crew were able to shoot down several enemy airplanes, scored bomb hits on a Japanese heavy cruiser, and shot down Admiral Yamagata of the Imperial Japanese Navy. He was awarded the Navy Cross, two Silver Stars, the Distinguished Flying Cross, and various other decorations. Stevens was a fighter pilot in a four-engine reconnaissance aircraft.
32. Stevens to the author, 8 January 1997.
33. Letter to Paul Stevens, 27 December 1956, as Stevens left VAH-1 for new duties at Patuxent River, Maryland.
34. Stevens to the author, 8 February 1998. Stevens went on to command two aircraft carrier squadrons and an air wing. He logged over 17,000 flight hours during his Navy career and role as a corporate chief pilot in civilian life.
35. Joe Dorrington flew anti–submarine warfare missions in shore-based and float-equipped aircraft during World War II. He was selected early for the heavy-attack program, going first with Chick Hayward to VC-5 at Moffett Field in California and later with Dick Ashworth in VC-6 at Patuxent River, Maryland. During a tour in Washington, he was involved in the nuclear weapons business and made contacts that he freely admits enabled him to lobby successfully for command of the first A-3 squadron.
36. Bill Spiegel spent the early years of World War II in the surface Navy, participating in the Battle of the Coral Sea, and then the Guadalcanal, Tarawa, and Kwajalein campaigns. He was designated a naval aviator during the latter part of the war. Following two years of carrier duty, he attended postgraduate training and received his master's degree from MIT. Spiegel later commanded VAH-1. He participated in all phases of the heavy-attack program, as a bombardier/navigator and pilot in the P2V, and as a pilot with the AJ at Port Lyautey, then with

the A-3. His specialty in ordnance made him a key factor in the provision and proper utilization of the ASB-1 high-altitude bombing system in the AJ and A-3 aircraft. In his shore duty assignments, he was involved in the heavy-attack program and the ASB-1 bombing system, accumulating a continuous ten-year record with the heavy-attack program.

37. From the cruise book report of the USS *Forrestal* deployment in the Mediterranean in 1957.
38. Commander, U.S. Sixth Fleet, message 301605Z, August 1957.
39. Rear Adm. James D. Ramage, USN (Ret.), "Taking A-Bombs to Sea," *Naval History,* January/February 1995, 34. U.S. Naval Institute, Annapolis. Ramage graduated from the U.S. Naval Academy in 1939. He fought hard to get into carrier aviation and flew the vintage Douglas SBD Dauntless in combat during World War II. Known as an "operator," he has sometimes been identified as one who believes that if you did not fly an SBD during World War II, you are not a real naval aviator. But Ramage was a lot more than a dedicated, die-hard dive-bomber pilot. He was a conceptual thinker. A treatise he wrote in 1947 at the Naval War College is one of the early pieces stressing the need for naval aviation to move into the atomic weapons delivery business. Rear Adm. James D. Ramage, *The Atom Bomb and the Fast Carrier Task Force* (Newport: U.S. Naval War College, 1947).
40. Ramage to the author, 2 May 1996.
41. Ashworth, "Oral History."
42. Information about the A-3 aircraft operations in the Pacific is from a collection of papers submitted to the author on 27 January 1997 by Capt. Charles Chute, USN (Ret.). Chute served for five years in five different surface ships before completing flight training and serving in the Korean War in a jet fighter squadron. He joined VAH-4 in November 1958.
43. Capt. Frank Ault, USN (Ret.), to the author, 8 June 1998.
44. Vice Adm. Kent Lee, USN (Ret.), "Oral History," 287–89, U.S. Naval Institute, Annapolis. Kent Lee entered the Navy from high school, served as an enlisted man, was designated a naval aviator, and saw combat during World War II. After the war, the Navy provided him with an excellent education, and he became very involved in the nuclear weapons business as an instructor in Norfolk, as a delivery pilot, and later targeting weapons at the Strategic Air Command headquarters in Omaha, Nebraska. He progressed in rank to commander, Naval

Air Systems Command, and became a leading advocate of the F/A-18 Hornet carrier aircraft.
45. Capt. Richard Davidson, USN (Ret.), to the author, 1997. Davidson sincerely enjoyed the heavy-attack program. He started his flying career in patrol planes by choice, wanting to be associated with the "big stuff." By the time he was selected for the heavy-attack program, he was a young officer with more than 2,500 flying hours, including time in various carrier types. He was a fully qualified instrument pilot, having the experience that Chick Hayward must have had in mind when he started the heavy-attack program. He served as executive officer for Paul Stevens in an AJ squadron. He was a member of VAH-1 during its impressive deployment with the A-3 in 1957. Spiegel thought Davidson was "one of the best." His experience with the A-5 aircraft was limited since the airplane was in the inventory as a bomber for a relatively short period of time, but he later commanded a squadron using the reconnaissance version of the plane, the RA5C. Davidson was impressed with the crew concept in flying, half jesting that fighter pilots were psychologically unsuited for heavy attack, that they had giant egos and were trained to do everything by themselves. Upon retirement from the Navy, he joined Paul Stevens in the corporate aviation business.
46. Chute to the author, 1997.
47. Ibid. Loft maneuvers will be discussed in chapter 6.
48. Vice Adm. Richard Dunleavy, USN (Ret.), audiotape to the author, 27 May 1998.
49. Ibid.
50. Ibid.
51. Dick Dunleavy was one of the fortunate ones. Starting as the bombardier/navigator with Bill Spiegel in VAH-1, he progressed up the ladder, eventually commanding an A-6 attack squadron, a deep-draft ship, and the attack carrier USS *Coral Sea*. He later became deputy chief of naval operations for air warfare, the head of naval aviation in the Navy.

Chapter 5. Light Attack
1. The information about early efforts to gain a light-attack delivery capability is taken from Ramage, "Taking A-Bombs to Sea," 30ff.
2. Letters to the author from Capt. John Iler, USN (Ret.), 27 August 1996 and 10 July 1999. Also, phone conversation with Rear Adm. William Leonard, USN (Ret.), on 27 March 1999.

Notes to Pages 132–148   **277**

3. Letter to the author from Capt. Robert Hunt, USN (Ret.), 19 February 1997. In his early career, Hunt flew the SBD in World War II and spent two tours of duty as a test pilot at Patuxent River, Maryland. He gained extensive experience with both the A-4 and the FJ-4B aircraft as he commanded a squadron and an air group. His senior years were involved with carrier operations as a staff member and in command of the USS *Boxer* (LPH-4).
4. Feightner interview and audiotape.
5. Conversation with Feightner, 1998.
6. Hunt letter.
7. Letter from Comdr. Richard King, USN (Ret.), to the author, 17 January 1999. King was a U.S. Naval Academy graduate, who, like many of his classmates, spent the early years of World War II in surface ships. His career in naval aviation concentrated on night and all-weather flying.
8. From a collection of notes and papers prepared by Capt. William Chapman, USN (Ret.), and forwarded to the author under cover of letters, 1 and 3 January 1997 and 15 August 1999. Chapman is a Naval Academy graduate whose naval service included a tour of duty in the Soviet Union and duties on the staff of the commander of the U.S. Sixth Fleet in the Mediterranean, targeting nuclear weapons. Later, he spent four years with Attack Squadron 63 (VA-63), first flying the F9F-8 Cougar and then the FJ-4B Fury.
9. Ibid.
10. Ibid.
11. Ibid.
12. Hunt letter.
13. Information about the early days of the A-6 aircraft is taken from personal conversations in 1999 with Mr. George Spangenberg, who was the evaluator of aircraft programs in the Navy's Bureau of Aeronautics during the initiation of the A-6 program.
14. Conversations between the author and Rear Admiral Snead, USN (Ret.), 1999.
15. Information about the tactical employment of the A-6 is taken from a letter to the author, 26 March 1997, from Lt. Joel Febel, a member of the squadron during its first deployment to Vietnam. Upon completion of the deployment, Lieutenant Febel married. A few days later, the wings of his A-6 folded during takeoff from a shore station. His subsequent unbelievable recovery from the accident is a story in itself.

16. From an audiotape provided to the author by Douglas Lee Miller (former lieutenant, USN), an ROTC graduate from the University of Rochester. Miller spent eight years in naval aviation, almost all of it in the cockpit of the A-7E, deeply involved with the nuclear weapons delivery capability. He served as weapons training officer and weapons safety officer. Miller is my oldest son. We believe that we are the only father/son members of the Caterpillar Club, composed of people who have been forced to exit an aircraft in flight under emergency conditions. I ejected from a Grumman F9F-5 Panther jet in 1952 over the mountains in southern California. Doug's ejection from an A-7E Corsair II occurred about twenty years later off the Philippine Islands. We were fortunate that we incurred no injuries.
17. I was fortunate to command the U.S. Second Fleet, an operational command that controlled forces in the Atlantic only when special exercises were being conducted or when units were en route to and from the Mediterranean or Indian Ocean. In times of war, it would be a massive fleet, but in peacetime, it concentrated mostly on training operations. The command also held a NATO role under the supreme allied commander, Atlantic (SACLant). In that capacity, the fleet commander was known as the commander, Striking and Support Forces, Atlantic (ComStrikeForLant). Wearing that hat, I made occasional visits to the NATO command headquarters of the Northern NATO commander (CinCNorth) in Norway and the commander of the central region (CinCCent) in Belgium. During an early visit to CinCCent, I had official discussions with the commander-in-chief, a German general, about problems in the Central European Theater. The general pointed out that he needed more tactical air power. I told him that the Striking and Support Forces that I represented could not solve all his problems, but that we could certainly provide something in the way of support. That resulted in plans to have a carrier conduct operations from the Bay of Biscay, off Spain, and the North Sea, off Great Britain, sending naval elements into NATO air-control theaters for simulated conventional and nuclear attacks on "enemy" targets.
18. Vice Adm. Robert Dunn, USN (Ret.), "The Nuclear Bomb and Me," a paper prepared for this book. Bob Dunn was associated with nuclear weapons in one way or another for most of his Navy career. He is a Naval Academy graduate who held many command positions as he rose through the ranks to become the deputy chief of naval operations for air warfare, the head of naval aviation. At the time of the naval air participation in NATO exercises in central Europe in 1971, he was an

air wing commander in the Mediterranean. He represented the Navy at the planning conference for the exercises.

Chapter 6. Delivery Tactics

1. Ashworth, "Oral History," and conversation between the author and Ashworth, 15 December 1997.
2. Gallery, "Oral History," 30–35.
3. Conversation between the author and Ashworth, 15 December 1997.
4. Vice Adm. Thomas Walker, "Early VX-5," 1–3, a paper prepared for this book and forwarded to the author on 2 January 1997.
5. Ibid.
6. Ibid., 4.
7. Ibid.
8. Joseph Schwager, a close friend of the pilot, in a letter to the author, 15 May 1999.
9. Joseph Schwager, *LABS*, a paper dated 29 December 1997, prepared for this book.
10. Ibid., and an amplifying letter, 15 May 1999. Joe Schwager continued with his work in weapons development and delivery. He spent six years at the Lawrence Radiation Lab in Livermore, California, working in close contact with some of the finest leaders in nuclear weapons research, including Edward Teller. With encouragement from his contemporaries, he received his doctoral degree in physics. He participated in some weapons tests at Eniwetok, which motivated him to look for ways to deliver weapons that would not involve targeting of launch bases on the U.S. mainland. He concentrated on ways to use the Navy's submarine-launched ballistic missile, the Polaris. Two schemes were considered: configuring the missile like a mine; and launching or seeding it like a depth charge from surface ships, that is, by rolling it off the aft gunwale or fantail of a ship. The Air Force later became interested and considered the use of the Minuteman ICBM as a sea-launched weapon. Schwager had one more tour of duty with VX-5, concentrating on the delivery of conventional weapons. One interesting technique that he worked on was "loop bombing," which emanated from the OTS maneuver. He retired after twenty years in the Navy, taking his talents to the International Business Machines Corporation in New York. Ironically, his first assignment in civilian life was to digitize the analog computer Low Altitude Bombing System gear, the system on which he had worked so much while on active duty.

11. Ramage, "Taking A-Bombs to Sea."
12. From an audiotape of an interview by the author with Feightner, 22 January 1997. Feightner entered naval aviation in July 1941, earned his wings, and deployed directly to combat duty in the Pacific. He was credited with nine confirmed victories and four "probables" in air-to-air combat, earning four Distinguished Flying Crosses. He was a graduate of the second class at the Test Pilot School at Patuxent River, Maryland. He first became involved with nuclear weapon issues when he was at the Test Center in 1949–52. The project involved testing the Mark VII nuclear weapon on the F2H Banshee. Feightner is one of only twenty-three members of the Naval Test Pilots Hall of Honor.
13. Vice Adm. Donald D. Engen, USN (Ret.), *Wings and Warriors: My Life as a Naval Aviator* (Washington, D.C.: Smithsonian Institution Press, 1997), 165. Following a brilliant career in the Navy, Engen served the federal government as a member of the National Transportation Safety Board and head of the Federal Aviation Administration. He was the director of the Smithsonian National Air and Space Museum at the time of his death in 1999, while flying a glider. Don Engen was the consummate aviator.
14. Feightner audiotape.
15. Ibid.
16. Ibid.
17. Ibid.
18. Comdr. James Reid, "Sandblower," *Wings of Gold,* spring 1998, 24. Association of Naval Aviation, Alexandria.
19. Capt. Charles MacDowell, USN (Ret.), a paper dated 21 January 1999, prepared for this book.
20. Joel Febel, a paper about A-6 aircraft operations, dated 26 March 1997 and delivered to the author.
21. Douglas L. Miller, audiotape dated 21 April 1997.
22. Ibid.
23. Ibid.
24. Ibid.

Chapter 7. Ships
1. Normal Polmar, *Aircraft Carriers: A Graphic History of Carrier Aviation and Its Influence on World Events* (Garden City, N.Y.: Doubleday, 1969), 731–38.

2. Riley, "Oral History," vol. 1, 366–75. All material concerning Secretaries Forrestal and Johnson is taken from Riley's oral history. Riley was a member of the Naval Academy class of 1927. As he rose through the ranks of naval aviation, he became known as an excellent administrator and aviator. He became the naval assistant to the first secretary of defense, James Forrestal. He was a member of Forrestal's personal staff of six. As such, he was in a unique position to observe and participate in the events leading to Secretary Forrestal's dismissal by President Truman and the selection, and subsequent actions, of Louis Johnson as Forrestal's successor. Riley considered that the time he spent with Forrestal was one of the most broadening periods of his life. It was his first experience with a mind like Forrestal's. Riley thought that Forrestal was far more capable of being president of the United States than Truman. When Truman replaced Forrestal with Louis Johnson, Riley expected to be reassigned to other duties. Much to his surprise, Johnson kept him on to serve as the naval aide. As a result, Riley was able to make an excellent comparison of these two initial incumbents in the powerful position of secretary of defense.
3. Ibid. Truman disliked Johnson personally, and he had every right to do so. He would not have appointed Johnson in the first place had Johnson not demanded the job as his "pound of flesh." Truman was well aware of Johnson's burning ambition to replace him as president, and that this personal ambition colored everything Johnson thought and did. Johnson ran hard for the presidency all of the time he was secretary of defense. That was evident from his many speeches, his publicity machine, and most of all, in his deliberate slashing of presidential and congressional military programs under the guise of "cutting fat, not muscle." He knew how to curry public favor and get votes. He wanted the secretary of defense job simply because the Defense Department had the largest increment of the national budget. The job would give him the greatest opportunity to "save the taxpayers" mammoth sums and thereby build his election platform. Korea crossed him up—and put him forever out of the government.
4. Both Ela and Small were graduates of the Naval Academy, Ela with the class of 1938 and Small with the class of 1942. Both received postgraduate education, Ela in naval architecture and marine engineering and Small in naval engineering, design. Both became engineering duty officers. Atomic weapons had a tremendous impact on the nature and volume of their workload. Because of their wartime experience and

their personal capabilities, they moved into positions of authority relatively early in their careers. Ela became the head of the major ship design branch in the Navy's Bureau of Ships in 1950, just twelve years out of the Naval Academy. He also had an interesting tour as the deputy for development at the nuclear weapons laboratory in Sandia. Small was involved in many of the early post–World War II innovations in carriers, particularly those associated with the introduction of jet aircraft.

5. Small to the author, 28 December 1996.
6. Ibid.
7. Ibid.
8. Ela to the author, 9 May 1997.
9. Small to the author, 28 December 1996.
10. Ela letter, 9 May 1997, and paper, 25 June 1997, to the author.
11. Ibid.
12. Ibid.
13. "Early History of the Special Weapons Organization," Headquarters 8460th Special Weapons Group, Sandia Base, 13, 25. This paper covers 1946–48.
14. Rear Adm. Robert McNitt, USN (Ret.), *Nuclear Weapons for Naval Aviation,* a paper dated 4 December 1997, submitted to the author. McNitt is another of those outstanding Naval Academy graduates, class of 1938, whose timing was such that he received considerable combat experience during World War II, serving in destroyers and submarines. Following the war, he received his postgraduate degree from MIT and was then assigned to duty for over two years as the gunnery officer on board the new carrier, USS *Midway,* which was the premier ship for the nuclear weapons delivery mission at that time. In that assignment, he was responsible for the stowage and assembly of nuclear weapons on board.
15. Small to the author, 28 December 1996.
16. Ibid. Also, Ela letter of 9 May 1997, and paper of 25 June 1997, to the author.
17. Ela paper of 25 June 1997.
18. Ibid.
19. Small to the author, 28 December 1996.
20. Ela paper of 25 June 1997.
21. Douglas L. Miller, audiotape dated 21 April 1997.
22. Information about CVN-77 and the CVNX series is taken from the Retired Flag Officer Symposium, conducted by the Office of the Chief of

Naval Operations (N-88) in Washington, D.C., on 16 March 1999. Also, see Rear Adm. William Cross II, USN, "Knowledge, Strength, Agility," *Sea Power Magazine,* June 1999, 27–30. U.S. Navy League, Arlington, Va.

Chapter 8. Testing the Capability

1. Barlow, *Revolt of the Admirals,* 95–103.
2. Rear Adm. Wendell "Windy" Switzer was in command. He was a wonderful gentleman who made some significant contributions to the Navy and his country, starting with two sons who were naval aviators. Both were lost in fatal accidents involving naval aircraft.
3. The three readiness inspections were planned and conducted by the author.
4. Personal interview with Vice Admiral McGinn, 7 April 1998, when he was in the Pentagon serving as the director of naval air warfare.
5. Conversation with John Beling, 1998.
6. Conversation with Don Engen, 1998. Also, Donald D. Engen, *Wings and Warriors* (Washington, D.C.: Smithsonian Institution Press, 1997), 320–22.

Chapter 9. Targeting

1. John Meyer was no slouch as a military officer. He was one of those young men who left college as World War II loomed and learned to fly fighter aircraft. He deployed to Europe, survived extensive combat, and became a leader at a very early age. He is credited with being the seventh leading all-time Air Force ace, destroying many aircraft in the air and on the ground in both World War II and Korea. Then he became involved in strategic bombing. He was a terrific leader in combat, adopting a set of principles that are born in combat service. Integrity was high on his list, and he tested his people for that quality. He was unpopular with a few who did not like his tough standards or tactics, but if you looked deeply into his cold, steel-blue eyes, you could see a sense of humor that was always near the surface. I liked the man, and so did my predecessor at the JSTPS, Vice Adm. Kent Lee, who had been there with me in the early 1960s under Gen. Thomas Power. There was a world of difference between the two men.
2. I had the opportunity to talk with President Ford during a seminar in Chicago in 1997. During our discussion, I asked him why he had

chosen to serve in the Navy during the war. He replied that it seemed logical. Michigan was a pro-Navy state, and many of his friends had joined. Every young man was going to join something, and it just seemed logical to choose the Navy.

Ford's performance as a naval officer has not been publicized much. Blowing his horn about what he did in the service does not seem to be a part of his character. He was a top-quality officer. I asked him about his first assignment as a junior officer. He had been ordered to the USS *Monterey,* a light aircraft carrier that saw quite a bit of combat, as did most carriers during World War II. Upon reporting aboard, he was assigned to a battle station in "after steering," about the lowest position one can be assigned. You are relegated to a post in the lower bowels of the ship near the rudder. If a steering casualty occurs and none of the various emergency systems work to steer the ship, the person assigned to after steering takes over and maneuvers the rudder on orders from the bridge or station controlling the ship. It is not a prestige assignment.

The former president said he had not remained with that battle-station assignment very long. With more prodding I got him to admit that his next battle station was as the "officer-of-the-deck" (OOD), the most responsible assignment a young officer can receive. The OOD executes the orders of the commanding officer as the ship fights its way into or out of trouble. You do not need much more than that on your resume to indicate your high quality as an officer and the trust of your superiors. Many politicians, including several presidents of the United States, served in the Navy in World War II. None could have had better credentials than Ford's: "OOD underway."

The commanding officer of the *Monterey* during Junior Officer Ford's time on board was the late Vice Adm. S. H. "Slim" Ingersoll. His daughter still recalls her father saying that Ford was "the best OOD that he had in the ship." Ingersoll had "complete confidence in Ford, who seemed to know instinctively what to do, thereby allowing the commanding officer to follow the combat action more closely and concentrate on the ship's operations." Ford held a position requiring the highest trust in his ability to stay in control under fire.

3. Richard Rhodes, *The Making of the Atomic Bomb* (New York: Simon and Schuster, 1986), 640–41.
4. Michael Wheeler, *Early U.S. Nuclear Doctrine and Command and Control* (Washington, D.C.: Scientific Associates International Corporation, 1998), 31.

5. Discussion of the JSTPS is based on the author's personal experience, first in the Atomic Operations Division of the Joint Staff serving the Joint Chiefs of Staff, and then as the initial representative of the chief of naval operations ordered to duty in the JSTPS. That was followed several years later by a second tour, as the deputy director of the staff.
6. This account is based on several unofficial meetings of the author during the 1970s and 1980s with members of a Soviet delegation. These meetings were concerned principally with arms control and were conducted in both the United States and the Soviet Union as part of a program conducted by the United Nations Association. The author was frequently quizzed on the capabilities of the carriers, which were obviously of great concern to the Soviets.
7. Groves, *Now It Can Be Told*.
8. Conversations between the author and Dr. Henry Lowenhaupt in 1998.
9. Kevin C. Ruffner, ed., *Corona: America's First Satellite Program* (Washington, D.C.: CIA Center for the Study of Intelligence, 1995), 49–50.
10. Ibid., 63–96.
11. Ashworth, "Oral History."
12. From a paper from Joel Febel dated 26 March 1997 and submitted to the author for this book.
13. Hunt letter.
14. Febel paper.
15. Douglas L. Miller, audiotape dated 21 April 1997.
16. Ibid.
17. Ibid.

Chapter 10. The Past, the Present, and the Future
1. Vice Adm. Gerald E. Miller, USN (Ret.), "Who Needs Arms Control?" *U.S. Naval Institute Proceedings*, January 1986, 39.
2. Ibid., 41.
3. Ken Adelman, "The Real Reagan," *Wall Street Journal*, 5 October 1999. Ken Adelman was the director of the Arms Control and Disarmament Agency in the Reagan administration.
4. David Hoffman, "Arms Control Damaged by War," *Washington Post*, 23 May 1999.
5. Much of the material concerning the current status of nuclear weapons in carriers is taken from an interview on 7 April 1998 with Rear Adm.

(then) Dennis McGinn, when he was the director of the Air Warfare Division on the Staff of the Chief of Naval Operations in the Pentagon.
6. Ibid. Emphasis added.
7. Ibid.
8. Ibid.

Chapter 11. Reflections

1. Personal conversation between the author and Vice Adm. William P. Lawrence when the latter was superintendent, U.S. Naval Academy.
2. From many conversations with Don Engen during the years of a close friendship, I gained an appreciation for a man who was not only a superb naval officer, but also the consummate aviator. Despite his experience as a combat pilot in World War II, a highly successful test pilot and developer of tactics, and the pilot of many general aviation and commercial aircraft, Don got his kicks from sailplanes. He often talked about the thrill of "soaring," getting into the cockpit of a powerless aircraft and working updrafts until he was at great heights. His favorite vacation experience was to go to Nevada and soar. His demise at age seventy-five while flying in a sailplane that disintegrated at high altitude was a tragic loss. But in retrospect, he was doing what he loved to do when the accident occurred.
3. Hansen, *U.S. Nuclear Weapons*, 7.
4. Ibid.
5. From conversations on the subject with Adm. Noel Gayler, spring 1999.
6. Daniel Patrick Moynihan, *Secrecy* (New Haven: Yale University Press, 1998), 227.
7. Riley, "Oral History."
8. *Washington Times*, 18 April 1995.
9. David Hoffman, "Kremlin to Bolster Nuclear Stockpile," *Washington Post*, 30 April 1999; Toni Marshall, "Yeltsin Orders Plans for Battlefield Nukes," *Washington Times*, 30 April 1999.
10. Dunn, "Nuclear Bomb and Me."
11. Ambassador James R. Lilley, "The U.S. and China in the 21st Century," address to the Institute of World Politics, Washington, D.C., 20 April 1999.
12. Ibid.
13. Comments in *Time Magazine* about the selection of Einstein as the man of the twentieth century, on C-Span radio/television, 26 December 1999, Washington, D.C.

14. "The Millennium: The Planet," *Washington Times,* 27 December 1999.
15. Associated Press, "Clinton Predicts New Cures, Insidious Weapons in Next Century," *Washington Post,* 28 December 1999.
16. William E. King IV, *Biological Warfare: Are U.S. Armed Forces Ready?* (Arlington, Va.: Institute of Land Warfare, Association of the U.S. Army, 1999), 1.
17. Ibid., v.
18. *Chemical Warfare: A Real and Growing Threat* (Arlington, Va.: Institute of Land Warfare, Association of the U.S. Army, n.d.).
19. The munition, which looks like an ordinary shell, contains two non-lethal chemical compounds separated by rupture disks. When the shell hits a target, a fuse is ignited, causing a burster to rupture the disks, which allows the chemicals to unite and form a lethal chemical agent. Production, storage, and surveillance are simplified. There is no danger of nerve agent leakage, no corrosion of the munition due to the agent, and no degradation of the agent itself. Storage and transportation of the binary compounds is simple and safe because the compounds are handled separately.
20. From conversations in 1999 with Gen. Michael Davison, USA (Ret.). General Davison was with the infantry during the campaign through Anzio, northern Italy, and France during World War II. He was with the infantry again in the jungles of Vietnam and eventually commanded all U.S. Army forces in Europe. He would readily accept a "neutralizing" weapon as a replacement for the nuclear weapon that contaminates the battlefield.

Index

Bold page numbers refer to illustrations

509th Bomb Group, 13–15

A-1 aircraft. *See* Douglas A-1 Skyraider
A-3 aircraft. *See* Douglas A-3 Skywarrior
A-4 aircraft. *See* Douglas A-4 Skyhawk
Acheson-Lilenthal Plan, 68–69
Aegean Sea: carrier task forces: exercise, 153; replenishment ships, 1–3
AFOAT-1, 55
AFSWP. *See* Armed Forces Special Weapons Project
Agnew, Harold, 53
Air Defense Command, 114, 171
Air Development Squadron 3 (VX-3), 132, 136, 169–75; mission, 158, 169
Air Development Squadron 5 (VX-5): establishment, 122; LABS, 164–69; loft/toss bomb-delivery tactic, 159–61, 168; mission, 158, 159; over-the-shoulder bomb-delivery tactic, 159, 161–69
AJ aircraft. *See* North American AJ Savage
Alamogordo, New Mexico: Trinity test, 17–18, 45
Albuquerque, New Mexico: AFSWP, 91, 122; weaponeer training, 88. *See also* Kirtland Air Force Base
America, USS, 205
Ames, Michael, 170
Anderson, George, 201, 203

Antietam, USS, 194
APA-5 bombing system, 86
Argentina: aircraft carrier capability, 178
Arkansas (ship), 50–52
Armed Forces Special Weapons Project (AFSWP), 21, 70, 75, 91, 122; liaison with Project 27A, 187
Armstrong, Frank, 27
ASB-1 bombing system, 87, 114, 115, 158
Ashworth, Frederick Lincoln "Dick," 10–17, 30–33, 44–50, 78–80; as pilot of torpedo bomber, **11,** 154–55; as weaponeer during atomic bomb drop on Japan, 14–16, 80, 156, 187; command of VC-6, 79, 95, 165; comments on issue of setting military requirements, 63–64; concern for Navy above personal career, 78, 237; discussion of Nagasaki mission, 19–20; idea of carrier and nuclear weapon mix, 33, 39; member of OP-36, 20–21, 39, 42, 68; quoted on Jig Ramage, 106–7; role in Manhattan Project, 10–13, 21, 70; role in Operation Crossroads, 47–50, 52–53; secretary of MLC, 69–70, 91
Atlantic Fleet, 122, 132
Atlantic Ocean: aircraft carriers, 97, 222, 235
Atomic Energy Act (1946), 69, 70
Atomic Energy Commission (AEC), 58–59, 69–71, 189–90; and AFOAT-1, 55; custody of nuclear weapons, 70–71, 245; establishment of (1946), 32, 69; Military Liaison Committee, 69, 71, 91

289

290 Index

Attack Squadron 42 (VA-42), 145
Attack Squadron 72 (VA-72), 134, 135
Attack Squadron 75 (VA-75), 144–47, 225
Attack Squadron 147 (VA-147), 225
Attack Squadron 195 (VA-195), 125
Augusta, USS, 18
Ault, Frank, 88, 89, 119, 237
Austin, Frank, 173

B-17 aircraft, 155, 156
B-24 aircraft, 155, 156
B-25 aircraft, 27, 30, 34–35
B-29 aircraft: horizontal bombing, 155, 156; Norden bombsight, 156; plutonium bomb size limit, 41; tests, 11, 15, 32; used in bombing of Japan, 14, 15, 17, 26, 28, 42
B-36 aircraft: aircrew course, 122; in-flight refueling, 36; Navy vs. Air Force arguments, 28–29, 129, 247; Norden bombsight, 155; size of atomic weapons, 53; vs. Banshee, 129, 130
B-43 aircraft, 149
B-52 aircraft: airborne alert tactic, 37; in-flight refueling, 36; Norden bombsight, 155; nuclear weapons tests, 58, 158; size of atomic weapons, 53
B-57 aircraft, 149
B-61 aircraft, 149
B-66 aircraft, 223
B-70 aircraft, 109
Baldwin, Robert, 165
Barlow, Jeffrey, 200
Bedfellow nuclear weapon, 109–10
Beling, John, 205
Bennington, USS, 185
Bethe, Hans, 12
Bikini Atoll, Marshall Islands, Pacific Ocean: atomic bomb tests, 6, 7, **49,** 50–51
Biscay, Bay of, 112, 152
Blackburn, Tom, 101, 102, 139, 237
Blandy, W. H. P. "Spike," 5–6, 39, 236–37; Crossroads tests, 32, 47, 49, 51; head of OP-06, 42, 67
Bohr, Niels, 12
Bradbury, Norris, 58, 63, 64
Bradley, Omar, 29, 30, 84, 85
Brown, Charles "Cat," 104–7, 119
Brown, George, 208
Buchner, Francis, 59
Bundy, McGeorge, 208

Burke, Arleigh A., 6, 29, 212–13, 236, 247
Bush, George, 231, 232, 250
Bush, Vannevar, 69
Butler, George Lee, 25, 66, 253

Caldwell, Turner, 86
Central Intelligence Agency (CIA), 54, 55, 207, 217
Chance Vought A-7 Corsair, 148–50, **150**; carrier exercise, 153; nuclear weapons delivery tactics, 149, 175–77; nuclear weapons safety, 195; radar bombing training mission, 204; radar system, 149–50, 176; realistic combat radius, 149, 175; specifications, 128; target materials and training facilities, 225–26
Chance Vought F7U-3 Cutlass, 58–59, **59**
Chapman, Bill, 237
China: development of nuclear weapons, 243–44; during Korean War, 87, 253; relations with United States, 257–58
China Lake. *See* Naval Ordnance Test Station
Chute, Chuck, 112
Clinton, Bill, 259
Colby, William, 207
Cold War: end of, 252–53; government secrecy, 246; policy for use of nuclear weapons, 22, 25; role of naval aviation, 235
Composite Squadron 4 (VC-4), 131, 132
Composite Squadron 5 (VC-5), 79, 88, 94, 165
Composite Squadron 6 (VC-6), 79, 94, 96, 165
Composite Squadron 7 (VC-7), 80
Comprehensive Test Ban Treaty (CTBT), 218–20
Conant, James B., 69
Connolly, Thomas, 8, 117, 136, 237
Constellation, USS, 225, 226
Cooper, Ken, 189
Coral Sea, USS, 81, **84,** 132, 204
Cotter, Don, 207
Crommelin, John, 29
Cuban missile crisis (1962), 111, 253–54
Curtiss SB2C Helldiver, 155–56, **157**
CVN-77, 198, 234
CVNX-1 and -2, 198, 234

Davidson, Dick, 237
Davies, Thomas D., 81, 84
Denfeld, Louis, 35, 236
Department of Defense (DOD), 70–71, 207–8, 213, 244

Desert Storm, 258
Doolittle, James, 27, 30
Dorrington, Joe, 103–4
Douglas A-1 Skyraider, 121, 126–27, **127**, 172–74; "butt buster" flights, 126, 173–74; delivery tactics, 159, 160, 163, 164, 172; dive brakes, 156; low-level flights, 127, 172–73; Mark VII weapons, 121, 122–23; role in SIOP, 126, 214–15; specifications, 128; use in Korea and Vietnam, 126, 156, 215
Douglas A-3 Skywarrior, 99–109, **100, 111**; ASB bombing system, 87, 114, 115; "buddy bombing" with A-4, 174; compared with FJ-4B, 139; delivery tactics, 112, 168, 176; heavy-attack strategy, 139, 168, 176, 214; horizontal bombing, 158, 168; lay-down maneuver, 168, 176; role in SIOP, 214
Douglas A-4 Skyhawk, 133, 134–36, **135**, 174; in-flight refueling, 141; replacement for, 148–49; role in SIOP, 214; specifications, 128; weapons-effect testing, 59, 60
Douglas Aircraft Company, 99, 107, 159
Douglas SBD aircraft, 155–56
Douhet, Giulio, 48
Dunleavy, Dick, 237
Dunn, Robert F., 255–57

Einstein, Albert, 259
Eisenhower, Dwight D.: approval of SIOP, 214, 247–48; concern over weapons stockpile, 76, 207; Korean War, 24, 253; nuclear weapons policy and strategy, 24–25, 58, 71, 76, 213, 253
Ela, Keith "Deke," 75, 185, 237
Elliott, William, 125
Engen, Donald D., 170, 205, 237
England: B-66 aircraft, 223; during Berlin crisis, 253; Soviet intelligence effort, 54. *See also* London
Eniwetok Atoll, Marshall Islands, Pacific Ocean, 54, 57–59
Enola Gay (aircraft), 17, 19
Enterprise, USS, 111, 181, 192
Enthoven, Alain, 65
Entwistle, F. I., 122
Essex, USS, 108, **179**
Essex-class carriers, 180; A-3 aircraft, 107, 108; conversions to accommodate nuclear weapons, 180, 186–91, 194; FJ-4B Fury aircraft, 136

F-4 Phantom II fighter, 115–16
F-8 aircraft. *See* Ling Temco Vought F-8 Crusader
F9F-8 aircraft. *See* Grumman F9F-8 Cougar
F-14 Tomcat fighter, 151
F-84 Thunderjet aircraft, 73, 121, 125, 171
F-105 Thunderchief, 125
Farrell, Thomas, 20
Fat Man bomb, 17–19, 41, **42**; dropped on Nagasaki, 18; estimated yield, 45; production, 25–26, 41; size, 54, 100; wooden mockup, 91–92
Febel, Joel, 237
Fechteler, W. M., 123
Feightner, E. L. "Whitey," 85–86, 132, 169–73, 237
Ferebee, Jim, 89
FJ-4B aircraft. *See* North American FJ-4B Fury
Florida: JSTPS educational effort, 208. *See also* Jacksonville
Ford, Gerald, 207, 229–30
Ford Foundation, 208
Forrestal, James, 39, 71, 183, 248
Forrestal, USS, 99, 191–94, **192**, 205; A-3 aircraft, 102, 107
Forrestal-class carriers, 94, 108–9, 181, 201
France: aircraft carrier capability, 178; NATO forces, 256. *See also* Normandy
Franklin D. Roosevelt, USS, 2–3, 81, 87, 131, **203**

Gallery, Daniel V., 33–35, 141, 237
Gates, Thomas, 247
Gayler, Noel, 66, 169–70, 237, 246, 255
George Washington, USS, 214
Germany: Berlin crisis (1948), 23, 24, 253; race for atomic reaction, 40; World War II: aerial bombing, 45; World War II: defeat, 12
Glasser, Otto, 99, 100
Global Positioning System (GPS), 165, 233
Goodpaster, Andrew, 66, 251, 253, 255
Gorbachev, Mikhail, 230, 231, 250
Graves, Ernest, 72
Great Britain: aircraft carrier capability, 178; NATO forces, 256. *See also* England
Greece: NATO forces, 256; Soviet expansion efforts, 24
Griffin, C. D., 124, 125

292 *Index*

Griffin, Don, 29, 236
Groves, Leslie, 10, 12, 14–21, 32, 40, 43–45; as head of AFSWP, 21, 70, 72, 75; personnel policies, 72, 239; security policies, 79, 243; target selection for Japan bombings (1945), 211, 216
Grumman A-6 Intruder: specifications, 128
Grumman A-6 Intruder aircraft, 141–48, **142**; as deterrent, 228; "hit on the first pass" requirement, 142–43, 237; night and all-weather capability, 144, 145, 174; nuclear role, 103, 134; role in SIOP, 225; side-by-side aircrew configuration, 116, 144, 148; weapons delivery tactics, 134, 146–48, 174–75
Grumman Aircraft Corporation, 146, 154
Grumman F9F-8 Cougar, 133, **133**, 138; specifications, 128
Guadalcanal, Solomon Islands, Pacific Ocean, 11, 154
Guam, Mariana Islands, Pacific Ocean, 13, 14
Guantanamo Bay, Cuba: training base, 134
Gullege, Doc, 237

Hansen, Chuck, 65
Hawaii: combat readiness testing, 200. *See also* Honolulu
Hayward, John Tucker "Chick," 7, 8, 32–33, 237; and AJ aircraft, 90, 94, 95, 97, 121; and P2V aircraft, 81, 83–85, 121; command of VC-5, 78–80, 88, 165, 242; personnel policies, 80, 103–4, 241, 242; views on Air Force and nuclear weapons mission, 48
Hearst, William Randolph, 84
Heavy Attack Squadron 1 (VAH-1), 101, 103–4, 241
Heavy Attack Squadron 4 (VAH-4), 107, 108
Heavy Attack Training Unit, Atlantic, Norfolk, Virginia, 113
Heinemann, Edward, 99–102, 126, 133, 237; and VX-5, 159, 168
Herzberger, Raymond, 85–86
Hill, Tom B., 14, 42, 47, 68
Hiroshima, Japan: bombing (1945), 8, 13–20, 31; bombardier, 89; damage survey, 6, 46–47; determination of bomb yield, 43–45; target selection, 211, 216; type of bomb, 17, 41
Honolulu, Hawaii: long-range navigational training flights, 88

Hornet, USS, 27, 30, 136, 180
Houser, William, 152
Hunt, Robert, 130–31, 134, 140, 237
Hyland, John J., 201, 203

Iceland: Reagan/Gorbachev actions, 230–31
Iler, John, 30
Independence, USS, 146–48
Italy: aircraft carrier capability, 178; NATO forces, 256. *See also* Sicily
Iwo Jima (island), Japan, 29

Jaap, Joseph A., 80, 237
Jacksonville, Florida: operational readiness inspections, 200–2
Japan: World War II, 8, 19, 26–28, 46–47, 158; Doolittle raid (1942), 27, 30; surrender, 19, 26, 46, 53, 211. *See also* Hiroshima; Kokura; Kyoto; Nagasaki; Okinawa; Tokyo
Johnson, Louis, 84, 85, 183–85, 248
Johnson, Lyndon B., 76, 248–49
Joint Strategic Target Planning Staff (JSTPS), 66, 206–8, 210, 213, 216–17, 222

Kennedy, John F., 214, 254
Kimball, Dan, 123
King, Ernest, 13, 14, 45
King, Richard "Ace," 136, 237
Kirtland Air Force Base, Albuquerque, New Mexico, 58
Kitty Hawk, USS, 181, 198
Kokura, Japan, 18
Korean War, 24, 87, 118–19, 200; impact on carrier operations, 238; number of deaths, 254; proposed nuclear radiation barrier, 87, 253; role of U.S. Navy, 192; U.S. lack of preparedness, 184, 248; use of A-1 aircraft, 126, 156
Kosovo, Yugoslavia, 250, 258
Kwajalein Atoll, Marshall Islands, Pacific Ocean, 49
Kyoto, Japan, 211

LABS. *See* Low-Altitude Bombing System
Langley, USS, 179
Larkin, Dick, 20
Lawrence, William P., 239–40
LeBlanc, Georges "Frenchy, " Jr., 58–62, 237
Lee, Kent, 111, 112
LeMay, Curtis, 200, 214, 248, 253–55

Leonard, William, 130, 237
Lexington, USS, 140, 179
Leyte, USS, 185
Libby, Willard F., 55
Liberty, USS, 205
Lilienthal, David E., 71
Ling Temco Vought F-8 Crusader, 148, **150**
Little Boy bomb, 17, 18, 40, **42,** 73
Lockheed P2V Neptune, 81–87, **83,** 89–90; bombardier/navigator training flights, 113; first launch (1948), **84**; heavy-attack program, 121, 245; P2V-3C version, 81, 85, 91, 94, 158, 165; reliability, 81, 95; specifications, 82
London, England: nuclear weapons damage survey, 43–44
Los Alamos National Laboratory, Los Alamos, New Mexico: AFOAT-1 mission, 55; AFSWP, 187; alleged theft of secrets, 244; atomic bomb development, 7, 10–12, 20, 40, 53, 63, 72; spying during World War II, 69
Low-Altitude Bombing System (LABS), 134, 164–69, 232

MacArthur, Douglas, 87, 253
MacDowell, Charlie, 237
Mandelkorn, Dick, 75, 237
Manhattan Project, 10, 17, 21, 32, 40, 54; security policies, 79, 243, 246; testing of atomic weapons, 47
Mao Tse-Tung: quoted, 258
Mark 12 nuclear weapon, 131, 137
Mark 28 nuclear weapon, 73–74, **74,** 139
Mark 39 nuclear weapon, 37
Mark 76 practice bombs, 161, 162
Mark IV nuclear weapon, 73
Mark V nuclear weapon, 63
Mark VII nuclear weapon, 63, **64,** 73, 91, 121; shapes, 163, 171; training bombs, 122–23, 131
Marshall, George C., 22
McDonnell-Douglas F/A-18 Hornet: specifications, 128
McDonnell-Douglas F/A-18 Hornet aircraft, **151,** 151–52, 228, 232–34
McDonnell F2H Banshee: specifications, 128
McDonnell F2H Banshee aircraft, 121, 125, 127–33, **129**; bomb-delivery tactics, 159, 160, 164; vs. B-36 aircraft, 129, 130; VX-3 demonstration, 170–72

McGinn, Dennis, 203, 233–35
McLean, William "Bill," 8
McMorris, Charles H. "Soc," 14
McNamara, Robert, 219–20, 224, 248–49, 254; and nuclear stockpile, 65, 76; expansion of Office of Secretary of Defense, 183; "whiz kids," 65, 219–20, 249
McNitt, Robert B., 189, 245
McQuilken, John "Red," 75, 187, 237
Mediterranean Sea: A-3 squadron, 103; aircraft carriers, 87, 98, 132, 222, 235; AJ aircraft, 97; antisubmarine warfare, 256; F2H-2B aircraft, 131; replenishment maneuvers, 1–3; U.S. Sixth Fleet, 104, 112, 153, 256–57
Meitner, Lise, 40
Meyer, John, 207–9
Midway, Battle of, 155
Midway, USS, 81, **93, 181**; FJ-4B aircraft, 137, 139; PV2 aircraft, 81, 83–84; stowage of nuclear cores, 189; VX-3 demonstration, 170–72
Midway-class carriers, 81, 90–91, 99, 120, 180; AJ aircraft, 94; FJ-4B Fury aircraft, 136
Military Liaison Committee (MLC), 69, 71, 91
Miller, Doug, 237
Miller, George, 36–39, 237
Mitchell, Billy, 48
Mitscher, Marc A., 90
MLC. *See* Military Liaison Committee
Moffett Field, California, 79, 81, 85, 94, 159
Moorer, Thomas H., 6–8, 38, 201, 203; member of Strategic Bombing Survey, 6, 46
Moscow, Russia: as SIOP target, 225
Moynihan, Daniel, 246
Murphy, J. N., 91

Nagasaki, Japan: bombing (1945), 8, 14–20, 31; damage survey, 6, 46–47; determination of bomb yield, 43–45; mushroom cloud, **16**; target selection, 18, 211, 216; type of bomb, 17, 41
National Security Agency (NSA), 66, 246
Naval Air Station, San Diego, California, 122–23
Naval Air Test Center, Patuxent River, Maryland, 94, 101, 129, 194; P2V-3C test flights, 85, 86; Service Test Division, 95, 97

Naval Ordnance Test Station (NOTS), Inyokern, California, 8, 32, 159–60, 168
Naval Proving Ground, Dahlgren, Virginia, 8, 10
Naval War College, Newport, Rhode Island, 5, 121
Nevada: test site, 54, 56, 57
Nimitz, Chester, 12, 13, 42, 45, 68
Nimitz, USS, **193**
Nimitz-class carriers, 181, 192, 198, 262
Nitze, Paul, 46
Nixon, Richard, 208, 229
Norden bombsight, 155, 156
Norfolk, Virginia: U.S. Navy facilities, 27, 113, 131, 132, 189, 204
Normandy, France: amphibious operations, 29
Norstad, Lauris, 17
North American A-5 Vigilante, 109–13, **110, 111**; specifications, 128
North American AJ Savage, 90–99, **92, 93**; accidents, 95–97, 243; ASB-1 bombing system, 87, 115, 132, 158; development, 86, 121; size problems, 95, 183, 184; specifications, 82; tankers, 138, 170, 171; test program partially bypassed, 93, 94–95, 101, 243
North American Aviation Corporation, 59–60, 91, 94, 141; Fat Man bomb mockup, 92; test pilots killed, 95–96
North American Defense Command (NORAD), 170
North American FJ-4B Fury, 136–41, **137**, 174; SIOP plan, 214; specifications, 128; weapons- effects testing, 59–61
North Atlantic Treaty Organization (NATO), 103, 131, 152, 247, 250
Norwegian Sea: carrier exercise, 153
NOTS. *See* Naval Ordnance Test Station

Office of the Chief of Naval Operations: OP-36 office, 6, 7, 20–21, 42, 67–68; Special Weapons Division, 122
Okinawa (island), Japan, 18, 29, 139, 140
Operation Crossroads, 32, 45, 47–52, **49**, 67, 76
Oppenheimer, Robert, 12, 20, 69–70; role of "Deak" Parsons, 7, 8, 10–11
Oriskany, USS, 124, 125, 186
Outlaw, Eddie, 85

P2V aircraft. *See* Lockheed P2V Neptune
Pacific Ocean: aircraft carriers, 29, 136–37, 139, 222, 225, 235; World War II, 6, 29, 42–43
Parker, E. N. "Butch," 213
Parsons, William "Deak," 7–8, 10–12, 77–79, 236; as midshipman, 43; as weaponeer during atomic bomb drop on Japan, 14–16, 80, 156, 187; death, 236; Manhattan Project role, 7, 10–12, 70, 75; member of OP-36, 7, 20–21, 39, 42, 67–68; role in tests at Bikini, 7, 47, 49, 187
Pearson, Drew, 33
Penney, Sir William, 43, 44
Pershing II missile, 231
Philippine Sea, USS, 123
Pittsburgh, USS, 43
Polaris missile, 6, 7, 213, 247, 248
Polaris submarines, 209–10, 220
Port Lyautey, Morocco, 95, 97, 98, 101
Poseidon missile, 248
Potsdam conference, 18, 45
Powell, Colin, 260
Power, Thomas, 200, 210, 212–13
Purdon, David, 96–97, 237

Quantico, Virginia: nuclear-weapons-delivery demonstration, 163–64
Quonset Point, Rhode Island: anti–submarine warfare mission, 134

RA-5C aircraft, 111, 112
Rabi, Isador, 12
Radford, Arthur W., 29, 90, 236
Ramage, James D. "Jig," 105–7, 120–25, 168, 202, 237; personnel policy, 106, 242; quoted on Korean War, 118
Ranger, USS, 179
Reagan, Ronald, 38, 230–31, 250
Regulus cruise missile, 31–32, 214
Richmond, Virginia: radar bomb-scoring site, 98
Rickover, Hyman G., 31, 236, 239, 240
Rivero, Horacio "Rivets," 6, 7, 47, 49, 68, 237; determination of bomb yields, 43–44
Roosevelt, Franklin Delano, 46, 54
Runyan, Don, 85
Russia: aircraft carrier capability, 178; relations with United States, 251. *See also* Moscow; Semipalatinsk; Vladivostok

Index **295**

Saipan (island), Mariana Islands, Pacific Ocean, 14, 29
Sandia Corporation, 59, 75, 99–100, 123, 186–87, 189
Saratoga, USS, 52, 102, 179, 201
SB2C aircraft. *See* Curtiss SB2C Helldiver
Schlesinger, James, 221, 222
Schwager, Joseph, 165, 166, 168, 237
Seaborg, Glenn, 71
Seeman, L. E., 54
Selmer, Robert, 159–60
Semipalatinsk, Russia: atomic explosion (1949), 56
Sherman, Forrest, 35
Sicily (island), Italy: amphibious operations, 29
Sidewinder missile, 8, 128
Sims, William S., **4,** 5, 143, 202
Single Integrated Operational Plan (SIOP), 126, 206–10, 214–15, 218–19; arms control, 229, 249; early targeting selection requirements, 233; impact on aircraft carrier operations, 204, 222–27, 257; nuclear weapons stockpile, 76, 226, 229
Sloatman, Jack, 123
Small, James D., 185, 237
Snark cruise missile, 223
Snead, Leonard "Swoose," 144, 237
Soviet Union: arms control, 229–31, 250; bomb tests, 54, 58, 62; Cold War, 22–25, 235, 246, 252–53; development of nuclear weapons, 55–56, 243–44; expansion of empire, 22–24; targets, 212, 216, 223, 225; thermonuclear weapons, 57, 58; U.S. intelligence efforts, 54, 216, 217; World War II, 19, 22, 25, 54, 69. *See also* Russia
Spaatz, Carl A., 23, 27
Spain: aircraft carrier capability, 178; NATO forces, 256
Spangenberg, George, 92, 237
Special Aircraft Service Stores (SASS), 186–89, 191, 193, 195, 196
Spiegel, William, 103, 237
Sprague, T. L., 122
Stevens, Paul, 101–4, 119, 237, 241, 242
Stimson, Henry, 211, 216
Strassman, Fritz, 40
StratCom, 212, 248
Strategic Air Command (SAC), 26–27, 36–38, 212–17; bombing competitions, 106, 114; creation of "strategic command," 212, 247–48; intelligence, 56, 215–17; readiness inspections, 200
Strategic Arms Limitations Talks (SALT), 46
Strategic Bombing Survey, 6, 46
Strategic Defense Initiative (SDI), 230, 253
Strauss, Lewis, 70
Sullivan, Gordon, 260
Sunday Punchers. *See* Attack Squadron 75
Sweeney, Charles, 15, 17, 20
Symington, Stuart, 84

Tactical Air Command (TAC), 27, 121
Talbot, Strobe, 230–31
Talent-Keyhole program, 216–17
TBF torpedo bomber, 154–55
Teller, Edward, 56, 58, 70, 244
Than Hoa Bridge, Vietnam, 148
Thompson, L. T. E. "Tommy," 8
Tibbets, Paul, 13, 15, 17, 20
Tinian (island), Mariana Islands, Pacific Ocean, 14, **15,** 17, 19, 20, 53
Titan ICBM, 229
Tokyo, Japan: attack (1942), 27; fire raid (1945), 19
Townsend, Bob, 237
Trapnell, Fred, 124
Trident SLBM systems, 22, 248, 251, 253, 261
"Trinity" test, 17–18, 20, 45, 51, 76
Truman, Harry S.: and Louis Johnson, 183–84; Berlin crisis, 253; Korean War, 87, 184, 253; nuclear weapons issue, 20, 22–24, 76, 87, 253; use of atomic bomb against Japan, 18, 24, 45, 211, 253
Turkey: A-1 flight, 173–74; NATO forces, 256

U-2 spy aircraft, 216
United Kingdom: development of nuclear weapons, 243–44. *See also* Great Britain
United States: aircraft carrier capability, 178–79; arms control, 229–31, 249–52; intelligence mission, 54–56, 215–17; interservice rivalries, 26–28, 34, 114, 152, 210, 247; nuclear weapons stockpile, 62, 64–67, 74, 229, 251–53, 255; relations with China, 257–58; relations with Russia, 251; Soviet intelligence effort, 54, 69
United States, USS, 28, 84, 182–85, 193

U.S. Air Force: creation of "strategic command," 212, 247; Fat Man bomb mockup, 92; intelligence capability, 55–56, 217; nuclear mission, 26–28, 34–35, 39, 90, 238, 247; rivalry with U.S. Navy, 26–27, 34, 109, 152, 247
U.S. Army, 26–28, 48, 55, 189
U.S. Army Air Forces, 23, 31, 41–42, 47, 48; B-29 bombers, 11; Norden sight, 156
U.S. Marine Corps, 26–29, 87, 142, 148
U.S. Military Academy, West Point, New York, 30, 239
U.S. Missile Defense Act (1999), 251
U.S. Naval Academy, Annapolis, Maryland, 4, 30, 43, 165, 239–40; class of 1942, 118; class of 1943, 119; class of 1960, 145
U.S. Navy: aircraft carrier nuclear weapons delivery capability, 61, 85, 91, 109, 228–29, 239; attacks on B-36 aircraft, 28–29, 129, 247; future of nuclear mission, 197–98; "gun club," 3–9, 11, 49, 236; heavy-attack program, 77–119; light-attack program, 120–53; nuclear weapons delivery tactics: loft/toss bombing, 159–63, 168, 174, 176, 177; nuclear weapons delivery tactics: Low-Altitude Bombing System, 164–69; nuclear weapons delivery tactics: over-the-shoulder bombing, 161–68, 171, 174–76; rivalry with U.S. Air Force, 26–27, 34, 109, 152, 247. *See also* Office of the Chief of Naval Operations
U.S. Pacific Fleet, 107, 121, 122, 124, 201
U.S. Sixth Fleet, 104, 107, 112, 153, 256, 257

VA-42. *See* Attack Squadron 42
VA-72. *See* Attack Squadron 72
VA-75. *See* Attack Squadron 75
VA-147. *See* Attack Squadron 147
VA-195. *See* Attack Squadron 195
VAH-1. *See* Heavy Attack Squadron 1
VAH-4. *See* Heavy Attack Squadron 4
Valente, Frank A., 54–55
Vance, Cyrus, 71, 230
Vandenberg Air Force Base, California, 220
VC-4. *See* Composite Sqaudron 4
VC-5. *See* Composite Squadron 5
VC-6. *See* Composite Squadron 6
VC-7. *See* Composite Squadron 7
Vietnam War: aircraft carriers, 146–48, 223; combat readiness tests, 200; command opportunity issue, 116–17; conventional weapons, 47, 125, 134, 145, 215; nuclear role, 203–4, 254; number of deaths, 254; role of F-105 Thunderchief, 125; use of A-1 aircraft, 126, 156, 215
Vinson, Carl, 29
Vladivostok, Russia: arms control negotiations (1974), 229–30
VX-3. *See* Air Development Squadron 3
VX-5. *See* Air Development Squadron 5

Walker, Thomas, 7, 8, 20, 122, 237; development of nuclear weapons delivery tactics, 159–60, 166, 168; sketches made by, **161, 162**
Wallop, Malcolm, 250
Weisskopf, Victor, 12
Wendover, Utah: Army air base, 11, 15, 17
Whitney, J. D., 125
Wigner, Eugene, 12
Withington, F. S., 124
World War I, 5, 154
World War II: aircraft carriers, 26, 90, 180, 238; early submarine patrols, 219; Germany, 12, 45; horizontal bombing, 154–56; Japan, 8, 19, 26–28, 46–47, 158; Japan: Doolittle raid (1942), 27, 30; Japan: surrender, 19, 26, 46, 53, 211; naval ordnance and gunnery, 5–6; replenishment ships, 1; Soviet Union, 19, 22, 25, 54, 69
Wrangell, USS, **203**
Wright, Jerauld, 32, 67, 68

Yalu River, China-North Korea, 87, 253
Yorktown-class carriers, 179–80
Youngs, Ted, 123–24
Yunck, Michael, 159–60